OBAMA, THE MEDIA, AND FRAMING THE U.S. EXIT FROM IRAQ AND AFGHANISTAN

Obama, the Media, and Framing the U.S. Exit from Iraq and Afghanistan

ERIKA G. KING
Grand Valley State University, USA

ASHGATE

© Erika G. King 2014

All rights reserved. No part of this publication may be reproduced, stored in a retrieval system or transmitted in any form or by any means, electronic, mechanical, photocopying, recording or otherwise without the prior permission of the publisher.

Erika G. King has asserted her right under the Copyright, Designs and Patents Act, 1988, to be identified as the author of this work.

Published by
Ashgate Publishing Limited
Wey Court East
Union Road
Farnham
Surrey, GU9 7PT
England

Ashgate Publishing Company
110 Cherry Street
Suite 3-1
Burlington, VT 05401-3818
USA

www.ashgate.com

British Library Cataloguing in Publication Data
A catalogue record for this book is available from the British Library

The Library of Congress has cataloged the printed edition as follows:
King, Erika G.
  Obama, the media, and framing the U.S. exit from Iraq and Afghanistan / by Erika G. King.
    pages cm
  Includes bibliographical references and index.
  ISBN 978-1-4094-2964-7 (hardback) -- ISBN 978-1-4094-2965-4 (ebook) -- ISBN 978-1-4724-0013-0 (epub) 1. Iraq War, 2003-2011--Mass media and the war. 2. Iraq War, 2003-2011--Press coverage--United States. 3. Afghan War, 2001---Mass media and the war. 4. Afghan War, 2001---Press coverage--United States. 5. Rhetoric--Political aspects--United States. 6. Obama, Barack--Oratory. I. Title.
  DS79.767.M37K57 2014
  070.4'4995670443--dc23

2013023960

ISBN 9781409429647 (hbk)
ISBN 9781409429654 (ebk – PDF)
ISBN 9781472400130 (ebk – ePUB)

Printed in the United Kingdom by Henry Ling Limited, at the Dorset Press, Dorchester, DT1 1HD

Contents

Acknowledgments   *vii*

    Introduction   1

1   Surging to Victory in the War on Terror   21

2   Disrupting, Dismantling, and Defeating Al Qaeda   45

3   War's Surge-then-Exit through a Skeptical Media Lens   77

4   Turning the Page on Operation Iraqi Freedom   115

5   War's Drawdown through a Censorious Media Lens   145

6   Framing War's Indecisive End   177

Bibliography   *189*
Index   *219*

Acknowledgments

This project would not have been possible without the aid and support of a number of people to whom I would formally like to express my gratitude. For almost two decades, I have had the pleasure of working at a university that places much value on faculty scholarship. I therefore offer thanks to the Department of Political Science, the Office of the Dean of Liberal Arts and Sciences, and the Office of the Provost at Grand Valley State University for granting me a sabbatical leave of absence with which to pursue my research. I also give heartfelt thanks to Professor Robert Wells, with whom I collaborated on an earlier analysis of President Bush, the media, and the Iraq War endgame—work which laid the groundwork for the present study.

I am also much indebted to the talented and hardworking staff of Ashgate Publishing—especially Senior Commissioning Editor for Politics Rob Sorsby, Senior Editor Aimée Feenan, and their team—who have provided invaluable editorial advice, guidance, and assistance. I appreciate in addition the incisive comments and suggestions of two anonymous reviewers.

My greatest debt is to my husband, Robert, whose patience, kindness, and ever-ready sense of humor have enabled me to keep everything in perspective. It is to him that I am honored to dedicate this book.

Introduction

Ten years and ten days after the terrorist attacks of September 11, 2001, President Barack Obama addressed world leaders at the opening session of the United Nations General Assembly in New York City, just a few miles from where the Twin Towers had been brought down on that fateful morning. His stated topic was the pursuit of peace in "an imperfect world" scarred by strife and human suffering. "Peace is hard," he repeatedly emphasized, and progress toward it had all too frequently been derailed. But urging his audience to do their utmost to attain that noble goal, Obama (2011a) proudly declared that under his watch "the tide of war is receding" and the two conflicts he had inherited were drawing to a close. By the end of the year, he announced, the final American troops would cross the border out of the sovereign nation of Iraq, and an increasingly capable Afghan government and security forces would begin to assume responsibility for their own future.

The decade that had preceded his remarks had been a most difficult one, Obama acknowledged, but 2011 had been a remarkable year of transformation as people from South Sudan to the Ivory Coast, Tunisia, Egypt, and Libya had risen up to claim those universal rights "embraced by this Assembly." And Osama bin Laden was also gone, and with him had been buried "the idea that change could only come through violence." Obama cautioned that in a world still facing dangerous convulsions, there was much yet to accomplish in pursuit of individual liberty and well-being. But even amid calls for change in places like Iran, Syria, and the West Bank, we had reason to hope that for increasing numbers around the globe, basic aspirations—"to live with dignity and freedom; to get an education and pursue opportunity; to love our families and our God. To live in the kind of peace that makes life worth living"—could now be met (Obama 2011a).

One month later, Obama reaffirmed the removal of all American forces from Iraq by the end of 2011, casting the decision as the fulfillment of his solemn campaign pledge to bring the war to a responsible conclusion "for the sake of our national security and to strengthen American leadership around the world." Again Obama noted that the end of the Iraq conflict reflected a broader U.S. military disengagement, and he once more proclaimed that "the tide of war is receding" as Qaddafi's death the previous day marked the imminent closure of NATO operations in Libya and troop withdrawals from Afghanistan would soon mean a transition to Afghan leadership. And finally, he was pleased to report, after a decade of war the United States could shift focus and concentrate on its greatest remaining challenge: domestic economic renewal. "The nation that we need to build—and the nation that we will build—is our own," he vowed; "an America that sees its economic strength restored just as we've restored our leadership around the globe" (Obama 2011b).

In remarks at Arlington National Cemetery on Veterans Day, Obama continued his message of war's denouement, presenting it through the prism of the hard work and heroic sacrifices of the thousands of military personnel who had served in America's twenty-first-century conflicts. As he admiringly observed, "Their service has been selfless. Their accomplishments have been extraordinary ... Because of their incredible efforts, we can stand here and say with confidence the tide of war is receding" (Obama 2011c). The following month in a speech to returning troops at Fort Bragg, North Carolina, the president warmed to this theme, declaring that one of the "most extraordinary chapters in the history of the American military" had finally come to an end. And the man who had risen to national prominence so roundly condemning the U.S. engagement in Iraq would now hail the accomplishments of its fighting forces in both wars as a triumph of the exceptional American character and spirit. Speaking directly to the veterans and their families, Obama offered this paean to their—and by extension, America's—selflessness, virtue, and resolve:

> Because of you—because you sacrificed so much for a people that you had never met, Iraqis have a chance to forge their own destiny. That's part of what makes us special as Americans. Unlike the old empires, we don't make these sacrifices for territory or for resources. We do it because it's right. There can be no fuller expression of America's support for self-determination than our leaving Iraq to its people. That says something about who we are.
>
> Because of you, in Afghanistan we've broken the momentum of the Taliban. Because of you, we've begun a transition to the Afghans that will allow us to bring our troops home from there. And around the globe, as we draw down in Iraq, we have gone after al Qaeda so that terrorists who threaten America will have no safe haven, and Osama bin Laden will never again walk the face of this earth. (Obama 2011d)

The Presidential Narrative of War

As Obama reflected on the meaning and import of America's post-9/11 wars, he was completing a long and occasionally winding rhetorical journey that began in the fall of 2002, when as an Illinois state senator he stepped forward to speak to an anti-war rally in Chicago and profess his support for combatting al Qaeda in Afghanistan while simultaneously decrying President George W. Bush's plan to invade Iraq. Drawing a distinction between righteous wars fought "in the name of a larger freedom" and one "based not on reason but on passion, not on principle but on politics," Obama (2002) began to formulate his own tale of America at war, adding his twist to the nation's on-going conversation about why it fights and what its conflicts have said about the country, its place in the world, and the perils it faces. Over the remainder of the decade, he would hone his discourse and craft a rationale for pursuing a war of necessity while ending what he pointedly labeled a most unfortunate war of choice.

Like the war scripts of previous presidents, Obama's story of America's current wars sought to weave a coherent narrative that explained when a resort to force of arms was both imperative and right—or, as in the glaring case of Iraq, at once unnecessary and misbegotten. It contained all of the elements that political communication scholar Robert Entman (2003: 417–19; 2004: 13–18) attributes to a political *frame*—it defined a problematic event and situation, identified causes and agents, conveyed a moral judgment that affixed innocence and blame, and endorsed a remedy or improvement. By carefully selecting, highlighting, distilling, and arranging these strands of information into a compelling storyline, it also presented a far from neutral version of reality, serving, in the words of researcher W. Lance Bennett (2012: 127), as a "meaning organizer" designed to promote a particular understanding and champion specific actions.

To that end, Obama's narrative of war employed a powerful rhetorical arsenal of dramatic words and soaring imagery intended to woo hearts as well as minds. Following the well-worn path of previous commanders-in-chief, he would draw upon cherished national myths and symbols—particularly the vision of America as that special nation set apart by unique history, institutions, and values—to provide a moral justification for its participation in the deadly and disruptive act of warfare.

As we shall see, Senator Obama's tale of why the United States had to fight in Afghanistan incorporated some core elements of Bush's rationale for war against al Qaeda, especially the notion of a virtuous country forced to defend itself against an enemy who hated the ideals it represents. But in its depiction of the language and tactics the U.S. should use in fighting terrorist foes it also differed in some significant ways from his predecessor's narrative, a divergence that became increasingly apparent as a newly-elected President Obama constructed his own arguments for how to win the battle against terrorism.

As I shall also examine in greater detail, the evolution of Obama's Iraq storyline followed a different trajectory. From the moment he first publicly reacted to Bush's proposed invasion of Iraq, Obama adamantly rejected both its moralistic underpinning and accompanying assertion that Saddam Hussein posed an imminent security threat to the U.S. Throughout his years as the junior senator from Illinois and then as the 2008 Democratic presidential nominee, he fleshed out his critique of Iraq but strayed little from his initial condemnatory frame. But as the official end of combat operations in Iraq drew near in the second summer of his presidency, Obama would modify his interpretation of what America had achieved, bringing it more closely into line with Bush's depiction of what the war represented.

Constructing a Resonant Presidential Narrative

Merely enunciating a presidential narrative, Entman (2003: 417–18; 2004: 6–8) reminds his readers, in no way guarantees that others will accept it as the prism through which they ought to view the event or issue. Presidential scholar George C. Edwards III (2009, ch. 3; 2012, ch. 2; 2003: 158–163) similarly writes that presidents—no matter how rhetorically skilled they might be—do not possess the power to command the public to attend to their appeals or support their construction of reality (also see Kernell 2007, ch. 7). How then might the commander-in-chief engage his national audience and capture its imagination in ways that further his national security goals?

Drawing on a wealth of previous research, Entman and Edwards argue that the president must first recognize the persuasive limits of the bully pulpit and eschew the illusory goal of changing minds and convictions. He should instead focus on *activating* existing attitudes and beliefs, channeling them into support by defining his initiatives or performance in readily accessible ways that clarify how they are congruent with what people value and hold to be self-evident. A frame's capacity to influence thus rests initially on what Entman (2004: 6) terms its *cultural relevance* and *resonance*—its ability to appeal to a society's shared ideals, aspirations, experiences, and self-image as well as its deeply-rooted fears and anxieties.

To achieve maximum impact, the tale the presidential frame tells and the connections it draws should be *salient*—that is, noticeable, understandable, memorable, and emotionally charged—to the broadest possible audience. Its narrative should, in short, strike a responsive public chord by drawing upon perceptions and opinions already stored in memory, bringing these habitual ways of thinking, or *schemas,* to the forefront of people's minds, and then linking them to desired outcomes. If this act of problem definition—or framing—is successful, large segments of the public should accept the president's position as compatible with their preferences and react accordingly (Entman 2004: 6–7).

By thus influencing *how* the citizenry think about and assess a political issue or situation, Edwards (2009: 63–67) contends, the president can aspire to set the political agenda, structure the terms of the debate in favor of his policies, and determine the premises on which the public evaluates them. From the perspective of the commander-in-chief, it is therefore essential that the creation of his frame and its accompanying narrative be undertaken with the utmost thought and care, particularly when American national security is at stake and he issues a clarion call for war.

American Exceptionalism and the Rationale for War

From Woodrow Wilson's resounding appeal to "make the world safe for democracy" to Franklin Roosevelt's call for the "liberation of Europe" to the Cold War and Vietnam mantras of "protecting the Free World" and containing communism, twentieth-century U.S. presidents sounded the rhetorical trumpet of war. America's two post-9/11 presidents have also readily assumed the mantle of framer-in-chief in a time of two protracted wars. While the immediate circumstances for waging each of these conflicts have varied, a common thread uniting their presidential war scripts has been reliance on a powerful foundational myth to explain what the nation represents and why it must heed the call to arms—American exceptionalism.

In its most basic form, the exceptionalist storyline goes as follows: Because of its founding ideals of liberty, equality, individualism, virtue, and duty, America stands, in the ringing words of Thomas Jefferson, as "the sole depository of the sacred fire of freedom" whose calling is to serve as a model for the world and lead others toward that light (see Lipset 1996; Domke 2004; Jackson 2005; Bacevich 2008b; Rojecki 2008; Toal 2009; Esch 2010). As international relations scholar Trevor McCrisken (2001: 65–66) notes, there are three interconnected elements of exceptionalist belief: The United States is a special nation with a divinely-ordained, uniquely virtuous role to play in human history; its actions reflect a distinctive commitment to the betterment of humanity through propagating core values of individual rights and dignity; and its path is always upward as it seeks perfection, destined to escape the cycles of decay and downfall that have befallen past great nations. Marking the 200th anniversary of the Constitution in his 1987 State of the Union address, President Reagan (1987) vividly expressed the staying power of this national vision: "The calendar can't measure America because we were meant to be an endless experiment in freedom—with no limit to our reaches, no boundaries to what we can do, no end point to our hopes."

The concept of America as a chosen nation, both distinct from and morally superior to all others, thus has deep roots in U.S. history and culture and is a worldview to which presidents from Washington to Obama have given full-throated endorsement. As diplomatic and military historian Andrew Bacevich (2008b:18) explains, "From its founding, America has expressed through its behavior and evolution a providential purpose. Paying homage to, and therefore renewing, this tradition of American exceptionalism has long been one of the presidency's primary extraconstitutional obligations." During times of war, presidents have been particularly inclined to embrace the vision of a shining city upon a hill, invoking their own variations of America's calling to provide a beacon of hope under the most stressful of circumstances. Bush's declaration at the U.N. two months after the terrorist attacks stands as a notable example:

> It is our task—the task of this generation—to provide the response to aggression and terror. We have no other choice ... We did not ask for this mission, yet there is honor in history's call. We have a chance to write the story of our times, a story of courage defeating cruelty and light overcoming darkness. This is a calling worthy of any life, and worthy of every nation. (Bush 2001b)

In the exceptionalist worldview, all American wars are noble ones where its enemies are treacherous and Americans are positioned on the right side of history. International conflict is therefore cast as a struggle between the forces of good and evil, not a contest over incompatible national interests. Bush's introduction of the phrase "axis of evil" in 2002 is illuminating, for it served the dual purpose not only of identifying U.S. adversaries as wicked, but also linking the contemporary conflict with a good war of the past by reference to the struggle against the Axis powers during World War II. Continuity of present policy with past triumphs is thus assumed, and as a moral force in world politics and the embodiment of universal values of human rights and liberty, the United States has a special responsibility to continue to lead.

As McCrisken (2001: 63–64) explains, exceptionalism undergirds two, often competing, views on how to translate that global leadership into foreign policy action: the U.S. as an exemplar nation versus the U.S. as a missionary nation. While the exemplary strand of exceptionalist thought advocates remaining somewhat aloof from the world's problems and leading by example, the missionary strand emphasizes more active intervention in the affairs of other nations, not to dominate but to help them achieve the political values and principles that America represents. But both forms of exceptionalism, McCrisken emphasizes, rest on the common assumption that the U.S. is dedicated to progress, improvement, and setting a standard of righteousness for all to emulate.

Secretary of State Hillary Clinton (2010) perfectly captured this sentiment in the following remarks to the Council on Foreign Relations:

> I think the world is counting on us today as it has in the past. When old adversaries need an honest broker or fundamental freedoms need a champion, people turn to us. When the earth shakes or rivers overflow their banks, when pandemics rage or simmering tensions burst into violence, the world looks to us. I see it on the faces of the people I meet as I travel, not just the young people who still dream about America's promise of opportunity and equality, but also seasoned diplomats and political leaders, who, whether or not they admit it, see the principled commitment and can-do spirit that comes with American engagement. And they do look to America not just to engage, but to lead … So let me say it clearly: The United States can, must, and will lead in this new century … For the United States, global leadership is both a responsibility and an unparalleled opportunity.

The U.S. thus becomes the benevolent world policeman in an environment of global danger and lawlessness, and it is the nation's calling as well as obligation to keep the peace. Even *realpolitik*'s strategic goals of U.S. primacy and security are thereby imbued with an aura of moral purpose (Rojecki 2008: 72).

American exceptionalism also contains what communication researchers Elizabeth Anker (2005), Richard Jackson (2005: 35–37), and Joanne Esch (2010) refer to as a belief in exceptional grievance. This idea is linked to Americans' notion of "chosenness," but emphasizes a unique sense of victimhood that reinforces its self-image as innocents on the world stage. The United States and its policies are not the source of conflict or war; its enemies are always the instigators, their motives invariably self-aggrandizing, lawless, and immoral. From the sinking of the battleship *Maine* to Pearl Harbor to 9/11, Americans are portrayed as the undeserving targets of irrational hatred and aggression, thus securing a ready justification for military responses against the perpetrators of evil deeds. As Esch (2010: 373) notes, "Reinforcing America's primary victim status at the hands of a vaguely defined enemy ... makes it possible for American military actions that are *prima facie* offensive to be understood as retaliatory."

A final consistent theme in the exceptionalist narrative is the superiority of American political and economic institutions, in particular the power of democracy and capitalism to bring about reform in repressive, corrupt, and inefficient regimes (Rojecki 2008). Exporting these institutions to other countries and rhetorically defending freedom, liberty, and free enterprise against all critics are essential to the exceptionalist vision of the American mission. Bacevich (2008b) and fellow historian Tony Judt (2008) also note the key role played by another American institution—the U.S. military—in this worldview. The bravery, sacrifice, and honor of its fighting forces stand as a representation of all that is special about the nation, and exalting and paying homage to its troops' heroic accomplishments becomes an essential element of presidential frames of war.

American exceptionalism's enduring cultural power is nicely demonstrated by the hold it continues to have over the nation's public imagination. Despite the worst economic downturn in a generation and two ongoing wars, an impressive eight out of ten Americans surveyed in a Gallup poll at the end of 2010 believed that because of its history and Constitution, "the U.S. has a unique character that makes it the greatest country in the world." Two-thirds also concurred that it has a special responsibility to be the leading nation in world affairs (Jones 2010). There is no greater illustration of exceptionalism's grip on the American mind than the lengths to which its two most recent presidents have gone to situate their justifications for war in the vision of the U.S. as the moral and institutional exemplar for the world.

Disseminating the Presidential Narrative

Even a compelling and resonant presidential narrative will not be successful, Entman (2004: 6) emphasizes, unless it is made easily available to vast numbers of citizens—and those individuals deign to take notice. A frame must therefore also achieve what he terms *magnitude* through prominent placement in the mass media and frequent repetition of the framing words and images. Edwards (2012: 47–61) concurs, stating that to reach the public effectively and sustain its attention a contemporary president must continually exploit the myriad communication outlets and platforms at his disposal as he reiterates his arguments in a world of message overload and constant opportunity for audience distraction and avoidance of unpleasant news.

The president, of course, is not the only performer upon the political stage who wishes to identify problems and offer solutions, and it is nowhere guaranteed that his will be *the* interpretation that wins widespread acceptance and establishes itself as dominant. Competing political messages tend to be abundant in contemporary America, as political opponents assiduously work to capture public attention and establish their perspectives as preeminent in the public mind. It is thus common for two—or even more—political frames to struggle for ascendancy and for the nation's response to remain divided (Entman 2004:13–17). Such *frame contests*, researchers note, are particularly common in the domestic policy realm but may occur in the sphere of national security policy as well (see Entman 2003: 418–419; Graber 2010: 303–310; Western 2005a, 2005b; Iyengar and McGrady 2007: 90–102).

There are occasions, however infrequent, where the dominant frame gains universal acceptance, remains unchallenged, and sets the preferred terms of public discourse and actions. Such was the case in the aftermath of the 2001 terrorist attacks, as the media and the public were mesmerized by the unanticipated, horrific events. All eyes turned to the commander-in-chief, and President Bush's tale of villainy, victimization, and retribution reverberated throughout a stunned and grieving nation and was unhesitatingly accepted across the ideological spectrum (King and Wells 2009, ch. 1; Jackson 2005, 2012). The official U.S. depiction of 9/11 so thoroughly fixed the meaning of the attacks and the need for a military response that it effectively blocked other American interpretations of what the event represented and removed from consideration all other possible actions, a phenomenon Ronald Krebs and his colleagues (Krebs and Lobasz 2007; Krebs and Jackson 2007) term *rhetorical coercion* (also see Entman 2003: 417; 2004, ch. 1).

But by the following year, as Bush extended his war-on-terror frame to encompass the invasion of Iraq, competing perspectives did push their way onto the public agenda. Although Congress deferred to the president and voted in favor of military action against Saddam Hussein, it did so only after some heated and well-publicized floor debates. And as events on the ground following Bush's premature declaration of victory gave lie to the presidential storyline of how the conflict was proceeding, the official narrative faced ever more impassioned challenges and heightened media scrutiny. For the remainder of his time in office, Bush would be forced to employ all the powers of the presidential megaphone to defend his interpretation of Iraq against staunch opponents and a rising tide of competing narratives (see King and Wells 2009, chs 2–5).

Edwards and Entman caution that there are other limits to the president's ability to disseminate his frame, not the least of which are the characteristics of the media conduits on which he depends to transmit his policy and performance narrative. Edwards's assessment that "setting the terms of debate is not a silver bullet" (2009: 68) rings particularly true for an ever-expanding media universe that exhibits a predilection for human interest stories and infotainment over less emotionally gratifying political events and issues and highlights the headline-grabbing but fleeting celebrity crises and scandals *du jour* over the persistent, thorny issues of governance.

Contemporary presidents may deliver more public statements about their agendas than at any time in recent history, but as researchers Matthew Esbaugh-Soha and Jeffrey Peake (2011: 4–14) emphasize, it has simply become more difficult for leaders to break through all the non-political media noise when, with the movement of a finger, anyone can instantaneously escape into a preferred fantasy world.

Compounding the president's message dissemination problems is the current tendency for even politically-attentive media organizations to emphasize political conflict and controversy over substantive analysis, highlight bad news, and push hyperbolic sound-bite advocacy and *faux* outrage over thoughtful, balanced policy debate. In a demanding, incessant, and highly competitive 24/7 news cycle where audiences increasingly gravitate to outlets that support their political convictions, presidents strive to adapt their messaging strategies to co-opt or bypass in ever more innovative ways what they see as the cynical and partisan filters of the traditional news gatekeepers (see Graber 2010: 96–101; Bennett 2012, ch. 4; Eshbaugh-Soha and Peake 2011: 4–14; Edwards 2003: 173–183; Baum 2003, ch. 1; Baum and Groeling 2010, ch. 1 and 9).

All is not lost for a president hoping to spread his narrative of war through the mainstream news outlets, however. Working in his favor are newspaper, broadcast, and cable journalists' standard operating procedures for covering national security stories, particularly in the early days of a conflict or crisis. Even in the post-9/11 era of media analysis, interpretation, and commentary where competing perspectives are readily presented, the voices granted fullest expression are drawn from a limited population of official U.S. sources and supposedly impartial experts (see Bennett, Lawrence, Livingston 2007, ch. 1 and 2; Bennett 2012, ch. 5 and 6).

From the 1970s to the present, researchers have uncovered a consistent pattern of U.S. national security reportage: Journalists calibrate their news judgments to the perceived level of their sources' political and policy clout and index their reports to the level of elite disagreement with the presidential frame (Bennett 2012: 15 and 21). The more powerfully positioned administration officials tend to garner the bulk of media focus, their perspectives ordinarily receive privileged treatment, and divergent points of view are usually presented only when they are part of ongoing debates within the Washington political establishment (see Mermin 1999; Zaller and Chiu 1996; Hallin and Gitlin 1994; Entman and Page 1994; Bennett 1994 and 2012, ch. 5 and 6; Entman 2004, ch. 4).

Media analyst Scott Althaus (2003) notes, for example, that there was significant reporting of elite oppositional viewpoints in the lead-up to the Gulf War as journalists exercised considerable discretion in proactively seeking out opponents and reporting their concerns—but, he emphasizes, these voices of dissent were limited to high-ranking, inside-the-Beltway sources. And once the war commenced in the winter of 1991 and those authoritative critics fell silent, the media frame followed the administration's script, effectively silencing the few who still dared to speak outside the boundaries of elite consensus (also see Entman and Page 1994; Hallin and Gitlin 1994).

Research also tells us that warning bells for the presidential war narrative appear when a military conflict drags on and/or unanticipated events occur outside normal institutional news routines. In such instances—the mounting post-invasion chaos in Iraq, for instance—congressional and other establishment critics become emboldened and the more the level of elite discord grows, the more likely the media are to unleash their adversarial role and highlight challenges to the president's storyline. Even under circumstances such as these, however, the power of a compelling narrative may prevail. In the dramatic and highly-publicized case of the Abu Ghraib scandal, the media and congressional foes deferred to the official frame when confronted with a sustained and energetic White House response that resonated with underlying public beliefs and values about the honor of America's fighting forces. As Bennett and his colleagues (Bennett, Lawrence, Livingston 2006, 2007) have documented, the Bush administration was successful in defining what happened at the Iraq prison as an isolated example of "mistreatment" by a few enlisted personnel rather than as evidence of a sustained policy of "torture."

The conclusion we can draw is that the president must be ever vigilant in constructing, disseminating, revising, and burnishing his narrative of war. While media deference to the prevailing national security frame is common as the nation marches off to war, over the course of a lengthy conflict such acquiescence becomes far from a given in the competitive and fragmented contemporary reportorial environment, as America's two post-9/11 presidents have—sometimes to their great frustration—been forced to recognize.

The Media's Narrative of War

Like the presidential narratives presented above, news reporting involves the act of storytelling—in this case, selecting from a vast array of events and issues a problematic situation worthy of notice, setting the scene and introducing the cast of characters, presenting an enticing plotline, and achieving some sort of satisfying conclusion. As Bennett (2012: 42–68) argues, the media tend to favor visually immediate, personalized and dramatized tales of trouble, conflict, and an attempt to restore order and normalcy—storylines, in other words, that have been found to resonate with the American audience. Often isolated from their complex historical and social context, these stories employ versatile themes that can be endlessly reconfigured to meet the audience demand for entertainment as well as information. Should the public tire of one plot, Bennett (2012: 48) writes, a twist in the script and a surprise ending can easily be inserted, as illustrated by the recent media shift to storylines that highlight unsympathetic, scheming politicians' increasing failure to provide solutions to the nation's pressing problems.

The media's 9/11 narrative demonstrates the preference for drama, emotion, conflict, and overcoming chaos. Numerous studies have documented how closely the media plotline in the aftermath of the 2001 attacks hewed to Bush's compelling frame: a virtuous, innocent, and unsuspecting country unjustly and savagely preyed upon by evil terrorists who hated it for the freedoms its people enjoyed and the liberty it represented, an act so heinous and destructive that the victimized nation's only recourse was to declare an open-ended war against the agents of terrorism and those regimes that supported them (see Domke 2004; Coe et al. 2004; Hutcheson et al. 2004; Domke et. al 2006; Jackson 2005; Entman 2003, 2004; Norris et al. 2003; Gershkoff and Kushner 2005; Nacos 2007; DiMaggio 2008).

Research has also shown that media elites were especially receptive to Bush's representation of an exceptional America, as editorial and opinion pieces in leading print and electronic outlets essentially parroted Bush's proclamations of U.S. virtue and condemnations of its evil enemies in the weeks after 9/11 (Rojecki 2008: 75–82; Domke et al. 2004: 237–238). In the months leading up to the 2003 invasion of Iraq, editorials and commentaries in the *New York Times* and *Washington Post* showed a similar reliance on the moralizing discourse of exceptionalism to justify America's need to confront the menace posed by Saddam Hussein, particularly in the wake of Secretary of State Powell's U.N. address on the existence of weapons of mass destruction (Rojecki 2008: 78–79).

But as previously noted, the tale of war the media choose to tell does not invariably echo the president's war script. As early as November 2001, for example, elite U.S. electronic and print outlets were beginning to downplay some of Bush's major war-on-terror themes and highlight their own competing interpretations of the conflict against al Qaeda (Kuypers et al. 2008, 2012). Unfavorable events on the ground, increasing dissensus among Washington elites, and the passage of time provide further important incentives for media departures from the official war narrative. Political communication scholars Matthew Baum and Tim Groeling (2010: 10–11, 34–36, 168–173) highlight the presidential/media framing disconnect as they present three testable propositions about the connections among presidential war rhetoric, the often harsh reality of war, and the media's response—the *Elasticity of Reality* hypothesis, the *Framing Stickiness over Time* hypothesis, and the *Negativity* hypothesis.

At the beginning of an overseas conflict, Baum and Groeling argue, the White House possesses a substantial information advantage that usually results in media acceptance of its rationale for war, but as time moves on and ambiguous or negative events intercede, that presidential edge recedes as journalists have the opportunity to assess the reliability of his assertions. The Elasticity of Reality hypothesis thus posits that the greater the gap between the administration's initial frame and what the media determine to be reality, the larger the likely shift, over time, to a more unfavorable depiction of war-related events and the president's interpretation of them (Baum and Groeling 2010: 34–35). The Negativity hypothesis—that journalists ordinarily prefer negative to positive coverage of political events—serves to buttress this tendency toward a skeptical and cynical media war storyline.

The Framing Stickiness hypothesis adds an important caveat: As subsequent events reinforce the revised media frame, the more entrenched it will become and the harder to dislodge. Even in light of new evidence that challenges the current conventional media wisdom, journalists will cling to the assumptions of their prevailing narrative and become increasingly resistant to any additional revisions (Baum and Groeling 2010: 35–36).

In a comprehensive quantitative analysis of presidential rhetoric and television news coverage of Iraq from May 2003 to November 2007, Baum and Groeling (2010, ch. 7) found ample verification of their hypotheses as media accounts initially paralleled Bush's highly optimistic frame of what the U.S. was achieving but then increasingly diverged from his storyline as dismal events in the war began to contradict his accounts. Even when the Iraq surge began to reap some benefits, the broadcast networks maintained a critical tone, shifting to a more positive storyline only after sustained evidence of progress. Although the more conservatively partisan Fox News reacted less intensely to negative events early in the conflict and more strongly to the good news emanating from the surge, it too followed this general pattern.

Political communication researchers Rebecca Glazier and Amber Boydstun (2012: 434) also offer three interrelated hypotheses about the dynamics of the presidential/media framing relationship in an international crisis. The first hypothesis, *Different Framing Dynamics*, posits that the president will adopt a consistent, positively-toned frame whereas the media will employ more critical frames as time elapses. The *Different Use of Frames* hypothesis states that the president will emphasize those few frames most favorable for his administration while the media will utilize a wider framing array. And the *Declining Frame Alignment* hypothesis predicts that the level of presidential/media framing alignment will decrease over time as the media tone trends more negative.

In their quantitative analysis of *New York Times* and *Wall Street Journal* coverage of the 9/11 attacks, the war on terror, and the Iraq War between September 2001 and December 2006, Glazier and Boydstun also found evidence to confirm all three expectations. Whereas Bush employed a consistent and focused set of frames predominantly about terrorism, journalistic accounts displayed a broader framing range and more varied narratives. The media frames were also significantly more likely to veer into negative depictions of the administration and its actions than Bush's predominantly positive storylines. And just as predicted, the initially high congruence between the tone and substance of presidential and media frames declined significantly over the five years of the study (Glazier and Boydstun 2012).

A closer examination of the shifting media frame of Iraq provides an excellent example of how these propositions played out in the early years of the war. Once Bush trained his war discourse on regime change in Iraq in early 2002, the media, still eagerly adopting his depiction of the insidious worldwide terrorist threat to America, privileged the White House viewpoint and were heavily reliant on evidence provided by the administration (Gershkoff and Kushner 2005; Livingston and Bennett 2003). As congressional expressions of concern on both sides of the aisle grew louder in the summer of 2002, journalists certainly highlighted them, but once Congress bowed to the president and elite disagreements subsided, the media again marched essentially in lockstep with the presidential argument that victory in Iraq was essential to winning the global war on terror (Entman 2003; 2004, ch. 5; Massing 2004; Bennett 2012: 162–166; Glazier and Boydstun 2012). It was only after post-invasion reports from Iraq continued to diverge dramatically from the administration's rosy "mission accomplished" scenario, and the much-hyped WMD could not be located, that the media storyline followed a different course and offered a decidedly more negative tale (Entman 2004: 115–116; Farnsworth and Lichter 2006: 92–93; Baum and Groeling 2010, ch. 7; Glazier and Boydstun 2012: 440).

In research conducted with Robert A. Wells (King and Wells 2009, ch. 2–5), however, I uncovered an important exception to the general pattern of increasing divergence between the media and presidential frames of war: The more unfavorable media narrative never extended to criticism of Bush's underlying rationale for military action against global terrorist foes. Even as journalists rejected Bush's justification for the invasion of Iraq and his assessment of how it was progressing, his overarching paradigm of the need for an open-ended war on terror was not called into question. Neither mainstream journalists nor the Washington establishment—nor, in fact, the young Illinois politician gearing up to run for his party's nomination to the U.S. Senate—constructed a narrative that countered Bush's well-entrenched frame that this generation must wage a defining battle against the terrorist menace. As Jackson (2011) and McCrisken (2012) have documented, Bush's apocalyptic assertion that America was now fully engaged in civilization's fight against untrammeled evil remained the nation's accepted truth even as his justification for Iraq as the epicenter of that battle came under heightened scrutiny and attack.

While the media's tilt toward negativity was evident in coverage of post-invasion Iraq, the idea of a virtuous, innocent, and exceptional nation undergirded journalists' more positive take on Bush's wider war-on-terror script. This uncontested aspect of the president's war frame endured even as the gap between the media and presidential narratives on other aspects of the Iraq story increased. It is thus apparent that when covering a war, the contemporary media do not operate in constant attack-dog mode, but neither do they act merely as supine transmitters of the White House war narrative. Continued investigation of the circumstances surrounding shifts in journalists' tales of war seems warranted as we search for patterns in media reportage of America's two twenty-first-century conflicts.

Framing War's Denouement

In any war, there comes a time when the public conversation inexorably moves from making the case for war and examining its progress to consideration of how it will end, what victory will look like, and how success should be defined. It is also the occasion to reflect on the conflict's big picture, assess what all the sacrifice in blood and treasure meant, and contemplate what the future might hold. Presidents thus have as much need for a compelling endgame narrative as they do for a resonant storyline that explains why the United States had to go to war in the first place.

Framing the outcome of a war presents more significant challenges than it did only a few decades ago, as President Bush seemed to acknowledge even before he ordered U.S. troops to Afghanistan in October 2001. Preparing the public for a lengthy and difficult engagement, he noted that war against the terrorist aggressors would be "unlike any other we have ever seen"—a different kind of conflict fought "without battlefields or beachheads" against a "new kind of enemy" and a "new kind of evil" (Bush 2001a). A year and a half later, even as he celebrated the overthrow of Saddam Hussein, he cautioned that the battle of Iraq was but the first step in a long road to victory in the war on terror (Bush 2003). Bush would leave office unable to claim a definitive military victory in either battlefront, but to the end remained insistent that the troop surge in Iraq was achieving its stated goals and that "al Qaeda is on the run in Iraq, and this enemy will be defeated" (Bush 2008a). It would be left to his successor, the only U.S. commander-in-chief to inherit two ongoing international conflicts, to put his own rhetorical imprimatur on the concluding chapters of those wars.

The media are also major players in the discourse of war's denouement, and the narratives they construct likewise play a key role in determining how a nation interprets the conflict's meaning and whether the public decides, in the end, that the burden of war was worthwhile. Evidence from previous research provides strong hints that in the case of the U.S. departure from Afghanistan and Iraq, the media would not hesitate to provide their own definitions of what America had achieved and impose their interpretations of what the two conflicts were all about.

Theoretical Framework and Plan of the Book

The winding down of America's two post-9/11 wars in the early months of Obama's presidency provides an excellent opportunity to examine the intersection of U.S. presidential and media frames of war as the nation strove to close the book on its current conflicts and turn instead to other looming challenges of the new century. There is much evidence to analyze from Obama's first two and a half years in office as he made full use of the presidential bully pulpit to promote his strategies for achieving closure in both wars and present his version of why America fought and what it had accomplished. As Obama highlighted his initiatives and honed his narratives, leading U.S. media outlets were also highly attentive to his war-related public remarks, thereby providing much news content to examine.

Two Case Studies of Elite and Media Discourse

In this volume I present two case studies of the framing of war's denouement. To provide adequate data for analysis, I have concentrated on the eight weeks surrounding two key foreign policy moments in Obama's first term: his December 2009 primetime address on the new way forward in Afghanistan and his August 2010 announcement of the end of U.S. combat operations in Iraq. Using the research technique of qualitative content analysis of Obama's speeches, primetime addresses, weekly radio addresses, interviews, and remarks to reporters during the designated time frames, I searched for the broad themes the president developed; his underlying assumptions, beliefs, and values; the symbols, images, histories, and myths he employed; and the storylines he crafted to explain and justify his course of action to extricate the nation from each conflict. I focus in particular on analyzing three facets of Obama's frame of war: first, the thematic evolution of his narratives for both conflicts; secondly, the amount of congruence with Bush's underlying war-on-terror frame; and thirdly, the level of reliance on the foundational myth of American exceptionalism to undergird his interpretations of the outcomes in Iraq and Afghanistan.

Also utilizing qualitative content analysis, I compare Obama's narratives of the U.S. exit from both conflicts to the endgame themes and storylines in the news and commentary of five leading U.S. media outlets—the *New York Times*, *Washington Post*, Associated Press (AP), NBC News, and Fox News—during the two time periods specified above. My first objective is to determine whether there was a general pattern of media subservience to or independence from Obama's war frame as both conflicts were drawing to a close; my second objective is to discover whether the five media organizations settled on common themes and drew similar conclusions or embarked instead upon differing interpretive paths.

There are, of course, hundreds of media outlets in the complicated and fragmented contemporary media ecosystem. Because my purpose is to conduct an intensive investigation of the thematic content of media presentations, I have sacrificed breadth for depth of information and thus limit my sample to a small number of U.S. outlets with significant national scope and reach during two time frames when media attention to the wars was high. I therefore make no claim that my sample is scientifically representative either of other leading media outlets or the myriad smaller news organizations across the country. I do, however, feel confident that I have selected outlets whose news and commentaries reach enormous numbers of average Americans while also catching the attention of national decision-makers.

The *Times* and *Post* are widely recognized as offering the most comprehensive national and international news coverage in the U.S., and the stories they present frequently set the news agenda for other media outlets and are closely monitored by the national political establishment. The AP, a not-for-profit news cooperative owned by its 1,500 newspaper members, supplies a steady stream of national and international news to thousands of newspaper, radio, television, and online outlets and therefore reaches large numbers of readers across the nation on a daily if not hourly basis (Project for Excellence in Journalism 2012).

Although the viewership of network television news has declined in recent years, its nightly and morning audiences are still vast, and television remains the source of foreign affairs news for most Americans, with NBC commanding the largest average evening audience. The cable news networks have also grown in viewership, and even though their numbers fall below those of the broadcast networks, their constant reports and commentaries constitute a significant portion of today's news offerings, with Fox News attracting a distinctly larger audience than its two cable competitors. These broadcast and cable television outlets also maintain a significant online presence and, like the *Times* and *Post*, update their websites throughout the day, frequently with breaking news from the AP (Project for Excellence in Journalism 2012).

Theoretical Framework and Research Questions

My analysis of presidential and media discourse surrounding the winding down of the two wars is informed by the hegemony, indexing, and cascading activation models of the government/media nexus. The *hegemony* model posits that ruling elites seek to secure consent to the established political order by constructing their preferred version of reality, embedding it in a society's underlying myths and core principles, and diffusing it through official statements and actions. They rely on "cultural workers," especially the media, to reproduce, amplify, and renew dominant meanings and values and secure public acquiescence to their ascendant worldview (Gramsci 1971; Carragee and Roefs 2004: 221–222; Jackson 2011; also see Herman and Chomsky 2002; McChesney 2002). The goal is to achieve political and cultural consensus through persuasion and argumentation rather than coercion; language and narrative, Richard Jackson (2011: 391) notes, thereby become an instrumental means for defining and interpreting events as the deep cultural grammar of a society finds expression in resonant promotional appeals.

In this model of hegemonic discourse, journalists act essentially as agents of those in power, privileging primarily the voices of the ruling group as their reportage relies on official statements and claims—the elites' manufactured reality about a situation or issue—more than on actual events themselves. Although political figures may disagree with one another, such infighting is merely over specific political means rather than important political ends, and leaders quickly close ranks against threats to their underlying beliefs and values as they affirm the congruence of desired political goals with what a society—and an acquiescent media—holds dear, accepts as common sense, and "knows" to be true. But hegemony theorists also note that a "crisis of hegemony" may occur in exceptional historical moments, weakening the influence of dominant ideologies and values. Such rare instances demonstrate that hegemony can be challenged and altered, and that the media may become the sites for the ensuing discursive battles (Artz and Murphy 2000; Condit 1994; Gitlin 2003; Hall et al. 1978).

The *indexing* model places greater emphasis on differing perspectives within the dominant political class. Contemporary elites, the model holds, frequently disagree about public policies and their implementation, and when such disputes erupt, the media provide the vehicle for transmitting divergent views. Controversy and conflict provide desirable storylines for journalists and the greater the level of discord among the powerful, the more these disagreements are presented in news reports. Thus, as Bennett and his colleagues (Bennett et al. 2007: 49–51) note, the media calibrate, or index, their coverage to the level of elite dissensus (also see Althaus 2003; Cook 2005; Bennett 2012: 15, 21; Entman 2004, ch. 1). But in so doing, the media privilege respected official voices, highlighting the perspectives of the politically well-entrenched and silencing non-establishment figures. This model thus rests on the notion of a delicate symbiosis between political officials and journalists as the latter compete for political access and a compelling storyline and the former seek a relatively uniform and deferential transmission of their policy initiatives.

Bennett et al. (2007: 75–77) have modified the indexing model to account for what they call *event-driven news* that originates from unanticipated events that occur outside of the routinized interactions between journalists and elites. In such instances, news organizations have greater leeway to exercise more independent—and often negative—judgments as highly-trained, professional journalists bring to bear their own analytical skills. But even in such cases, the official perspective tends to appear quickly as reporters look to those voices they deem authoritative to interpret the incidents. Entman (2003; 2004: 15–20) offers a similar perspective that he terms the *cascading activation* model, noting that while a national security frame ordinarily descends from the White House to the rest of the political system and the public, challenges to the president's dominant narrative—what he labels *counterframes*—may gain traction if a competing interpretation better explains events on the ground *and* captures non-administrative elites' and the public's habitual ways of thinking about those occurrences.

The three models thus differ in the extent to which they emphasize discord among political elites. But all stress the ability of leaders to establish the political agenda by constructing compelling narratives that are congruent with a society's deeply-held beliefs, core values, and sense of national identity. As Entman (2004: 17) argues, the more resonant a presidential frame—that is, the more it is in line with a nation's core principles and self-image—the less likely elites outside the administration are to challenge it, and the more likely the media are to accept the uncontested White House narrative. As in the hegemony model, the perspectives most likely to prevail under the indexing and cascading activation models are those enunciated by the most powerful players, a discursive advantage in the realm of foreign policy that ordinarily (but, importantly, not always) adheres to the current administration (see also Livingston and Bennett 2003).

The present study was also guided by Baum and Groeling's (2010) and Glazier and Boydstun's (2012) analyses of presidential and media frames of Iraq and the war on terror. As discussed above, their hypotheses highlight the variable of time, positing that even though the early stages of a conflict provide the president a significant rhetorical advantage and a wealth of positive coverage, there will be a shift to increasing media skepticism if the reality of war continues to differ substantially from the sanguine presidential narrative. And once the media have arrived at a more negative interpretation, it will tend to persist even in the face of improving conditions on the ground. Hence the divergence between the presidential and media frames of war should increase as years pass without definitive indicators of success, a prediction that held true for the years prior to the implementation of the surge in Iraq.

My research questions about media frames of the Iraq and Afghanistan denouements thus center on whether journalists' responses to Obama's endgame narratives followed the expected pattern of media suspicion and negativity even in light of the diminishing violence during the first two years of Obama's term and the positive news that American combat troops would soon be coming home. The research presented above suggests several propositions to test:

- Obama's endgame frames for Afghanistan and Iraq will highlight the positive elements of what the wars represented and accomplished, and focus on future prospects for the region, especially the spread of democracy and enhancement of U.S. security.
- The media endgame frames will be distinctly less sanguine as they privilege negative, event-driven news from the region; emphasize Washington-based political disagreements; and continue to question the wars' implementation.
- Neither Obama nor the elite U.S. media will contest Bush's wider war-on-terror narrative as the wars draw to a close; the frame of a virtuous and innocent nation forced to engage in a life-and-death contest against those who wish to destroy all the good it represents will remain America's received wisdom.

Overview of the Chapters

To understand Obama's frame of the U.S. exit from Iraq and Afghanistan, it is helpful to review George W. Bush's narrative of why America had to go to war, what had been achieved over the course of his presidency, and the prospects for success. I therefore begin this study with an overview of Bush's tale of how the war on terror would conclude in light of his surge policy for Iraq. To set the stage for my analysis of the media response to Obama's war narrative, Chapter 1 also summarizes how leading media outlets framed the Iraq surge and their assessments of whether victory was on the horizon as Bush completed his final term and enunciated his endgame narrative.

Chapter 2 presents the first case study of Obama's war rhetoric—his narrative of Afghanistan and America's struggle against the terrorists who attacked the U.S. on 9/11. Commencing with a brief summary of Obama's initial statements on why the nation had to fight the attackers and what the battle would entail, I outline his arguments for war through his time in the U.S. Senate and on the presidential campaign trail. My primary focus, however, is on the storyline Obama constructed as president to explain and justify his new policy to successfully conclude the war. What endgame themes did he utilize, how did he weave them together into a compelling call for action, and how did his war script evolve over the course of his first year in office? I also examine the extent to which he relied upon Bush's conception of the war on terror and how he incorporated the notion of American exceptionalism into his tale.

Chapter 3 examines the media's general narrative about Afghanistan during the early months of the Obama presidency as well as journalists' reactions to his new strategy. More than seven years into the war on terror, how did the media assess the status of the conflict and the prospects for victory? Would the five media outlets converge on the same themes, and would their storylines exhibit the skepticism that Baum and Groeling's hypotheses predict? In other words, would the media reportage and commentary follow the presidential lead or would the media tale of Afghanistan diverge significantly from the new president's carefully-constructed story of the war and its conclusion?

In Chapter 4 I turn to an analysis of Obama's frame of Iraq, once again presenting a brief overview of his earlier rhetoric but concentrating primarily on the evolution of his presidential narrative about the conflict he had derisively labeled America's "war of choice." What was President Obama's Iraq storyline as he assumed office, and how did his narrative develop over the first two years of his presidency? By the time Obama officially announced the end of combat operations in Iraq, had he arrived at any common rhetorical ground with his predecessor's depiction of the conflict and what it represented or did he maintain his initial, highly censorious interpretation? And I again examine how Obama tied the concept of American exceptionalism into his tale of why the nation fought and what it had achieved in the war.

As I discuss in Chapter 5, Obama's 2010 announcement of the U.S. troop drawdown in Iraq primed media organizations to pay attention to a conflict they had been ignoring since Bush's surge policy began to yield positive results in late 2007. But an increase in media attentiveness says little about the content of their coverage, and thus I address the following questions: Would the media outlets parrot Obama's storyline about the meaning of the conflict and the withdrawal of American combat forces? Given the war's difficult history, would journalists choose to focus on its chaotic past and still contentious present, or would they shift their storyline to the future prospects for Iraq? Would predictions about the persistence of media negativity also hold true even as the U.S. turned the final page on an unpopular war?

In the final chapter I draw together the results of my two case studies of Obama's and journalists' narratives of the Iraq and Afghanistan endgames and seek to determine what conclusions might be reached about the relationship between presidential and media frames of war's denouement. On the basis of the evidence provided by these two recent examples, is it possible to suggest any wider patterns that could illuminate the concluding narratives of whatever international conflicts the U.S. might confront in the near future? The search for that answer begins with George W. Bush's frame of war's outcome in Iraq and the media's response to his tale of how the surge would allow America to emerge victorious in the new century's defining ideological battle.

Chapter 1
Surging to Victory in the War on Terror

Bowing to the harsh realities of an increasingly chaotic Iraq and ever louder calls to pursue a different path in the war, President George W. Bush announced his new way forward in a January 10, 2007 primetime address to the nation. He opened his remarks with these determined words: "Tonight in Iraq, the Armed Forces of the United States are engaged in a struggle that will determine the direction of the global war on terror—and our safety here at home. The new strategy I outline tonight will change America's course in Iraq, and help us to succeed in the fight against terror" (Bush 2007a). For Bush, Iraq had always been ground zero in the existential struggle against America's terrorist adversaries, and his final two years in office would involve an intensive rhetorical push to remind the nation of why it was essential to maintain its resolve and emerge victorious.

As he had for the previous half decade, Bush presented a complete and comprehensive war narrative that conflated the conflict in Iraq with the global battle against those who had attacked the U.S. on September 11, 2001. His tale of a virtuous America so unjustly targeted and its ensuing contest against the forces of evil and repression continued unabated as he now tweaked his storyline to account for the proposed shift in strategy for Iraq. Consisting of three interrelated themes—military victory in Iraq was still attainable and vital to winning the wider conflict against terrorism; defeat would be catastrophic; and General David Petraeus, the new commander in Iraq, would chart the course to success—Bush's revamped Iraq script intertwined dire warnings about current conditions with a decidedly hopeful vision of future possibilities (see King and Wells 2009: 157–163).

Keeping America Safe in the War on Terror

To promote his strategy of increased force levels in and around Baghdad—a policy that observers quickly labeled a "surge"—Bush first highlighted the intimate connections among the deteriorating situation in Iraq, the ominous specter of global terrorism, and the dangers still confronting American national security. Dreadful consequences, he proclaimed, would come from a refusal to heed his call:

> Failure in Iraq would be a disaster for the United States. The consequences of failure are clear: Radical Islamic extremists would grow in strength and gain new recruits. They would be in a better position to topple moderate governments, create chaos in the region, and use oil revenues to fund their ambitions. Iran would be emboldened in its pursuit of nuclear weapons. Our enemies would

have a safe haven from which to plan and launch attacks on the American people. On September 11, 2001, we saw what a refuge for extremists on the other side of the world could bring to the streets of our own cities. For the safety of our people, America must succeed in Iraq. (Bush 2007a)

The president also repeated a key underlying argument from his initial 9/11 narrative about the profound gulf in worldview the attacks laid bare: "The challenge playing out across the broader Middle East is more than a military conflict. It is the decisive ideological struggle of our time. On the one side are those who believe in freedom and moderation. On the other side are extremists who kill the innocent, and have declared their intention to destroy our way of life" (Bush 2007a). In his State of the Union address two weeks later, Bush reminded his vast audience that America was still a nation at war, confronted by the "shoreless ambitions" of the terrorist enemy, a war that would not end until the terrorists' "radical vision" had been eliminated:

> Our enemies are quite explicit about their intentions. They want to overthrow moderate governments, and establish safe havens from which to plan and carry out new attacks on our country. By killing and terrorizing Americans, they want to force our country to retreat from the world and abandon the cause of liberty. They would then be free to impose their will and spread their totalitarian ideology ...
>
> In the sixth year since our nation was attacked, I wish I could report to you that the dangers had ended. They have not ...
>
> This war is more than a clash of arms—it is a decisive ideological struggle, and the security of our nation is in the balance. (Bush 2007b)

As he announced the surge, Bush's appeals thus remained firmly ensconced in what McCrisken (2001) terms the missionary strand of exceptionalist thought: The need for the U.S. not merely to eliminate those evildoers who currently threatened its security but also to provide the conditions that would allow the core values of democracy, human dignity, and equal opportunity to take root and grow. Only by so doing, Bush consistently argued, would American security be guaranteed and its mission to stand as an example for the world be fulfilled.

While the core elements of his initial war-on-terror frame remained in place, Bush did adjust his updated Iraq storyline to include a brief acknowledgment of problems with the invasion's rationale as well as missteps in the war's prosecution. His primary emphasis, however, was on leaving the past behind and exhorting all Americans to voice support for his plan to achieve a successful outcome in Iraq. An exemplary nation, he implied, could do no less than muster all its military and psychological resources toward the goal of keeping America—and the world—secure from harm even as events in Iraq had thus far failed to turn out as anticipated. America's destiny, Bush insisted, was still in its hands. Witness this passage from his State of the Union address:

> This is not the fight we entered in Iraq, but it is the fight we're in. Every one of us wishes this war were over and won. Yet it would not be like us to leave our promises unkept, our friends abandoned, and our own security at risk. Ladies and gentlemen: On this day, at this hour, it is still within our power to shape the outcome of this battle. Let us find our resolve, and turn events toward victory. (Bush 2007b)

In a press conference the following month, Bush repeated his warning of the horrendous domino effect that would cascade across the globe were the United States to fail to act at this critical juncture:

> [T]o step back from the fight in Baghdad would have disastrous consequences for people in America … The Iraqi government could collapse, chaos would spread, there would be a vacuum, into the vacuum would flow more extremists, more radicals, people who have stated intent to hurt our people … What's different about this conflict than some others is that if we fail there, the enemy will follow us here. (Bush 2007c)

And in his Coast Guard commencement speech that May, Bush directly addressed those still inclined to question the link between the battle in Iraq and the war on terror. Citing newly declassified intelligence data from 2005, the president described how Osama bin Laden had possibly enlisted the assistance of a key al Qaeda operative in Iraq to help organize and plan attacks against the U.S. Other similar threats still loomed, he continued; it was therefore up to members of Congress to step up and take appropriate action:

> The question for our elected leaders is: Do we comprehend the danger of an al Qaeda victory in Iraq, and will we do what it takes to stop them? However difficult the fight in Iraq has become, we must win it. Al Qaeda is public enemy number one for Iraq's young democracy, and al Qaeda is public enemy number one for America as well. And that is why we must support our troops, we must support the Iraqi government, and we must defeat al Qaeda in Iraq. (Bush 2007h)

Although the president remained careful not to promise specific results, his public remarks never wavered from the idea that success was possible in Iraq. And as the months passed, his pronouncements gradually became more positive. In March he pleaded for breathing time, noting that while it was going to require a "sustained, determined effort to succeed," there were some "early signs that are encouraging" (Bush 2007e). The following month he reported that even though the new approach brought risks, "day by day, block by block, Iraqi and American forces are making incremental gains" (Bush 2007f). By July, even when faced with a report that the Iraqis were failing to meet a number of political and economic benchmarks, Bush stated that he saw the "satisfactory performance on several of the security benchmarks as a cause for optimism" (Bush 2007j). And by late summer, he felt sufficiently confident to declare that U.S. troops were taking the fight to "the extremists and radicals and murderers throughout the country" and were "seeing the progress that is being made on the ground" (Bush 2007k).

But even though he presented an increasingly sanguine narrative as the year wore on, Bush never clearly articulated the precise timing or exact parameters of success in Iraq, content instead to fall back upon the words he had first uttered in the aftermath of the 9/11 attacks: "Victory will not look like the ones our fathers and grandfathers achieved. There will be no surrender ceremony on the deck of a battleship" (Bush 2007a). The particulars of victory were not what mattered in Bush's endgame narrative; of far more importance was its relentlessly optimistic tone as he never failed to play upon exceptionalist sentiments that progress and improvement are core elements of America's national destiny (see McCrisken 2001) and that strategic miscalculations in the war would inevitably be made right.

Mindful of a congressional backlash against his surge policy, Bush did speak out vehemently against House and Senate proposals to redeploy the troops and block funding for the war. At best, he argued, these efforts would undermine American fighting forces' ability to accomplish their mission; at worst, they would leave the nation vulnerable to further terrorist attacks. Imposing a "specific and random" date for troop withdrawal would, he bluntly noted, "endanger our citizens, because if we leave Iraq before the war is done, the enemy will follow us here" (Bush 2007e). He also warned that an arbitrary withdrawal date would be a betrayal to the U.S. military. Such a move would "pull the rug out from under the troops," Bush declared in August, "just as they're gaining momentum and changing the dynamic on the ground in Iraq" (Bush 2007k).

Integral to Bush's surge narrative was also the idea that winning the war would enhance the spread of democracy, an outcome that would make the world, and America in particular, a safer place both now and in the future. A democratic upsurge throughout the Middle East, he explained, would lead those nations to renounce terrorism, the hate-filled ideology that gave rise to violence, and the leaders who sought to spread it. As Bush proclaimed in his January address to the nation, "Victory in Iraq will bring something new in the Arab world—a functioning democracy ... A democratic Iraq will not be perfect. But it will be a country that fights terrorists instead of harboring them—and it will help bring a future of peace and security for our children and our grandchildren" (Bush 2007a). Here again, the exceptionalist idea of American commitment to human rights, liberty, and the betterment of mankind—and the nation's duty to ensure the global propagation of these values—undergirded the president's national security discourse (see Jackson 2011; McCrisken 2012).

Petraeus as Savior of the Surge

The novel component of Bush's Iraq surge narrative was the starring role it assigned to General David H. Petraeus, the man he had chosen to become the new U.S. commander in Iraq. Under the president's reconstituted storyline, Petraeus essentially became the embodiment of the surge as his character, competence, and credentials were paraded before the public. With his Princeton PhD in International Relations, authorship of the Army's counterinsurgency field manual, command of the 101st Airborne Division's drive to Baghdad, and appointment as head of the Multi-National Security Transition in Iraq, the general was cast as the leading military expert on counterterrorism and the ideal choice to lead the surge. For a president whose own approval ratings had seen a steady decline, it was a perfect opportunity to transfer the media and public spotlight to this captivating new national figure who represented the best and brightest that an exceptional America had to offer.

Bush even ceded authorship of the plan on the ground to Petraeus, admonishing members of the House of Representatives in mid-February that the anti-surge resolution they had been debating would mark the first time in history that Congress had voted to send a new commander into battle and then turned around and opposed "*his plan* that is necessary to succeed in that battle" (Bush 2007d, emphasis added). From that point on, Petraeus owned the surge as he and the new way forward in the war were irrevocably fused in the president's official war discourse. As Bush chastised congressional Democrats the following month for erecting a legislative roadblock to the surge: "Yet at the very moment that *General Petraeus's strategy* is beginning to show signs of success, the Democrats in the House of Representatives have passed an emergency war spending bill that undercuts him and the troops under his command" (Bush 2007e, emphasis added). Again referring to the surge strategy as "General Petraeus's plan," the president exhorted Congress and the public over the summer to give the commander "time to see whether or not this works" and "a chance to come back and tell us whether *his strategy* is working" (Bush 2007g and 2007i, emphasis added).

Congressional Democrats agreed in May to drop a withdrawal timetable from a supplemental funding request for the war in exchange for an agreement that Iraq meet a series of political and security benchmarks. The legislation specified that the president was to submit a report on Iraq's progress by September 15; it also stipulated that Petraeus and the U.S. Ambassador to Iraq, Ryan Crocker, testify before Congress in advance of Bush's report. Since Bush had given every indication that he would defer to Petraeus's assessment of Iraq, the commander's testimony would in effect become the de facto presidential report and a make-or-break moment for the future of the surge strategy (King and Wells 2009: 194).

In response to a reporter's question at a July press conference about what the general's forthcoming report to Congress might contain, President Bush used the opportunity to promote his storyline of Petraeus as savior of the surge: "I'm going to wait to see what David has to say. I'm not going to prejudge what he may say. I trust David Petraeus, his judgment. He's an honest man. Those of you have interviewed him know that he's a straight shooter, he's an innovative thinker" (Bush 2007j).

So thoroughly was Petraeus intertwined with the surge itself, so completely had he become the face of the new strategy, that even the liberal advocacy organization MoveOn.org highlighted his pivotal role with a full-page anti-surge advertisement in the *New York Times* on the first morning of the commander's September testimony. The ad displayed a photograph of the uniformed general above the provocative caption, "General Petraeus or General Betray Us?" and the accompanying text accused the commander of "cooking the books for the White House" (Moveon.org 2007). The none-too-subtle implication was that he was acting merely as the president's shill, unwilling to admit the unfortunate truth that Iraq was "mired in an unwinnable religious civil war." A reporter's request for Bush's reaction to the MoveOn ad provided him with a perfect opening to recapitulate this important component of his surge narrative. In one brief verbal stroke, Bush was able to castigate the Democrats and their allies while defending his commander, the honor of America's fighting forces, and the surge itself:

> I thought the ad was disgusting. I felt like the ad was an attack not only on General Petraeus, but on the U.S. military. And I was disappointed that not more leaders in the Democrat Party spoke out strongly against that kind of ad … It's one thing to attack me; it's another thing to attack somebody like General Petraeus. (Bush 2007m)

By conflating the persona of Petraeus with the surge, Bush had staged an impressive rhetorical coup: Well before the general delivered his September testimony, any negative depiction of the surge strategy had become tantamount to attacking the honor and integrity of this icon-in-the-making. Even MoveOn acknowledged Petraeus as "the architect of the escalation of troops in Iraq," further cementing his role as the key player in the unfolding drama of the surge while also solidifying Bush's martial frame of the wider war against terrorism.

Constructing an Oppositional Narrative

Months before Bush announced his new surge strategy, Democrats—and a smattering of high-profile Republicans—had argued that the only way to proceed was to extricate the U.S. from Iraq, and a number had gone public with their own proposals for a withdrawal of forces. In the wake of the president's primetime announcement on the troop buildup, opponents redoubled their rhetorical efforts, unveiling a loosely coordinated counterframe that consisted of three general themes: Iraq was not part of the wider war on terror (and was, in fact, detrimental to that effort), the conflict was unwinnable, and the only reasonable course of action was to initiate a drawdown policy.

For a number of Iraq critics, a grave concern was that the war had imperiled America's ability to sustain the war on terrorism. Speaker Nancy Pelosi's (D-CA) February remarks on the House floor encapsulated the arguments that the conflict in Iraq had taken the nation's eye off the real threat and that as a result, terrorism continued to fester and spread, and U.S. security remained in jeopardy:

> The war in Iraq continues to detract from our ability to fight the war against international terrorism effectively. We need to finish the job started more than five years ago in Afghanistan against al-Qaeda and the Taliban, and address other conditions around the world in which the appeal of terrorism breeds. The longer it takes to resolve the situation in Iraq, the longer resources and attention will continue to be diverted from the war on terrorism. (Pelosi 2007)

Pelosi's congressional colleagues also raised the issue of America's diminished capacity to respond to other potential military contingencies around the world. As outspoken Iraq opponent Rep. John Murtha (D-PA) stated in an April press release, "Our military readiness has deteriorated to levels not seen since Vietnam and our ability to fight future threats is severely compromised. Yet the President refuses to address this most vital issue" (Murtha 2007). Thus even as Democrats repudiated Iraq as part of the war on terror, they did not call into question the White House's assumption of the need to maintain a war footing against terrorist foes.

A chorus of leading Senate Democrats added their voices to the critical narrative of Iraq, publicly rejecting the notion that a military option was still viable. Patrick Leahy (D-VT) and Carl Levin (D-MI) labeled the war a "failure"; Hillary Clinton (D-NY) derided the Bush surge as a "dead end"; Joseph Biden (D-DE) declared the strategy was "doomed to fail"; and majority leader Harry Reid (D-NV) declared to reporters in April that "this war is lost." Opponents of the surge focused on the conflict's degeneration into a bitter civil war with American forces caught in the middle of an intense sectarian conflict, a bloody struggle, they claimed, that the weak and corrupt Iraqi government neither would nor could combat. The U.S. needed instead to pursue a political resolution. As a letter to President Bush from Democratic leaders Pelosi and Reid bluntly stated:

> Surging forces is a strategy that you have already tried and that has already failed. Like many current and former military leaders, we believe that trying again would be a serious mistake. They, like us, believe that there is no purely military solution in Iraq. There is only a political solution. Adding more combat troops will only endanger more Americans and stretch our military to the breaking point for no strategic gain. (Pelosi and Reid 2007)

And as the financial costs of the war escalated, surge critics raised an additional problem—the negative budgetary implications of the Iraq conflict, especially its contribution to the U.S. budget deficit and the limitations it placed on Congress's ability to fund important domestic programs and meet other pressing national priorities (Herzsenhorn 2007).

But even as the war's congressional opponents constructed a coherent tale of why the surge was doomed to fail, they were unable to fashion a unified policy alternative to Bush's new military strategy. In Entman's (2004: 14–17) terms, not only had they failed to mount a resonant counterframe specifically about the surge, they had also exhibited no willingness to contest the notion of open-ended war against the twenty-first-century menace of terrorism. A January headline in the *New York Times* prophetically stated: "Democrats are United in Opposition to Troop Increase, but Split over What to Do About It" (Rutenberg and Healy 2007). As Jackson (2005: 19; 2011) noted, the Democrats' rival discourse questioned only the wisdom of where and how the war on terror should be contested; it never rejected the underlying assumption that America must fight its terrorist adversaries and do so in the most efficient way possible (see King and Wells 2009, ch. 6). While Democrats continued to spar with the administration over Iraq in the weeks before Petraeus's September testimony, they continued to do so within the hegemonic discourse of the war on terror.

Media Representations of the Surge

In the months leading up to Bush's January surge announcement, media reports had been filled with all the problems confronting the conflict in Iraq, a storyline that had picked up steam as the 2006 midterm elections returned the Democrats to power in Congress, a result widely interpreted as a referendum on the president's failed policies in Iraq. The December 2006 release of the congressionally-commissioned Iraq Study Group's report on the status of the war also served to drive negative coverage, as journalists highlighted its somber opening sentence that "The situation in Iraq is grave and deteriorating" and emphasized its call for "a change in the primary mission of U.S. forces ... that will enable the United States to begin to move its combat forces out of Iraq responsibly" (Iraq Study Group Report 2006; see King and Wells 2009, ch. 5).

Although the president assured the nation that his administration would take the ISG recommendations very seriously and noted "the urgency of getting it right in Iraq" (Bush 2006), the media emphasized the deteriorating situation and the growing expressions of concern on both sides of the congressional aisle. Not surprisingly, therefore, national print and broadcast outlets' reactions to Bush's January remarks initially displayed far more skepticism than praise as journalists clung to their now-established storylines that Iraq remained a violence-riddled quagmire and that the president and Democrats in Congress were locked in a bitter conflict over how to proceed. But reporters and commentators continued to refrain from interrogating the seemingly settled discourse on the necessity of a military response to terrorism as they focused instead on the far narrower critique of the proper strategic path to follow in that wider conflict. The media were following the path of the Democratic opposition in acquiescing to the Bush frame of a war on terror while vigorously contesting its implementation.

The day after Bush's primetime address, *New York Times* chief Washington correspondent David Sanger emphasized the political wrangling and offered his own none-too-sanguine take on how Bush's Iraq surge plan might fare:

> Democrats in Congress are drawing up plans for what, at a minimum, could be a nonbinding resolution expressing opposition to the commitment of more forces to what many of them say they now believe is a losing fight. They will be joined by some Republicans, and may attempt other steps to block Mr. Bush from deepening the American commitment. Not since Richard Nixon ordered American troops in Vietnam to invade Cambodia in 1970 has a president taken such a risk with an increasingly unpopular war. (Sanger 2007)

An AP story the following day noted that the president's surge strategy "was slammed as desperate and even dumb" by many on Capitol Hill (Baldor 2007), and the *Washington Post* reported that even some key Republicans were not on board with Bush's proposal:

> More than 30 years after Vietnam, John. W. Warner (R-VA) is once again watching as generals propose additional troops. But this time, he's not staying silent. In a rebuke to President Bush, Warner is leading an effort to have the U.S. Senate declare a lack of confidence in the administration's plans to send 21,500 additional soldiers into the Iraqi war zone. (Shear 2007)

As noted earlier, congressional critics of the surge continued to voice their disapproval throughout the spring and summer of 2007, and media organizations responded with ample reports of their condemnations of Bush's plan and their calls to redeploy U.S. troops. Much of this coverage focused on Democratic efforts to force Bush to set timelines for a drawdown. A prime example was a late January *Times* story that noted congressional Democrats had begun to lay the constitutional groundwork for an effort to block the surge in forces and "place new limits on the conduct of the war there, perhaps forcing a withdrawal of American forces" (Hulse and Shanker 2007). Intertwined with the storyline of congressional disapproval was the theme that the death knell of the surge seemed likely and that in its place a troop drawdown appeared increasingly inevitable. In May, for instance, the *Post* quoted a spokesperson for Senator Reid as saying, "Sounds to me like the president has a Plan B after all, and that it includes timelines for withdrawal of U.S. troops" (Abramowitz and Baker 2007).

As the troop increase got underway in late winter, news reports were also filled with descriptions of continuing problems on the ground in Iraq, especially a rising tide of sectarian violence. Journalists presented doubts military officials voiced about the surge's prospects; correspondents stationed at the Pentagon and in Iraq also offered their predominantly negative assessments of how the surge was still falling short of its intended goals. The related interpretation that the surge was "too little, too late" was common in early spring newspaper articles. "Placed in charge this late in the game, Petraeus should not have to carry the burden of Iraq's probable failure," a late February report in the *Post* grimly stated (Sewall 2007), a sentiment echoed in numerous elite media accounts.

In April, NBC anchor Brian Williams reported that "U.S. military sources tell NBC News they're worried about new threats to American troops and the president's surge strategy"; Pentagon correspondent Jim Miklaszewski confirmed that "It's been one of the bloodiest weeks in four years of war. More than 500 Iraqi men, women and children killed, hundreds more wounded" (Williams and Miklaszewski 2007a). Two months later, NBC reported that no improvements on the ground were yet apparent. As Williams bluntly stated, "the so-called U.S. troop surge to secure Baghdad is not working." Miklaszewski concurred, declaring that "Four months into the surge, and the outlook is grim" (Williams and Miklaszewski 2007b). In a similar vein, military correspondent and best-selling author Thomas Ricks of the *Washington Post* quoted retired Army General Barry McCafferty's reference to the surge as "a fool's errand" and an unnamed U.S. intelligence officer's conclusion that as a result of the surge, "we are being led to failure" (Ricks 2007a). An April AP report also observed that most Americans called the surge "a hopeless effort," a far cry from the success so passionately touted by the president (Sidoti 2007).

By late spring, however, some members of the press were beginning to report "mixed results" from the surge (Tyson 2007). A typical glass half-full *and* half-empty assessment was provided by this report in the *Post*:

> If there is one indisputable truth regarding the current offensive, it is this: When large numbers of U.S. troops are funneled into areas, security improves. But the numbers only partly describe the reality on the ground. Visits to key U.S. bases and neighborhoods in and around Baghdad show that recent improvements are sometimes tenuous, temporary, even illusory. (Raghaven 2007)

As evidence of declining violence continued to grow over the summer, the theme that the war was lost was undercut, and media accounts shifted to other problems still confronting Iraq, including Iraqi failures to meet political and economic benchmarks. As the AP reported in late August, "Military efforts to stabilize the country have made strides in recent months, but political progress has lagged" (R. Burns 2007), a sobering evaluation that continued to haunt the Bush administration's claims that conditions in Iraq were improving on all fronts.

The media theme that Iraq was placing an enormous strain on U.S. military preparedness and on the fighting forces themselves also remained a nagging constant over the year. In early March, the *Times* reported that "any extension of the troop buildup would add to the strain on Army and Marine forces that have already endured years of continuous deployments." The article went on to point out that another stress point was the decreasing amount of time active duty units were allowed between deployments (Cloud and Gordon 2007). According to the *Post* in early September, senior Pentagon officers had warned that extra brigades flowing to Iraq had "stretched the military beyond the breaking point" and the chief of U.S. Central Command was worried that Iraq was "undermining the military's ability to confront other threats, such as Iran" (Baker et al. 2007).

As news out of Baghdad continued slowly to improve, editorials and opinion columns in the *Times* and *Post* also gradually began to reflect the more optimistic reports about declining violence in Iraq. In March, a *Times* opinion piece by several Brookings Institution scholars noted "a glimmer of hope from the surge" (Campbell et al. 2007); by July, their colleagues presented a distinctly more positive scenario under the heading "A War We Just Might Win" (O'Hanlon and Pollack 2007). In a similar vein, neoconservative columnists Robert Kagan (2007) and Frederick Kagan (2007) also penned increasingly sanguine assessments of the surge's successes as the spring wore on.

Numerous op-ed pieces in both newspapers did remain highly critical of the surge. *Times* columnists Frank Rich, Maureen Dowd, and Paul Krugman, among others, consistently voiced skepticism about the new strategy, and *Times* editorials presented particularly harsh evaluations, as exemplified by a July editorial calling for the withdrawal of U.S. forces "without any more delay than the Pentagon needs to organize an orderly exit" ("The Road Home" 2007). But these commentaries notwithstanding, a more mixed judgment about what the surge had already accomplished and what it still might achieve became increasingly apparent even in *Times* opinion pieces. Even Iraq's harshest critics in the media refrained from carefully questioning the fundamental underlying assumptions of Bush's war on terror and focused instead on far narrower and more strategically-based condemnations.

Throughout 2007, *Post* editorials had tended to be more cautious in their surge critiques and more likely to include both positive and negative assessments. As one July editorial warned, while Bush might be guilty of wishful thinking on Iraq, Congress should at least give his generals "the months they asked for to see whether their strategy can offer some new hope" ("Wishful Thinking on Iraq" 2007). By September, the *Post*'s editorial board was optimistic enough to characterize the surge strategy as "the least bad plan" ("The Least Bad Plan" 2007), an increasingly positive editorial trend that continued into the fall.

The Dire Consequences of Losing in Iraq

In its first analysis of Bush's January surge address, the *Times* highlighted the president's warning about what losing in Iraq would entail: "In defying mounting pressure to begin troop withdrawals, the president reiterated his argument that the consequences of failure in Iraq were so high that the United States could not afford to lose" (Sanger 2007a). Two weeks later, the paper reported that in his State of the Union address Bush had again raised the "nightmare scenario" of an Iraq "overrun by extremists on all sides," declaring that "violence in the country would turn contagious, spread beyond Iraq's borders and inflame the entire Middle East" (Sanger and Rutenberg 2007).

In the months following his surge announcement, President Bush continued to argue forcefully that failure to achieve America's goals in Iraq would entail disastrous consequences for U.S. and world security, and the media routinely repeated his words of warning. As an AP article in early February stated, "Those who favor Bush's plan and many who oppose it are in striking agreement that the consequences will be dire if it flops" (C. Woodward 2007a). As the media theme that progress was being made started to gather additional force and news accounts of the surge began to reflect a more optimistic tone, journalists accentuated the frightening consequences of prematurely withdrawing the newly deployed troops. The following selection from a July the *Times* report provides a clear example:

> General Lynch, a blunt-spoken, cigar smoking Ohio native who commands the Third Infantry Division, said that all the American troops that began an offensive south of Baghdad in mid-June were part of the five-month-old troop buildup, and that they were making 'significant' gains in areas that were previously enemy sanctuaries. Pulling back before the job was completed, he said, would create 'an environment where the enemy could come back and fill the void.'
>
> He implied that an early withdrawal would amount to an abandonment of Iraqi civilians who he said had rallied in support of the American and Iraqi troops, and would leave the civilians exposed to renewed brutality by extremist groups. (J. Burns 2007a)

A *Post* editorial published several days earlier similarly argued that, though withdrawal advocates would like to minimize the chances of disaster following a precipitous U.S. withdrawal, the hope that America could avoid a full-blown civil war, conflicts spilling beyond Iraq's borders, or genocide was at best an exercise in naïveté, and at the very least Congress owed it to the American public to allow the new strategy a chance to succeed ("Wishful Thinking on Iraq" 2007). A June *Times* opinion column by well-regarded military analysts Peter Rodman and William Shawcross also provided a similarly stark assessment of the consequences of failure in Iraq:

> There should be no illusion that defeat would come at an acceptable price. George Orwell wrote that the quickest way of ending a war is to lose it. But anyone who thinks an American defeat in Iraq will bring a merciful end to this conflict is deluded. Defeat would produce an explosion of euphoria among all the forces of Islamic extremism, throwing the entire Middle East into even greater upheaval. The likely human and strategic costs are appalling to contemplate. (Rodman and Shawcross 2007)

The unsettling specter of a looming humanitarian disaster in Iraq gained increasing traction as Petraeus's congressional testimony approached and the general highlighted the possibilities of such a dreadful situation. Commenting on the potentially horrific outcome of an early U.S. withdrawal for that nation's civilian population, Petraeus quipped in a mid-August *Times* story, "If you didn't like Darfur, you're going to hate Baghdad" (J. Burns 2007b). The general seemed well aware that the exceptionalist vision of America would not tolerate a storyline of the world's most powerful democracy standing helplessly by as yet another humanitarian crisis unfolded.

Framing Petraeus's Congressional Testimony

Over the course of the year, Bush's decision to link the policy strategy of the surge with his new commanding general in Iraq had paid handsome benefits in the amount and tone of media representations of both Petraeus and the decision to deploy additional forces to Baghdad. From the time the president announced the general's nomination, journalists applauded the wisdom of his decision. In late January, for example, an article in the *Post* noted that political and military leaders alike characterized Petraeus as "the best man to salvage the Iraq effort" (Ricks 2007a); a month later, another of the paper's reporters gushed, "If anyone can save Iraq, it's David H. Petraeus, the ultimate can-do general" (Sewall 2007). National media outlets were unanimous in their praise, frequently employing the accolades "brilliant" and "the best general in the army" to describe the new commander. Throughout the spring and summer, numerous news articles also referred to the surge as the "Petraeus Plan." The exceptionalist conception of the American military had become part and parcel of U.S. national identity even for skeptical voices in the media.

Journalists were well aware of how reliant an unpopular president was on his newly-anointed commander to sell the surge. As Ricks (2007b) wrote in a July *Post* report, "Bush has mentioned Petraeus at least 150 times this year in his speeches, interviews and news conferences, often setting him up in opposition to members of Congress." Some of these accounts explicitly noted just how far Bush had sunk in public opinion polls, as illustrated by this excerpt from an early September article in the *Times*:

> Only 5 percent of Americans—a strikingly low number for a sitting president's handling of such a dominant issue—said they most trusted the Bush administration to resolve the war ... Asked to choose among the administration, Congress and military commanders, 21 percent said they would most trust Congress and 68 percent expressed most trust in military commanders. (Meyers and Thee 2007)

As the best known military leader in the nation, if not the most trusted and respected, it is therefore no wonder that on the eve of his September testimony before Congress, the media spotlight indeed shone brightly upon General Petraeus.

In comparison, Ambassador Crocker was essentially relegated to the shadows, his testimony warranting little more than a footnote in media accounts as supporting evidence of what the hearings' star player enunciated.

In an earlier study of how the *New York Times, Washington Post*, Associated Press, and NBC News portrayed the new commander and the surge over the course of 2007, Robert Wells and I (2009, ch. 6) discovered that, by the end of the summer, these leading national news outlets eagerly awaited Petraeus's testimony, anticipating that the fate of the surge would rest on his report. As a *Times* editorial one week prior to his congressional appearance breathlessly put it, the general's report "could be the most consequential testimony by a wartime commander in more than a generation" ("Hiding Behind the General" 2007). The media assumed that the hearings would entail a clash of titanic forces as Petraeus faced an opposition intent on peeling away "enough nervous Republicans to create a veto-proof majority in favor of a withdrawal" (Sanger and Shanker 2007). What journalists ended up reporting was a one-sided contest between a heroic figure and his outgunned political opponents—a clash that was over almost before it began. The *Post*'s awestruck account of the general's appearance left little doubt of who had emerged as the clear victor:

> The best historical analogy for Gen. Petraeus's appearance before Congress yesterday might be found in the days of the Roman Republic.
>
> Then, returning generals wearing laurel wreaths and purple robes and riding in chariots were greeted at the city gate by senators and led through a 'Triumph' ceremony that included trumpeters and the slaying of white bulls.
>
> There were no animal sacrifices in the Caucus Room yesterday, but Petraeus— even the name is a felicitous echo of the Latin 'patronus' (protector)—enjoyed the modern equivalent: Taking his place on a raised platform in the middle of the room, the general, with four stars on each shoulder and a chest full of ribbons, was surrounded by more than 50 cameras and lawmakers lining up to pay respects.
>
> The lawmakers used their allotted questioning time to heap linguistic laurels on the visiting general, and to a lesser extent, U.S. Ambassador to Iraq Ryan Crocker: 'America's finest ... Our nation's most capable ... The capability, the integrity, the intelligence and the wisdom ... Nothing but admiration.'
>
> And that was from the Democrats. (Milbank 2007)

As the following passage indicates, the AP's depiction was no less adulatory:

> A Congressional hearing that lawmakers called the most important of the year opened like a rock concert Monday, with crackling anticipation and screeching

feedback from acoustic speakers. Yes, this show turned out to be David Petraeus, unplugged. Calm, measured, unflinching, the Iraq war commander walked lawmakers through the latest turns in the unpopular war, stopping well short of promising victory but asking the nation to give escalation a chance. (C. Woodward 2007b)

And with only a little less dramatic flair, the *Times* provided this interpretation of the encounter:

If it is true that a battle's outcome is determined before the first shot is fired, then Gen. David H. Petraeus won the first day of hearings before his microphone was turned on ... It turned out that the military was not on trial on television, but the Democrats were. The Bush administration let the popular and respected military commander make the case for maintaining troop levels, forcing opponents to tiptoe around the general's rows of medals and gleaming four stars. (Stanley 2007)

Another *Times* report added that the "epic confrontation" expected between opponents of the war and its front-line leaders did not materialize because only a few Democrats "seemed inclined to dispute with much vigor the assessments provided by a commander with medals on his chest and four stars on his shoulders" (Cloud and Shanker 2007).

Coverage of the hearings in NBC News emphasized the drama in the verbal exchanges between Petraeus and his would-be inquisitors, displaying a calm and stoic professional soldier more than holding his own against all incoming volleys. An excellent example is provided by correspondent Miklaszewski's description of the general's terse "I wrote this testimony myself" response to the charge that he was merely fronting for Bush: "A four-star general used to taking enemy fire, Petraeus shot back at his critics who accused him of shaping his Iraq strategy to appease the White House" (Miklaszewski 2007). For the media, it was yet another compelling example of advantage: Petraeus. For students of contemporary political discourse, it also was yet another example of advantage: White House national security narrative.

Media reports also repeated Petraeus's claims that security conditions were improving in Iraq as well as his grim warning of the "devastating consequences" of a more rapid pullout (Baker and Weismann 2007). His ability to work in 160 mentions of al Qaeda during his two days of testimony provided an additional boon to the president's Iraq-as-war-on-terror narrative, an accomplishment that did not go unnoticed in NBC's coverage (Williams 2007b). As it turned out, demonstrating military success was all that was required to maintain GOP support, and an article in the *Post* noted that the general's cautiously optimistic testimony was just the "political lifeboat" that nervous congressional Republicans needed to save them from being forced to repudiate the president's surge policy (Baker and Weismann 2007). As *Post* columnist E.J. Dionne (2007) surmised, with Petraeus's testimony, "Bush has pacified two of the three constituencies he needed to quiet if he was to continue with his policy—Republicans in Congress and the leading Republican presidential candidates."

According to media reports, Petraeus's suggestion that a U.S. drawdown to pre-surge levels would likely occur by the summer of 2008 also served to reassure some Democratic dissenters in the House and Senate. As NBC's David Gregory put it, "By recommending a withdrawal of surge troops beginning in December, Petraeus may have satisfied both sides of the aisle" (Gregory 2007). He also seemed to have satisfied the American public, as a Gallup poll taken during the week of his testimony indicated that Petraeus's favorability ratings jumped from 52 to 61 percent (Gallup 2007a).

The President, the Media, and the Surge

For the national media, Petraeus's testimony marked a decisive rhetorical and policy victory for the president, and journalists were essentially unanimous in their conclusion that, in the words of the *Times*, Bush and his communication team had finally been able to "take control of the debate on Iraq" (Stolberg and Myers 2007). It seemed clear to all members of the press that the surge strategy would prevail and that the Democrats could do little more than observe and grumble from the sidelines. And with the triumph of that media perspective, interest in interrogating the underlying assumptions of the wider war on terror essentially vanished from news reports and commentaries.

A relieved and clearly more confident President Bush addressed the nation the day after Petraeus and Crocker completed their testimony. Framing this moment as a definitive turning point in Iraq, he began his address with a dramatic flair: "In the life of all free nations, there come moments that decide the direction of the country and reveal the character of its people. We are now at such a moment" (Bush 2007l). Affirming that the surge was working, Bush embraced Petraeus's troop level recommendations, and to underscore his agreement with the general, the president made reference to him eight times.

Bush also left little doubt about the identity of the enemy in Iraq, incorporating the phrases *war on terror, terrorists*, and *al Qaeda* 20 times into his primetime address. In contrast, he mentioned *sectarian violence* a mere three times and *insurgency* only once. The president also introduced a new concept—*return on success*—the idea that "the more successful we are, the more American troops can come home," thereby suggesting that he, too, had a military strategy for withdrawal from Iraq, but only after the troops "defeat the enemy" (King and Wells 2009: 181). And in his conclusion, Bush returned to his oft-repeated theme that America's stake in Iraq was nothing less than winning the global battle against terrorism: "Some say that the gains we are making come too late. They are mistaken. It is never too late to deal a blow to al-Qaeda. It is never too late to advance freedom. And it is never too late to support our troops in a fight they can win" (Bush 2007l).

In media accounts across the board, congressional Democrats were depicted as divided and defeated in the wake of the Petraeus–Crocker testimony. The *Post*, for instance, noted that "amid division, some Democratic leaders appeared glum" (Baker and Weisman 2007), and the *Times* stated that "the struggle to settle on a party alternative illustrates the problems Democrats are having finding a way to take on the president that unites their party and avoids criticism that they are weak on national security" (Hulse 2007). NBC's *Today Show* host Meredith Vieira posed this query to correspondent Tim Russert: "So, essentially he [Bush] has won, Tim, hasn't he?" Russert responded that, "in terms of prosecuting this war the way he wants to, absolutely. General Petraeus's plan has become the Bush Strategy" (Vieira and Russert 2007). Once again journalists demonstrated a clear preference for privileging political conflict, controversy, and gamesmanship over wider, and far thornier, issues of the role and meaning of contemporary warfare. And in the media's storyline, Bush had emerged as the clear victor in the strategic contest over the surge as evidence mounted that violence was decreasing.

When No News is Good News for the Surge

Media coverage of the surge and the general who led it decreased significantly in the aftermath of the September hearings. While the Project for Excellence in Journalism found that Iraq comprised nearly 25 percent of the total news media hole during the month of Petraeus's testimony, by December the war accounted for a mere 6.2 percent of all news coverage. And media attention to the conflict sank still further in the first two months of 2008 as journalists geared up for what promised to be an exciting and dramatic presidential contest (Pew Research Center 2008a).

The declining media interest in Iraq appeared to reflect several developments. First, it now seemed apparent that the surge strategy had prevailed and would successfully withstand any congressional challenge; thus the newsworthiness of the Iraq policy debate was severely diminished even as Democrats tried to maintain their faltering opposition. Secondly, as the fall brought fewer casualties in Iraq, events on the ground there also became a less important media story. And finally, by late 2007 the elite media were beginning to conclude that America's exit from Iraq would be a *fait accompli* in the not-too-distant future (King and Wells 2009: 182).

By the end of September, the media storyline of the Democrats' failure to overturn the surge policy had been set, and their unsuccessful—and largely symbolic—attempts to impose funding cuts on the war merely fed into the media's newly-dominant narrative of the surge's progress. And with the triumph of the process-based, surge-is-working frame came neglect of the entire subject of Iraq, a development that elicited this sarcastic October op-ed piece by *Times* columnist Thomas Friedman: "Boy, am I glad we finally got out of Iraq. It was so painful waking up every morning and reading the news from there. It's just such a relief to have it out of our mind and behind us … Huh? Say what? You say we're still there?

But how could that be—nobody in Washington is talking about it anymore?" (Friedman 2007)

As the year came to an end, the narrative that the surge was accomplishing its intended goals held sway in elite media accounts, a perspective buttressed by a year-end headline-grabbing report from Petraeus that violent attacks in Iraq were down by 60 percent since June (King and Wells 2009: 181–184). Public opinion polls taken late in 2007 also fed into the surge success frame, with Gallup reporting that the number of respondents who thought the surge had improved the situation in Iraq increased from 22 percent in July to 40 percent by December. Gallup also found that 48 percent of the public believed the military effort in Iraq was going well or very well, an increase of 18 percentage points over February of that year (Gallup 2008a).

Could the U.S. Now Claim Victory in Iraq?

For all its efforts to promote the surge and the general who led it, however, the Bush administration was unable to alter the public's fundamental attitudes about Iraq or eliminate all media criticism of the war's achievements and probable outcome. Throughout 2007, public attitudes about America's ultimate failure or success in Iraq remained evenly divided, and there was no significant shift on whether U.S. troops should stay or be withdrawn (Pew Research Center 2007a). And aggregate American views about whether the decision to go to war was an error remained stable during the year, with 57 percent claiming both in January and December that the decision to invade Iraq had been a mistake (Gallup 2008b).

It is also important to note that even though surge critics constituted a minority of media voices, there were dissenting accounts in the months after Petraeus testified before Congress, with some high-profile columnists and commentators continuing to raise larger problems with the U.S. mission in Iraq. Andrew Bacevich, for instance, charged in a January 2008 *Post* op-ed piece that Bush's quip America was now "kicking ass" in Iraq was "pure fantasy." Reality, he asserted, was far more complicated and problematic, and the underlying dilemma of the war remained unchanged: "Continue to pour lives and money into Iraq with no end in sight, or cut our losses and deal with the consequences of failure" (Bacevich 2008b). It was a warning that Bacevich was far from alone in delivering.

The perceived tactical success of the surge and the popularity of its commanding general could therefore not eradicate all underlying public concerns about whether victory was even possible or placate those elite critics who ardently believed the U.S. never should have gone to war in Iraq in the first place. The Gallup News Service captured the import of these public and media trends when it concluded in mid-October that the surge and Petraeus's testimony had "bought time, but not support" to President Bush on the issue of the Iraq War (Gallup 2007b).

But as the violence declined both on the ground in Iraq and in news accounts of the war, the media, Congress, and the public began to turn their attention to presidential politics and worrisome economic issues as a growing mortgage crisis and recession began to crowd out Iraq for news space. And in the case of Iraq, no news was good news for the Bush administration, especially as journalists neglected to investigate the precise nature of the causal linkages between diminishing sectarian violence and the surge in U.S. troops.

Iraq as War on Terror

President Bush began his January 2007 primetime address on the surge by embedding Iraq in the wider war-on-terror frame he had constructed to justify the post-9/11 decision to invade Afghanistan. And just as Bush's rationale for war rested on Saddam Hussein's putative role in promoting terrorism, the Democrats' opposing narrative relied on uncoupling Iraq from the global battle against terrorist aggressors. Left unchallenged was the underlying notion that America had to wage a war against the terrorists. And because congressional critics did not make it a basic component of their opposition to the surge, the media also left the president's terror narrative—and America's largely-forgotten war in Afghanistan—essentially unexamined. Consensus continued to reign on terrorism as the greatest existential threat of the contemporary era, and in the absence of elite conflict over this issue, the media were content to ignore it. And as the political battle over Iraq cooled, attention to Bush's central front in the war on terror dipped as well (King and Wells 2009: 187).

Throughout 2008, a lame-duck president tried to remind an ever more indifferent public and media about the importance of succeeding in Iraq. But he was bucking some powerful trends as Iraq accounted for only 4 percent of the total news hole during the first three months of the year and public attention was increasingly diverted to domestic economic issues (Project for Excellence in Journalism 2008a, 2008b). Even General Petraeus's May congressional testimony hardly made a ripple in the news once it appeared he had nothing dramatic to announce. And in the absence of "important" news from the war front, media organizations began to withdraw reporters from Iraq and shutter their news bureaus in Baghdad (Londono and Paley 2008).

While Iraq and terrorism receded as paramount public and media concerns, the president continued to promote the importance of combating terrorist adversaries. Bush devoted nearly 50 percent of his final State of the Union address to the topic of foreign policy, with particular emphasis on the still-looming threat of terrorism around the globe. Echoing rhetorical themes from earlier years— and situating Iraq among a number of countries striving to cast off the yoke of terrorism and heed democracy's call—he noted both the justness of the cause and the significance of the stakes:

> We are engaged in the defining ideological struggle of the 21st century. The terrorists oppose every principle of humanity and decency that we hold dear. Yet in this war on terror, there is one thing we and our enemies agree on: In the long run, men and women who are free to determine their own destinies will reject

terror and refuse to live in tyranny. And that is why the terrorists are fighting to deny this choice to the people in Lebanon, Iraq, Afghanistan, Pakistan, and the Palestinian Territories. And that is why for the security of America and the peace of the world, we are spreading the hope of freedom. (Bush 2008a)

Highlighting what the surge had accomplished in Iraq, Bush noted that prior to its implementation America's enemies were succeeding "in their efforts to plunge Iraq into chaos." While acknowledging that work still remained to be done, he proudly declared that as a result of the increase in forces the U.S. had "achieved results few of us could have imagined just one year ago"—an overall reduction in violence, a decline in terrorist attacks, and lower civilian casualties in Iraq. He addressed remaining skeptics with these blunt words: "Ladies and gentlemen, some may deny the surge is working, but among the terrorists there is no doubt. Al Qaeda is on the run in Iraq, and this enemy will be defeated" (Bush 2008a). For America's 43rd president, Iraq had become irrevocably fused to the war on terror, and up until the day he left office he used all the powers of his fading bully pulpit to secure the narrative that the surge was key to success in the war against terrorist foes.

Speaking to a friendly audience at Wright-Patterson Air Force Base in March 2008, Bush emphasized the surge's role in promoting Iraqi freedom and democracy. He observed that America's military achievements had been accompanied by "a political transformation." It might feel like "distant history," he continued, "but it was only five years ago that Iraq was one of the most brutal dictatorships on Earth—a totalitarian nightmare where any election was a sham, and dissenters often found themselves buried in mass graves." Once again he admonished those who doubted the wisdom of the surge, and once more he conflated it with America's battle against its terrorist adversaries—with the unsettling specter of Iran added in as well:

> No matter what shortcomings these critics diagnose, their prescription is always the same—retreat. They claim that our strategic interest is elsewhere, and that if we would just get out of Iraq, we could focus on the battles that really matter. This argument makes no sense. If America's strategic interests are not in Iraq – the convergence point for the twin threats of al Qaeda and Iran, the nation Osama bin Laden's deputy has called 'the place for the greatest battle,' the country at the heart of the most volatile region on earth—then where are they? (Bush 2008b)

Throughout the year, Bush often returned to the theme of the surge's accomplishments, noting in a July radio address, for example, that Iraq's "sustained progress" was the result of the surge. He also announced that the U.S. had been able to reduce the troops' tours of duty to 12 months and bring home all five of the surge combat brigades. He even suggested that further troop reductions might soon be forthcoming (Bush 2008c). By November, it was clear that Bush interpreted the surge's results as vindication of his policy in Iraq. Whether intentional or not, he had replaced the "we" pronoun in his State of the Union address with "I" as he recounted the policy review that resulted in the surge. As he told the troops at Fort Campbell, "So I reviewed our strategy and changed course. Instead of retreating, I ordered more troops into Iraq. And to lead the surge, I chose a former commanding general of the 101st Airborne—the man formerly known as Eagle Six, General David Petraeus" (Bush 2008d; King and Wells 2009: 207–208).

In a December radio address to the nation, the president cited the surge as the proximate cause that would enable the withdrawal of U.S. combat forces from Iraq by 2011 under the new Status of Forces Agreement (SOFA). The departure of American forces would in no way signal defeat or surrender, he insisted, and ended his remarks with these encouraging words: "The war in Iraq is not yet over—but thanks to these agreements and the courage of our men and women in Iraq, it is decisively on its way to being won." He also made reference to the ongoing war on terror, declaring that it was still being fought on two fronts—Afghanistan as well as Iraq (Bush 2008e).

Bush also addressed the United States Military Academy and Army War College in December, delivering formal perorations on his foreign policy accomplishments. These included reshaping America's approach to national security in the wake of the 9/11 attacks, strengthening U.S. counterterrorism capabilities, and transforming the military so as to wage the war on terror (Bush 2008f and 2008g). Two weeks earlier, in an interview with ABC's Charles Gibson, Bush had been asked to comment on the one thing he was proudest of as president. He unhesitatingly replied, "I kept recognizing that we are in a war against ideological thugs and keeping America safe" (Gibson 2008).

On January 15, 2009, President Bush delivered his farewell address to the nation. He began with thoughts of the 9/11 terrorist attacks, mentioning Iraq and Afghanistan only within the context of his primary national security achievement—preventing another terrorist attack on American soil. He drove home the idea that Iraq must be seen as part of "a broader struggle between two dramatically different systems," emphasizing one last time the Manichean worldview that underlay his entire war-on-terror strategy: "Good and evil are present in this world, and between the two there can be no compromise" (Bush 2009).

For the president who had labeled Iraq the central front in his country's war on terror, the 2007 troop surge became the defining policy decision of his second term. To retreat in defeat, he asserted in his interview with Charlie Gibson, would have compromised the basic principle that "when you put kids into harm's way you go in to win." And to America's parents he gave this resounding promise: "I'm not going to let your son die in vain; I believe we can win in Iraq; I'm going to do what it takes to win in Iraq" (Gibson 2008). But as Bush ended his term in office insisting that Iraq was a battle the U.S. was poised to win, he also emphasized that the wider struggle against terrorism was ongoing. "Our enemies are patient and determined to strike again," he declared; "We must resist complacency. We must keep our resolve. And we must never let down our guard" (Bush 2009). And as he noted, it would now be up to his successor to carry on the fight. There was no question in his mind that even a Democratic administration would continue to focus on the nation's battle against terrorist foes and that the media and the public would not dispute the necessity of winning that existential conflict.

* * *

In his final months as president, George W. Bush's Iraq-as-war-on-terror frame took center stage in his public utterances. Even as public and media attention turned to pressing economic concerns and the 2008 presidential campaign, Bush continued, as he had since the attacks of 9/11, to highlight national security issues, particularly the threat still posed by terrorist adversaries and Iraq's decisive role in that on-going battle. His storyline of a virtuous, freedom-loving country attacked for its ideals and fundamental values still struck such an intensely responsive chord across the U.S. that Bush constantly sought to enfold his less resonant argument about winning in Iraq within the ascendant discourse of success in the wider struggle against terrorism.

As we shall see in the following chapter, neither Obama nor his Republican opponent John McCain challenged Bush's fundamental assumption that America had to wage a global war on terror. Both candidates, in fact, strongly affirmed their support for military engagement of the terrorist threat; their disagreement was over Iraq's significance in that struggle. While Barack Obama's election did represent a victory for the oppositional narrative on Iraq as a distraction from America's major security task, it also represented a significant victory for Bush's narrative of an innocent and exceptional nation forced to confront its worldwide terrorist enemies (King and Wells 2009: 209–210; Jackson 2011; McCrisken 2012). Bush's post-9/11 hegemonic national security discourse was thus poised to prevail even as one of the most outspoken foes of the Iraq War captured the presidency.

The elite media also continued to privilege the prevailing war-on-terror frame, echoing the candidates' unified stance on combatting international terrorism while highlighting their differences on Iraq. For America's journalists, however, national security had faded as a decisive campaign issue in the face of a deepening economic crisis and sustained evidence that the surge was accomplishing its intended goals. As Democrats relinquished their storyline that the war in Iraq was lost and failed to mount a successful rebuttal to Bush's frame of the surge's success, journalists acceded to the presidential narrative. The media then quickly abandoned Iraq and aimed their spotlight on other pressing problems. But they never repudiated the narrative that underlay all of Bush's Iraq rhetoric; reporters and commentators simply shifted their political spotlight from foreign to domestic issues.

One month before leaving the White House, Bush gave the following brief assessment of the driving focus of his two terms in office: "As President, I've had no higher responsibility than waging this struggle for the security and liberty of our people. After 9/11, I vowed that I would never forget the wounds from that day—and I'm not. *That day defined my presidency, and that day changed the course of history*" (Bush 2008g, emphasis added). As a new president was sworn in, a lingering question remained: Would Bush's vision of why America had to fight and what the nation had accomplished in its two post-9/11 wars outlast his presidency?

For Andrew Bacevich the answer was obvious. Declaring in a webcast interview that "the real winner in this election will be President Bush himself as his defective strategy carries over into the next presidential administration," Bacevich noted that both Obama and McCain were committed to a "fundamental strategy of global war" against terrorism and merely disagreed on the "operational priorities" of Iraq versus Afghanistan (Bacevich 2008c). Author Bob Woodward similarly reported that one of the architects of the surge, retired General Jack Keane, believed that once General Petraeus had been appointed commander in Iraq, "U.S. strategy in the Middle East would be locked in, no matter who won the 2008 presidential race" (B. Woodward 2008: 411).

Researchers now have evidence from several years of the Obama presidency to guide us as we seek a more complete response to this query. I therefore turn to my two case studies of how President Obama and the national media framed the U.S. exit from Afghanistan and Iraq, and in so doing seek a greater understanding how the 44th president and America's leading journalists interpreted the meaning and import of both wars.

Chapter 2
Disrupting, Dismantling, and Defeating Al Qaeda

From the moment he first spoke publicly about the terrorist attacks of September 11, 2001, Barack Obama framed President Bush's military response as both necessary and just—and one that he too would readily have undertaken. "After witnessing the carnage and destruction, the dust and the tears," he declared the year following the first U.S. air strikes in Afghanistan, "I supported the administration's pledge to hunt down and root out those who would slaughter innocents in the name of intolerance, and I would willingly take up arms myself to prevent such tragedy from happening again" (Obama 2002). And even as he vehemently criticized Bush's move toward war with Iraq as intemperate and foolish, Obama was careful to indicate that he did not oppose all wars, equating the fight against al Qaeda with two of America's most noble conflicts—the wars to remove the "scourge of slavery" and eradicate Nazi evil (Obama 2002).

In his keynote address to the 2004 Democratic National Convention, U.S. Senate candidate Obama took advantage of the national spotlight to underscore his contention that the deployment of military might was sometimes necessary to keep America safe and secure. "Let me be clear," he argued in reference to the 9/11 attackers, "we have real enemies in the world. These enemies must be found. They must be pursued. And they must be defeated" (Obama 2004).

After his election, Senator Obama continued to voice strong support for the fight against international terrorism and embed it in America's more than 200-year struggle to preserve its cherished ideals and values. In remarks to the Chicago Council on Foreign Relations in late 2005, he embraced Bush's martial lexicon, expressing approval of the "war on terrorism" and asserting that radical Islamic terrorists posed grave threats both to U.S. security and "our way of life" (Obama 2005). But while he concurred with the Bush administration that military power was key to America's anti-terrorism efforts, Obama insisted that Iraq had proven to be a deadly and dangerous distraction from waging an effective war against those who had actually sought to destroy the nation, and that only by extricating itself from that misguided Iraqi conflict could the U.S. hope to prevail over its true terrorist foes (Obama 2005).

A Defining Moment

Addressing the Chicago Council on Global Affairs in late 2006, Obama doubled down on his earlier assertions about the need to combat international terrorism.

He began his speech with words that foreshadowed Bush's September 2007 surge address: "Throughout American history, there have been moments that call on us to meet the challenges of an uncertain world, and pay whatever price is required to secure our freedom" (Obama 2006). The 9/11 attacks, he proclaimed, had created just such a defining moment, and it was now America's duty to do whatever it took "to hunt down those responsible, and use every tool at our disposal—diplomatic, economic, and military—to root out both the agents of terrorism and the conditions that helped breed it" (Obama 2006). The man who would shortly seek his party's nomination for the presidency had thereby placed himself squarely on the rhetorical frontlines of America's war against the forces of global terrorism. He was also carefully positioning his national security discourse firmly within the contours of Bush's ascendant war-on-terror narrative.

In his declaration of candidacy in early 2007, Obama framed the terrorist attacks as the galvanizing incident that had inspired a nation to unite against a new and deadly enemy. While the war in Iraq had sorely tested that unity of purpose, he stated, it was not too late to recapture America's common spirit of sacrifice and resolve. And he issued this stirring call: "Most of all, let's be the generation that never forgets what happened on that September day and confront the terrorists with everything we've got. Politics don't have to divide us on this anymore—we can work together to keep our country safe" (Obama 2007b).

Throughout that spring and summer, Obama more firmly situated the menace of terrorism within wider, interconnected dangers—from dramatic climate change and pandemic disease to the proliferation of weapons of mass annihilation—that could "no longer be contained by borders and boundaries." Old ideologies and outdated strategies, he argued, had led the U.S. to focus its anti-terrorism efforts on the single nation of Iraq, an approach with tragic consequences. But the globalized world of the twenty-first century and all its attendant problems called for a different mindset and recognition of a new reality—that "the security of the American people is inextricably linked to the security of all people" (Obama 2007d). America must therefore not abandon its preeminent role on the global stage, tempting though that might be to those grown weary of its misadventures in Iraq. The mistakes of the past six years had made the nation's current task more difficult, Obama acknowledged, but the threats of this century would only worsen were America to cede its claim of leadership in world affairs. "We must neither retreat from the world nor try to bully it into submission," he declared; "we must lead the world by deed and example" (Obama 2007d and 2007e).

Obama thus called upon American leaders to confront these new challenges with solutions that reflected the power of the nation's ideals, arguing that the 9/11 attacks had presented the U.S. with an opportunity to demonstrate that "the American moment" had not passed, that it could once again "lead the world in battling immediate evils and promoting the ultimate good" (Obama 2007d and e). That latter goal would be realized only when a new president rejected the current administration's "false choice between the liberties we cherish and the security we demand." Holding true to America's core values by rejecting torture and protecting individual rights, Obama maintained, would allow it once again to "set an example for the world," turn tragedy into triumph, and "write a new chapter in our response to 9/11" (Obama 2007f). Exceptionalism's dual conception of America as both the exemplar of liberty and democracy's ardent missionary had found a new and most eloquent proponent.

For Obama as for Bush, an idealized vision of American national values and character formed the basis of his national security discourse (see Jackson 2011; McCrisken 2012). Both men envisioned an exceptional nation whose ideals of freedom, human dignity and rights, opportunity, and commitment to progress set it apart from the rest of the world. Obama split ranks with his predecessor over his belief that the actions of the Bush White House had violated these most cherished values but was very much on the same page when it came to the perception that the terrorist threat was formidable and ongoing and that fighting the terrorist foes was inherently just. And his emphasis on correcting past mistakes in the conduct of the war served, as Jackson and McCrisken argue, both to highlight the exceptionalist claim that America always strives to perfect its actions and to further solidify the dominance of the war-on-terror frame by eliminating any incompatibility with the nation's fundamental principles.

Obama's bottom line was that military force was essential to combat the terrorists who posed a threat to his country's security. "Just because the President misrepresents our enemies does not mean we do not have them," he bluntly stated in late summer 2007; "The terrorists are at war with us." The problem was not that the U.S. was employing force of arms against the terrorist extremists; it was that it had been fighting the wrong enemy (Obama 2007f). The U.S. had to focus on its true foes, and Obama left no doubt that as commander-in-chief he would "not hesitate to use military force to take out terrorists who pose a direct threat to America." But this would require a smarter, more comprehensive and integrated approach than had been employed thus far. Military strength had to be combined with economic, political, and diplomatic strategies, Obama insisted; "We need to integrate all aspects of American might" (Obama 2007f).

In a July 2007 *Foreign Affairs* article titled "Renewing American Leadership," Obama repeated his call for the U.S. to provide "visionary leadership" in meeting the complex new threats of the twenty-first century. Again he argued that America needed to refocus its efforts on Afghanistan and Pakistan—"the central front in our war against al Qaeda"—so that "we are confronting terrorists where their roots run deepest." He also warned once more that time was running short; "Success in Afghanistan is still possible," Obama wrote, "but only if we act quickly, judiciously, and decisively." His anti-terrorism resolve remained unwavering. The U.S. had to defeat al Qaeda; "There must be no safe haven for those who plot to kill Americans" (Obama 2007e).

As the 2008 Democratic presidential nominee, Obama repeatedly pressed the case for focusing U.S. efforts on those who had attacked it on September 11. Expanding his argument that military strength would not suffice as the sole deterrent of terrorism, his analogy of choice now became America's lengthy Cold

War struggle against communism. In a July 2008 foreign policy address in Kabul, Afghanistan, Obama forcefully argued that U.S. security and freedom were under assault, just as they had been in the aftermath of World War II when faced with a powerful and ideological foe similarly "intent on world domination." The enemy might have changed in the intervening decades, but today's threats were no less ominous, the battles that lay ahead no less arduous. In both instances, he claimed, America's adversaries possessed "the power to destroy life on a catastrophic scale," and in neither case would there be a "single decisive blow that could be struck for freedom" (Obama 2008c).

Because America could no longer "be protected by oceans or the sheer might of our military alone," Obama held that it needed "a new overarching strategy"— one akin to the multifaceted plan George C. Marshall conceived six decades earlier to rebuild war-devastated Europe. Citing Marshall's admonition that the "whole world of the future hangs on a proper judgment," Obama called for the United States to join overwhelming military strength with wisdom and good sense, thereby shaping events "not just through military force, but through the force of our ideas; through economic power, intelligence and diplomacy" (Obama 2008c). The missionary and exemplary strands of exceptionalist thought had become inextricably intertwined in Obama's national security rhetoric.

Unfortunately, Obama went on to lament, America's current leaders had not devised an approach capable of meeting "the challenges of a new and dangerous world." Precious years and lives had therefore been wasted as the terrorist leaders remained at large, free to plot ever more carnage while the conditions that allowed extremism to fester went unchecked (Obama 2008c). He thus reserved his most impassioned words for Bush's failure to "answer the call of history" and face down the true threat of international terrorism. Instead of harnessing "America's might and moral suasion" to the cause of a secure, free, and prosperous future, the Bush administration had squandered "thousands of American lives, spent nearly a trillion dollars, alienated allies and neglected emerging threats—all in the cause of fighting a war for well over five years in a country that had absolutely nothing to do with the 9/11 attacks" (Obama 2008c).

In a widely-quoted July 14 *New York Times* op-ed piece, Obama (2008b) had written that "the central front in the war on terror is not Iraq, and it never has been," a charge he repeated almost verbatim the following day in Kabul. With the blunt pronouncement that "This is a war that we have to win," Obama declared that the U.S. could not afford four more years of a strategy that was out of step "with this defining moment," and he pledged as president to "make the fight against al Qaeda and the Taliban the top priority that it should be" (Obama 2008c). In a speech in Berlin, Germany later that month, Obama again cast the battle against global terrorism as this generation's paramount ideological struggle. Reminding his audience that "the Cold War born in this city" was waged not for land or treasure but for the hopes and dreams of a populace yearning for freedom, he equated the actions America had taken in the Berlin air lift with its current mission to "defeat terror and dry up the well of extremism that supports it" (Obama 2008d).

But this century's new dangers were too great for America to confront alone, he warned. Only by working in concert with allies could the U.S. rout the terrorists in Afghanistan and dampen the fires of terrorism through an effective worldwide campaign to fulfill the "aspirations shared by all people: that we can live free from fear and free from want; that we can speak our minds and assemble with whomever we choose and worship as we please" (Obama 2008d). Obama therefore urged European allies not to turn inward, not to shrink from important global responsibilities, but to renew the resolve to "remake the world once again." As he continued:

> If we could create NATO to face down the Soviet Union, we can join in a new and global partnership to dismantle the networks that have struck in Madrid and Amman; in London and Bali; in Washington and New York. If we could win a battle of ideas against the communists, we can stand with the vast majority of Muslims who reject the extremism that leads to hate instead of hope. (Obama 2008e)

By the time of the 2008 presidential election, Obama had constructed a compelling and resonant narrative of what the 2001 terrorist attacks represented and why it was essential for the U.S. to refocus on the struggle against global terrorism. Much of it was congruent with the Bush frame of 9/11: America, an innocent, freedom-loving nation unjustly attacked by extremists who were intent on destroying its way of life and the ideals it represents, was forced to defend its very existence through force of arms. Because this battle represented a transnational clash of ideologies against those who had no interest in compromise or conciliation, it would be lengthy and difficult, perhaps even open-ended. The U.S. and its allies would therefore need to maintain the fight and develop a comprehensive, long-term global strategy for removing the agents of terrorism (see King and Wells 2009, chs 1 and 7).

As noted above, an exceptionalist conception of America—that unique among nations past and present the U.S. has a dual providential purpose to serve as a moral example and lead the fight against evil—also undergirded both leaders' views of the global battle against terrorism (see Lipset 1996; Bacevich 2008; Rojecki 2008; King and Wells 2009; Toal 2009; Esch 2010; Jackson 2011; McCrisken 2012). It is thus no accident that throughout his public remarks on why the U.S. had to continue the struggle against al Qaeda, Obama paid homage to America's virtuous past wars and those who served in them. In his first statement on Afghanistan, for example, Obama (2002) noted that his grandfather had enlisted the day after Pearl Harbor was bombed, and that he had fought "in the name of a larger freedom, part of that arsenal of democracy that triumphed over evil." Obama continually emphasized the righteous nature of America's earlier wars, arguing that they had been waged to "uphold our most deeply held values and ideals" and bring forth the promise of an ever brighter future (Obama 2006).

What seemed to set the U.S. apart from all others, Obama declared in his 2004 keynote address, was the opportunity it provided for each individual, no matter how humble his beginnings, to achieve his potential and fulfill aspirations that elsewhere he might not have dared even to dream about. Citing his own personal history and improbable journey to the national stage, Obama presented himself as the embodiment of that American dream: "I stand here knowing that my story is part of the larger American story, that I owe a debt to all of those who came before me, and that in no other country on Earth is my story even possible" (Obama 2004). In Obama's conception as in Bush's, the U.S. stood as a beacon of hope for all people who longed for a better tomorrow—"Hope in the face of difficulty, hope in the face of uncertainty, the audacity of hope: In the end, that is God's greatest gift to us, the bedrock of this nation, a belief in things not seen, a belief that there are better days ahead" (Obama 2004; see also Toal 2009).

This belief in the individual, in the limitless possibilities to which everyone might aspire, is what the terrorists had sought to destroy, Obama argued. And America had to maintain the fight until it eradicated not only the terrorists themselves but the circumstances that gave rise to the anger, hopelessness, and despair off which they fed. It was the nation's solemn duty to remove the breeding grounds for extremism and lead the battle for peace, opportunity, and a better future for all mankind. As Obama had declared shortly after announcing his candidacy for president, "I still believe that America is the last, best hope of Earth ... The American moment is here. And like generations before us, we will seize that moment, and begin the world anew" (Obama 2007d).

Although Bush and Obama painted comparable portraits of an exceptional America and provided similar explanations for why it was attacked and how it had to respond with force of arms, the Obama frame of the battle against terrorism differed from Bush's in three specific respects that centered on how the fight should be implemented. First, Obama insisted that the U.S. military response hone in on the real terrorist culprits, not other foes who, brutal and ruthless though they might be, were not involved in the 2001 attacks or the spread of terrorism. America therefore had to extricate itself from Iraq. Secondly, Obama emphasized the non-martial aspects of the struggle against terrorism and the need to formulate a comprehensive economic, diplomatic, and intelligence strategy. Military strength alone could not combat the conditions that allowed terrorist extremism to incubate and thrive.

Obama's third departure from the Bush anti-terrorism narrative centered on the nature of America itself and what the nation and its core values represented to the rest of the world. Because the United States had to lead as much by moral example as by military might, Obama argued, its recent willingness to compromise basic democratic ideals and practices in the name of fighting terrorism had seriously undermined its efforts. The U.S. needed to reverse its policies on torture, extraordinary rendition, and indefinite detention so that America could again be worthy of its calling to defend democracy and fight the evil that threatens it. Once again, his rhetoric served to buttress the exceptionalist conception of a virtuous nation as well as the dominant storyline that war against terrorist adversaries did not contradict the nation's most cherished principles.

As president, Obama would have to oversee the formulation and implementation of the comprehensive anti-terrorism strategy he had so ardently spoken about as a candidate; he also faced the daunting rhetorical task of persuading a war-weary nation that to win the struggle against its terrorist foes, it would have to deploy additional forces, recommit scarce resources, and sacrifice additional lives to a conflict that would soon attain the dubious distinction of America's longest war. It was already apparent, however, that he would not seek to repudiate Bush's central thesis that an open-ended, militarized response to the existential menace of terrorism was essential, nor would he seek to re-write his predecessor's exceptionalist narrative of the American mission to stand as a righteous model for the world to emulate.

Winning America's War of Necessity

"Our nation is at war against a far-reaching network of violence and hatred," President Obama (2009a) declared in his inaugural address, and with those somber words he elevated the war in Afghanistan to a major foreign policy crisis that required immediate attention. He would shortly begin to lay out the parameters of a new strategy to bring the war to a successful conclusion and in so doing craft his own presidential narrative about why it was essential to win the fight against the terrorists. As we shall see, the completed Afghanistan storyline contained Entman's (2003, 2004) basic framing functions: defining a problematic situation, identifying causes and agents, conveying a moral judgment, and endorsing a remedy. It was also a tale, the new president hoped, that would inspire a citizenry battered by an economic collapse to refocus on a monumental threat to its national security that America had—at great peril—failed to confront.

Throughout his public comments in 2009, Obama incorporated six major themes into his narrative: 1) Afghanistan as a just and necessary war; 2) learning from America's failed war on terror; 3) a new approach to combating terrorism; 4) America's fighting forces as exemplars of the nation's exceptionalism; 5) surging and exiting from Afghanistan; and 6) constructing a new definition of victory. For more than 10 months, Obama concentrated on his first three themes, carefully laying out the nature of the U.S. commitment in Afghanistan and the argument for why it was essential to develop a new strategy. In early November, in response to a deadly shooting rampage on a U.S. Army base, he focused on the heroism and sacrifices of America's military, and at the beginning of December, he finally unveiled his new way forward, explained why it was the path America had to follow, and laid out the metrics for success. I shall examine each of these themes in turn, and then present the final narrative that the president constructed to explain and defend his Afghanistan policy. In so doing, I shall demonstrate that even as the U.S. prepared to exit from the conflict, Obama's rhetorical construction of America at war reflected far more continuity than change from his predecessor's frame of a global war on terrorism.

A Just and Necessary War

As of the date of Obama's inauguration, America had been at war against al Qaeda for close to seven and a half years, and throughout the remainder of 2009 he sought to remind the public of the magnitude of the atrocities that had been committed against unsuspecting and blameless civilians. "The United States of America did not choose to fight a war in Afghanistan," Obama explained in his March 27 remarks on the conflict: "Nearly 3,000 of our people were killed on September 11, 2001, for doing nothing more than going about their daily lives" (Obama 2009l). In a much-heralded June speech in Cairo, he informed a global audience that America did not go to war in Afghanistan "by choice, we went because of necessity ... Let us be clear: al Qaeda killed nearly 3,000 people on that day. The victims were innocent men, women and children from America and many other nations who had done nothing to harm anybody. And yet al Qaeda chose to ruthlessly murder these people ..." (Obama 2009q). And as he announced the troop surge on December 1, Obama reiterated the reasons why the U.S. had been compelled to fight:

> We did not ask for this fight. On September 11, 2001, 19 men hijacked four airplanes and used them to murder nearly 3,000 people. They struck at our military and economic nerve centers. They took the lives of innocent men, women, and children without regard to their faith or race or station ...
>
> As we know, these men belonged to al Qaeda—a group of extremists who have distorted and defiled Islam, one of the world's great religions, to justify the slaughter of innocents ... (Obama 2009ee)

Obama believed that given the nature of the attacks and the enemy that had conceived and executed them, America had no choice but to respond with a declaration of war against al Qaeda. At the State Department shortly after he took the oath of office, the new president proclaimed that "America will be unyielding in its defense of its security and relentless in its pursuit of those who would carry out terrorism or threaten the United States" (Obama 2009b). Job one, Obama assured the Marines at Camp Lejeune in late February, would always be preserving "the safety of the American people," and the first line of defense was to unleash the full might of U.S. military force (Obama 2009g).

Even a cursory reading of Obama's public statements indicates that he did not hesitate to affix the label *war* to America's battle with the terrorists, and examples abound throughout his first year in office. "Our nation is at war," he declared in his inaugural address; "We're still at war with terrorists in Afghanistan and Pakistan," he said at the National Defense University in March; "We are indeed at war with al Qaeda and its affiliates," he stated in national security remarks two months later; and to the Nobel audience in Oslo at the end of the year he again repeated the phrase, "We are at war" (Obama 2009a, 2009j, 2009p, 2009ff). In a

March interview, Bob Schieffer, host of CBS News's *Face the Nation*, had posed the following query to the president: "This has really now become your war, hasn't it?" Obama offered this curt and pointed rejoinder: "I think it's America's war," and he immediately emphasized that "It's the same war that we initiated after 9/11, as a consequence of those attacks on 3,000 Americans who were just going about their daily round" (Obama 2009m).

But as observers soon noted, within days of his inauguration Obama had quietly but decisively done away with his predecessor's sweeping *global war on terror* catchphrase. In an interview with the Arab television network Al Arabiya on January 27, he seemed eager to reframe Bush's terror discourse in narrower and more focused terms. Asked to comment on his disinclination to use the broad terror narrative of his predecessor, Obama agreed that "the language we use matters," and that his administration would be careful to distinguish between organizations like al Qaeda that espoused violence and those that merely had policy disagreements with the U.S. (2009c).

In an early February interview with CNN's Anderson Cooper, Obama again addressed his discursive drawdown of Bush's war-on-terror lexicon, stating that while it was important to recognize that "we have a battle or a war against some terrorist organizations," it did not amount to a limitless war against unknown, amorphous enemies and the fear their tactics engendered (Obama 2009d). The U.S. had identified a specific enemy—al Qaeda and those who continued to shelter and support it—and it was essential, Obama insisted, to concentrate all of the nation's efforts on this particular foe. By failing to focus on the real enemy, America had hobbled its anti-terrorism efforts and put its security at risk. The Bush White House had engaged for far too long in what had become a policy of drift and delay (Obama 2009b). And because of its often careless choice of language, the previous administration had also alienated many who had originally rallied to America's cause. As he went on to emphasize, "Words matter in this situation because one of the ways we're going to win this struggle is through the battle of hearts and minds" (Obama 2009d).

In his inaugural address, Obama sought an apt replacement for Bush's signature phrase that would do justice to the U.S. engagement in Afghanistan. He thus spoke not of the war on terror but, as previously noted, of war against a "far-reaching network of violence and hatred." Two days later, he referred to "our enduring struggle against terrorism and extremism," and in his speech on Afghanistan in late March, he described the conflict as a "campaign against extremism" (Obama 2009a, 2009b, 2009l). In remarks on national security in late May, he said America must "take the fight to the extremists" who attacked it on 9/11; to his worldwide audience in Cairo, Obama declared that the U.S. had to "relentlessly confront violent extremists who pose a grave threat to our security"; and in his primetime address on the troop surge, he spoke of "the struggle against violent extremism" (Obama 2009p, 2009q, 2009ee).

Although he seemed unable to settle on a resonant sound bite to describe America's fight against al Qaeda, one fact was readily apparent: President

Obama refused to employ his predecessor's preferred terminology of a war on terror. And over the course of the year, even the terms *terrorist/terrorism* would increasingly be replaced by the apparently less politically encumbered labels of *extremist/extremism*. In his December West Point address on his new strategy for Afghanistan, it is noteworthy that Obama employed the former terms only three times, while the latter appeared a total of nine times (Obama 2009ee).

Obama believed that America had been attacked because of the noble principles it held so dearly, and he sought to ensure that neither intemperate language nor questionable actions would undermine the moral basis of the nation's leadership. "To overcome extremism," he declared in a February address before a joint session of Congress, "we must also be vigilant in upholding the values our troops defend, because there is no force in the world more powerful than the example of America" (Obama 2009f). A few weeks later, in remarks at the National Defense University, Obama enumerated the ideals that made America the model for the world. "The true strength of our nation," he told the audience, "comes not from the might of our arms or the scale of our wealth, it comes from the power of our ideals: democracy, liberty, equality, justice, and unyielding hope" (Obama 2009j).

The Bush administration's war-on-terror rhetoric had cast too wide a net, Obama maintained, and one very troubling consequence was that it had led many to assume America was at war with Islam itself. He was therefore careful to reassure Muslims around the world that he did not equate an entire religion with the abhorrent deeds of a small minority of violent jihadists. The extremists who promoted conflict "by distorting faith," he stated in a speech to the U.N. General Assembly, had been "discredited and isolated" because they offered "nothing but hatred and destruction" (Obama 2009u). America and Islam "are not exclusive," he insisted in his Cairo address: "Instead, they overlap, and share common principles—principles of justice and progress; tolerance and the dignity of all human beings" (2009q).

While he viewed America as that exceptional nation whose ideals "still light the world," Obama acknowledged that over the course of its history the U.S. had sometimes violated its most fundamental principles. But America's general path had been a righteous one, and using its values "as a compass," it had moved consistently to overturn past wrongs (Obama 2009p). It was therefore time to recognize that the U.S. had gotten off course in its battle against terrorism, and admit that the force of its example had been significantly undercut by some of the tactics it had employed (Obama 2009a). For too many people both at home and abroad, he argued, the war-on-terror rhetoric seemed to condone even the harshest methods of extracting information as well as the abrogation of individual rights in the name of preserving national security.

Having proclaimed in his inaugural address that "we reject as false the choice between our safety and our ideals," Obama acted quickly to underscore his rhetorical shift with policy changes, announcing the closure of the Guantanamo Bay detention facility within the year, the termination of harsh interrogation techniques, reforms in U.S. military commissions, and an end to the CIA's secret prisons. The executive orders he had just signed, the president stated on January 22, "should send an unmistakable signal that our actions in defense of liberty will be just as our cause, and that we the people will uphold our fundamental values as vigilantly as we protect our security. Once again, America's moral example must be the bedrock and the beacon of our global leadership" (Obama 2009b). His goal of eliminating the gap between unsavory wartime words and actions and the nation's guiding principles had finally, the president was pleased to declare, been accomplished.

The week before his March address on Afghanistan, Obama was interviewed by Steve Kroft on CBS's *60 Minutes*. Kroft asked the president about his reaction to former Vice President Cheney's charge that Obama's willingness to shut down Guantanamo and change the way prisoners were treated and interrogated was actually making America weaker and more vulnerable to another attack. Obama's reply was swift and uncompromising: "I fundamentally disagree," he stated; "I think he's drawing the wrong lesson from history." As the president continued,

> The facts don't bear him out ... That attitude, that philosophy has done incredible damage to our image and position in the world. I mean, the fact of the matter is after all these years how many convictions actually came out of Guantanamo? How many terrorists have actually been brought to justice under the philosophy that is being promoted by Vice President Cheney? It hasn't made us safer. What it has been is a great advertisement for anti-American sentiment. Which means that there is constant effective recruitment of Arab fighters and Muslim fighters against U.S. interests all around the world. (Obama 2009k)

The attacks of 9/11 had been "an enormous trauma to our country," Obama admitted in his Cairo address in early June, and the fear and anger that it provoked were "understandable." But that could not justify acting "contrary to our ideals" (Obama 2009q). As he remarked in his December Nobel Peace Prize acceptance speech,

> I believe the United States of America must remain a standard bearer in the conduct of war. That is what makes us different from those whom we fight. That is a source of our strength. That is why I prohibited torture. That is why I ordered the prison at Guantanamo Bay closed. And that is why I have reaffirmed America's commitment to the Geneva Conventions. We lose ourselves when we compromise the very ideals that we fight to defend. (Obama 2009ff)

In his Oslo remarks, Obama capped off his 2009 comments on Afghanistan by reflecting on whether there could ever be a truly "just war." Noting that he was living testimony to the moral power of the civil rights movement's policy of non-violence, the president nonetheless defended the use of force under certain horrific circumstances. Fighting to end the carnage wrought by the Third Reich was one such instance; responding with military might to the unprovoked murder of thousands on 9/11 was another (Obama 2009ff).

To an audience that had gathered to celebrate the ideal of peace, Obama outlined his philosophy of war. It was grounded in theologian Reinhold Niebuhr's (1952) conception of the darker side of human nature and based on the hard truth that violent conflict had been part of the human condition since the dawn of man and would remain so for the foreseeable future. There thus were occasions when war—or the threat thereof—was the only option to redress a grievous wrong, make right a massive injustice. Paraphrasing the man he had deemed one of his favorite philosophers (see Brooks 2007), Obama stated categorically that "Evil does exist in this world." As a consequence, "A non-violent movement could not have halted Hitler's armies. Negotiations cannot convince al Qaeda's leaders to lay down their arms. To say that force may sometimes be necessary is not a call to cynicism—it is a recognition of history, the imperfections of man and the limits of reason." Obama concluded with "I face the world as it is," noting that, when man's inhumanity to man led to the slaughter of innocents and the suffering of many, "the use of force was not only necessary but morally justified" (Obama 2009ff; see also Kaplan 2009).

While Obama believed that there were times when the ultimate expression of "human folly" could be quelled only through military might, he was also quick to warn that no matter how much a country might be compelled to resort to force of arms, "War promises human tragedy ... War itself is never glorious, and we must never trumpet it as such." Nations that used the "instruments of war" to preserve the peace therefore bore the responsibility of ensuring that the outcome of a just war was also an equally just and lasting peace (Obama 2009ff).

Obama expanded his ideas about why America had to fight in a pre-Christmas interview with PBS *News Hour* host, Jim Lehrer. He began by recapitulating the general theme of his Nobel speech—that "this is a dangerous world where real evil exists out there and that compels us to occasionally make very difficult decisions about using force—that we shouldn't glorify war, but we should accept that there are times where we have to defend our nation, protect our values." He then noted this was the precisely the same argument he had been presenting from the time of his 2002 Chicago address, through his years as a U.S. senator and the months as a candidate for the presidency:

> It is very important for ... those of us who desperately want peace—who see war as, at some level, a break-down, a manifestation of human weakness—to understand that sometimes it's also necessary. And you know, to be able to balance two ideas at the same time; that we are constantly striving for peace, we are doubling up on our diplomacy, we are going to actively engage, we are going to try to see the world through other people's eyes and not just our own ...
>
> We're going to do all those things. And then there are going to be times where there is a Hitler; there are going to be moments like 9/11 where, despite our best

efforts, things have still ... emerged that are of such danger not only to us but our ideals and those things that we care for, that we've got to apply force ... (Obama 2009hh)

Learning from the Failed War on Terror

The Bush administration's greatest failure, Obama had consistently alleged since the fall of 2002, was its misconceived war in Iraq. While war could be justified under certain circumstances such as the 9/11 attacks, Obama repeatedly argued, a war lacking an appropriate rationale ought never to be undertaken. During his first months in office he would highlight the faulty intelligence the U.S. had utilized and the opportunities it had wasted by insisting that war against Saddam Hussein was the most effective means of fighting terrorism. Iraq had been waged "at enormous cost in lives and resources," he declared, but despite everything the U.S. had poured into the conflict, the primary goal of defeating terrorism had remained elusive (Obama 2009ee).

For six years, Obama maintained, the administration had denied U.S. troops in Afghanistan the support the conflict demanded. Starved of appropriate resources because of Iraq, the military situation in Afghanistan had become "increasingly perilous" (Obama 2009l). Al Qaeda had grown stronger and had even managed to gain some degree of legitimacy in certain quarters as America's moral authority waned in response to the extreme rhetoric and tactics of Bush's war on terror. Years of contentious, partisan wrangling over Iraq and terrorism had also taken a severe toll on America's sense of national unity and purpose (Obama 2009ee). And in the meantime, Middle Eastern stability had been severely damaged (Obama 2009g). American security was thus increasingly at risk.

It was therefore time, Obama concluded, to take two essential strategic steps. First was "to begin to responsibly leave Iraq to its people," and devise an exit strategy grounded in "a clear and achievable goal shared by the Iraqi people and the American people: an Iraq that is sovereign, stable, and self-reliant" (Obama 2009a, 2009g). The resources the U.S. had been squandering in Iraq could then be deployed against America's real terrorist foes, and the lessons it should have learned could now be applied to the second step—waging a smarter, more effective war in Afghanistan.

Obama's new strategic approach was accompanied by an important change in the tone and content of his rhetoric about America's "war of choice." His criticisms of Iraq became more muted as he turned his focus to the future and began to flesh out his own resolution to the wars in Iraq and Afghanistan. Adopting a reproachful rather than an angry voice, he noted in a February interview with the Canadian Broadcasting Corporation that as a consequence of the war in Iraq, America "took our eye off the ball. We have not been as focused as we need to be on all the various steps that are needed in order to deal with Afghanistan" (Obama 2009e). And two weeks later, in a primetime speech on Iraq that presaged his strategy for Afghanistan, Obama spoke of a "renewed cause for hope in Iraq" and outlined the drawdown strategy that would enable the U.S. to exit responsibly from the conflict there (Obama 2009g).

The implication, of course, was that his predecessor had focused on the wrong foe and had failed to devise a comprehensive strategy for dealing with terrorism. But as Obama stated in a PBS *News Hour* interview that evening, he had no desire to "relitigate" the wisdom of invading Saddam Hussein's country in the first place or enumerate the specific flaws in Bush's anti-terrorism policies. He did note that had the Bush administration stayed more focused on Afghanistan and the problems throughout the entire region, "we would probably be further along now than we are" in this "whole processes of dealing with extremists." But, he carefully added, "that's history" (Obama 2009h). Obama thereby suggested that little would be gained by continuing to place blame; it was time to learn from U.S. mistakes in Iraq, move forward in Afghanistan, and concentrate on how best to win the battle against extremism.

A New Approach to Combating Terrorism

In his inaugural address, Obama spoke of forging "a hard-earned peace in Afghanistan," and to anyone who might have doubted his intention to emerge victorious in the struggle against the terrorists, he issued a stern warning: "And for those who seek to advance their aims by inducing terror and slaughtering innocents, we say to you now that, 'Our spirit is stronger and cannot be broken. You cannot outlast us, and we will defeat you'" (Obama 2009a).

On multiple occasions he reiterated his deep personal commitment to preserving America's security. In announcing his new strategy for Afghanistan in March, he stated that "As President my greatest responsibility is to protect the American people" (Obama 2009l), and in remarks on national security in late May he added this emotional twist to keeping the American people safe: "It's the first thing that I think about when I wake up in the morning. It's the last thing that I think about when I go to sleep at night" (Obama 2009p).

The president also sought to erase any doubts about the magnitude of the still-looming terrorist threat. From its safe-haven in Pakistan, the "far-reaching network of violence and hatred" behind the 9/11 attacks was still at work plotting more carnage both in America and across the globe, he asserted. The U.S. thus had to develop a new regional strategy that encompassed both Afghanistan and its neighbor to the east. The situation in the region was "perilous," Obama warned, "and progress will take time." He reported that violence was up dramatically in Afghanistan, and that a deadly insurgency as well as a thriving opium trade had taken root there. The Afghan government was unable to deliver basic services, and al Qaeda and Taliban forces had been operating from bases embedded along the rugged, tribal border area (Obama 2009b). That America faced an international security challenge "of the highest order" had been amply demonstrated by recent al Qaeda-sponsored strikes in London, Bali, North Africa, Islamabad, and Kabul. Particularly painful, Obama noted, was the fact that 2008 had been the deadliest year of the war for U.S. forces (Obama 2009l).

The attacks of 9/11, Obama stated at the National Defense University in early March, "signaled the new dangers of the twenty-first century" (Obama 2009j). It was therefore especially tragic that the U.S. had thus far failed to deploy the "entire arsenal of American power" throughout the region or think through what it hoped to achieve there (Obama 2009h). And as if all this were not reason enough to be concerned, Obama also told an international audience in Prague that the terrorists posed a nuclear threat as well: "Al Qaeda said it seeks a bomb and that it would have no problem with using it" (Obama 2009o). It was a warning he would repeat as he spoke of the many challenges—the spread of nuclear weapons, emerging cyber threats, a dependence on foreign oil, poverty, disease, and the persistence of conflict and genocide—that were intertwined with the threat of terrorist extremism (Obama 2009j).

A constant theme in Obama's public statements on Afghanistan was that the mission, while essential, would be very difficult. In his March *60 Minutes* interview he offered the blunt appraisal that "Afghanistan is not going to be easy in many ways," adding that "this is not my assessment. This is the assessment of commanders on the ground" (Obama 2009k). Iraq, the president asserted, was actually an easier battleground than Afghanistan because of its better terrain and infrastructure, more highly educated population, and more secure border. "So this is going to be a tough nut to crack," he concluded, but immediately went on to add that it was "not acceptable for us simply to sit back and let safe havens of terrorists plan and plot" (Obama 2009k). Given the rapidly deteriorating situation in Afghanistan, a well-thought-out strategy, with clear, achievable goals that would elicit the strongest support possible from the American public was of the utmost urgency (Obama 2009g).

In remarks to assembled diplomats, Pentagon and State Department officials, and members of his national security staff on the morning of March 27, Obama outlined his "comprehensive, new strategy for Afghanistan and Pakistan," noting that "to defeat an enemy that heeds no borders or laws of war," the U.S. had to bring to bear all elements of American military, diplomatic, and economic power. "A campaign against extremism will not succeed with bullets or bombs alone," he cautioned. It would also be doomed to fail unless America worked in concert with its NATO allies, partners in the region, and other nations across the globe that had a stake "in the promise of lasting peace and security and development" (Obama 2009l).

A stronger, smarter, and more comprehensive strategy would have to begin with "a clear and focused goal," Obama asserted, and with much rhetorical flourish he specified that the U.S. aim should be to "*disrupt, dismantle, and defeat al Qaeda in Pakistan and Afghanistan.*" He continued, "That is a cause that could not be more just ... And to the terrorists who oppose us, my message is the same: We will defeat you" (Obama 2009l, emphasis added). Some variant of the phrase "disrupting, dismantling, and defeating" al Qaeda would now become Obama's equivalent of Bush's war-on-terror mantra. Rejecting the specific vocabulary of his predecessor, however, in no way meant that Obama repudiated the underlying rationale or goals that Bush had enunciated for America's war against terrorism.

Obama constantly stressed that America's goals in Afghanistan must be "achievable." The U.S. had no interest or aspiration to be there "over the long term," he said in an interview with PBS's Jim Lehrer in late February: "There's a long history, as you know, in Afghanistan of rebuffing what is seen as an occupying force, and we have to be mindful of that history ..." In recent years there had been too great "a sense of drift in the mission," and he had therefore ordered a "head-to-toe, soup-to-nuts review" of the U.S. approach. "Until we have a clear strategy, we're not going to have a clear exit strategy," he stated, again emphasizing that his goal was to get American troops "home as quickly as possible without leaving a situation that allows for potential terrorist attacks against the United States" (Obama 2009h). To underscore his new approach, and to distinguish it from Bush's open-ended war on terror, Obama also stressed that his administration would "set clear metrics to measure progress and hold ourselves accountable." Going forward in Afghanistan, he insisted, "We will not blindly stay the course," a none-too-subtle reference to his predecessor's war of choice in Iraq (Obama 2009l).

A major question still remained: What were the president's specific criteria for victory in Afghanistan? In a February interview with Peter Mansbridge of the Canadian Broadcasting Corporation, Obama struggled to respond to whether the U.S. could still be victorious there. "Well, I think Afghanistan is still winnable in the sense of our ability to ensure that it is not a launching pad for attacks against North America. I think it's still possible for us to stamp out al Qaeda to make sure that extremism is not expanding but rather is contracting," the president stated in rather ambiguous terms (Obama 2009e).

Jim Lehrer had also raised the issue of success in his interview with Obama. "As you know, Mr President," he began, "there's a traditional language for these kinds of conflicts, and it's victory, or it's loss, you win a war or you lose a war. Is there a victory definition for Afghanistan now ...?" Obama chose to reply not with clear standards for victory but by enumerating the minimal goals the U.S. had to achieve: making certain that Afghanistan was not a safe haven for terrorists, ensuring that al Qaeda and its allies would not again be able to launch attacks on America or other targets around the world, and providing the conditions necessary for the Afghan people to determine their own fate. The overarching goal, he added, "was to keep the American people safe" (Obama 2009h). The discourse of existential threat remained intact.

In response to Steve Kroft's related query on *60 Minutes* about what America's mission in Afghanistan should be, Obama first presented what he termed the number one priority—"Making sure that al Qaeda cannot attack the U.S. homeland and U.S. interests and our allies"—and then added that this was the same central mission that America had when it went in after 9/11: "And that is these folks can project violence against the United States' citizens. And that is something that we cannot tolerate" (2009k). It was becoming obvious that a more precise assessment of victory would have to await the results of the review process the Obama administration was about to undertake.

One week after Obama delivered his inaugural address, Secretary of Defense Robert Gates, the only Cabinet hold-over from the Bush administration, had stated in testimony before the Senate Foreign Relations Committee that Afghanistan presented America's greatest military challenge and that the Afghan theater should be the top overseas military priority. In words that echoed the new president's concerns about setting appropriate goals for the war, he offered the sobering assessment that "this is going to be a long slog, and frankly, my view is that we need to be very careful about the nature of the goals we set for ourselves" (Gates 2009a). And in a widely quoted rejection of his former boss's foreign policy paradigm, Gates went on to add, "If we set ourselves the objective of creating some sort of central Asian Valhalla over there, we will lose, because nobody in the world has that kind of time, patience and money" (Gates 2009a). It was thus no secret that success in Afghanistan would not include the creation of a Western-style democracy.

The Exemplars of an Exceptional Nation

In early November, in the context of a tragic and horrific shooting episode at the U.S. Army base at Fort Hood, Texas by an Army psychiatrist of Islamic faith, President Obama gave full voice to a theme that had run throughout all of his discourse on Afghanistan and the rationale for war: U.S. fighting forces as exemplars of the values and ideals that had defined America for more than two centuries.

At the memorial service for the 13 military personnel who had been killed, Obama began by noting that "this is a time of war," and that while "these Americans did not die on a foreign field of battle," their sacrifice had been as great at any on the field of combat. His remarks centered on all that the U.S. military had accomplished across the decades, and he eulogized those who had lost their lives in the carnage as the latest incarnation of exceptional heroes. This generation of fighting forces, he emphasized, "has more than proved itself the equal of those who've come before" (Obama 2009w). America therefore did not need to look to the past for greatness, because "it is before our very eyes." The troops gathered at Fort Hood and across the world "have served in tour after tour of duty in distant, different, and difficult places. They have extended the opportunity of self-government to peoples that have suffered tyranny and war ... —all Americans, serving together to protect our people, while giving others half a world away the chance to lead a better life" (Obama 2009w).

Obama thus used this mournful occasion to underscore the troops' contributions to preserving those uniquely American ideals that reflected all the good the country represented. "Your loved ones endure through the life of our nation," the president intoned in homage to American exceptionalism: "Every evening that the sun sets on a tranquil town; every dawn that a flag is unfurled; every moment that an American enjoys life, liberty, and the pursuit of happiness—that is their legacy" (Obama 2009w).

Obama also reminded a grieving audience that even though there might not be any obvious indicator of victory in today's wars, the measure of the troops' impact "is no less great. In a world of threats that know no borders, their legacy will be marked in the safety of our cities and towns and the security and opportunity that's extended abroad." The president concluded his remarks with these uplifting words: "It will be said that this generation believed under the most trying of tests; believed in perseverance, not just when it was easy, but when it was hard; that they paid the price and bore the burden to secure this Nation, and stood up for the values that live in the hearts of all free peoples" (Obama 2009w). A more fitting and eloquent testimonial to America's ingrained sense of national mission and virtuous identity would be difficult to construct.

The following morning, in remarks following a Veterans Day wreath-laying ceremony at Arlington National Cemetery's Tomb of the Unknowns, Obama again spoke emotionally of everything that generations of America's fighting forces had done for the nation, particularly to preserve its cherished values. "Above all else," he declared, "they believed in and fought for a set of ideals. Because they did, our country still stands; our founding principles still shine; nations around the world that once knew nothing but fear now know the blessings of freedom." And this, the president solemnly concluded, "is why we fight" (Obama 2009x).

Surging and Exiting from Afghanistan

When President Obama first spoke in late March 2009 of his new strategy for Afghanistan and Pakistan, he stated that he had already ordered the deployment of 17,000 U.S. troops the military commander in Afghanistan had requested to expand the fight in the border regions, provide additional security for the upcoming presidential election, and train Afghan security forces. He also noted that an additional 4,000 U.S. trainers would shortly be deployed as well. Obama furthermore promised that his administration would carefully monitor U.S. progress and commence a thorough review of whether it was employing "the right tools and tactics" to achieve the stated goal of disrupting, dismantling, and defeating al Qaeda (Obama 2009l).

Following his remarks on Afghanistan, Obama sat down for an interview with Bob Schieffer of CBS's *Face the Nation.* Pressed on the issue of what an increased U.S. troop presence could really accomplish, the president acknowledged that Afghanistan had never been "very favorably disposed towards foreign intervention." He also admitted that "there may be a point of diminishing returns in terms of troop levels" (Obama 2009m). Pledging not to undertake "an open-ended commitment of infinite resources," and studiously avoiding the term *surge* to describe his new strategy, Obama noted that "We've just got to make sure that we are focused on achieving what we need to achieve with the resources we have." And he concluded with the admonition that there had been a dangerous deterioration of conditions in Afghanistan over the last several years, and that "unless we get a handle on it now, we're going to be in trouble" (Obama 2009m).

As the review he had ordered in the early spring moved forward over the next seven months, the president essentially went silent on the particulars of how his administration would proceed in Afghanistan. In his public statements on the war over the summer of 2009, Obama took refuge in the general narrative he had already constructed, continuing his pattern of very circumspect comments about what America hoped to accomplish. At the VFW National Convention in Phoenix, for instance, Obama repeated the mantra of disrupting, dismantling, and defeating al Qaeda and its extremist allies through a comprehensive, regional strategy that focused on the remote tribal areas of both Pakistan and Afghanistan. He highlighted once more the multifaceted nature of America's approach. It was not enough to kill extremists and terrorists; the U.S. also needed to "protect the Afghan people and improve their daily lives." Acknowledging again the difficult days ahead, the president continued to stress how essential it was to maintain the fight. And he reverted to a well-worn phrase: "We must never forget: This is not a war of choice. This is a war of necessity" (Obama 2009t).

We know from Bob Woodward's (2010), Jonathan Alter's (2010), and David Sanger's (2012) riveting accounts of the behind-the-scenes deliberations on Afghanistan through the late summer and fall of 2009 that Obama's official silence masked a heated and frequently acrimonious series of debates both among the high-ranking members of the administration and between the president's civilian and military advisors over the direction of the war and how best to extricate the U.S. from the conflict. As we shall see in the next chapter, members of Congress from both sides of the aisle also debated the way forward in Afghanistan, and media coverage, fed by contentious congressional discourse as well as leaks from within the White House and Pentagon, reflected the often intense political discussions that ensued. But until the month prior to the official announcement of his new Afghanistan policy, Obama declined to offer more than occasional generalities about the way forward in the war.

In mid-November, the president embarked on an eight-day trip to East Asia. In a series of media interviews and press conferences from China and South Korea, he once again broached the topic of his strategy for Afghanistan. His prepared remarks as well as his responses to a variety of questions emphasized the reasons the U.S. had originally gone to war in Afghanistan, why it was essential to maintain the fight, and why a more focused and defined strategy was so imperative. While he refused to divulge the details of what this strategy would actually involve, he signaled that it would include a further troop deployment. And he used this global opportunity to reinforce his message of the American mission to serve as a model for the world and keep the globe secure so that the conditions for democracy might develop and thrive.

To a Chinese student in Shanghai, Obama asserted that the greatest threat to American security came from terrorist networks like al Qaeda and although these organizations might be small in number, they had "no conscience when it comes to the destruction of innocent civilians." And because of contemporary technology, he warned, if a terrorist organization were to get ahold of a weapon of mass destruction "and they used it in a city, whether it's in Shanghai or New York, just a few individuals could potentially kill tens of thousands of people, maybe hundreds of thousands" (Obama 2009y). With this statement, he basically dismissed the argument that the al Qaeda network was so diminished that it no longer posed a terrorist threat.

While in Beijing, Obama sat for interviews with several U.S. news outlets, and Afghanistan was a major focus of all the interviewers' queries. Followers of the president's rhetoric would quickly note that as he broached the subject of a troop increase, Obama would once more reject the term used to label his predecessor's revised strategy in Iraq and never utter the word *surge*. To Chip Reid of CBS's *Early Show*, the president said that he was still in the process of making a decision about how many more troops he would send to Afghanistan, but he emphasized that at this point, it was primarily a matter of fine-tuning a strategy that would be both successful and time limited. As to his specific objective, Obama remained vague, noting that he, his commanding general in Afghanistan, and the American public all shared the same overarching goal: "for us to be able to protect our homeland, protect our allies, protect U.S. interests around the world" (Obama 2009z).

On NBC's *Today Show*, Obama told correspondent Chuck Todd he was confident that within a few weeks he would be able to present to the American people "in very clear terms, what exactly is at stake, what we intend to do, how we're going to succeed, how much it's going to cost, how long it's going to take." Todd did report that one option definitely off the table was reducing the U.S. troop presence in Afghanistan any time soon. But in response to a question that sought some specifics on his new strategy for Afghanistan, the president again reverted to his familiar script:

> Part of, I think, the task here is making sure that Afghanistan is sufficiently stable so that we can make that handoff. So my goal is ... creating a situation in which our footprint is smaller and Afghan security forces can do the job of keeping their country together. They're not there yet. They need help from us. And that's exactly what our strategy is going to be designed to do. (Obama 2009aa)

To Todd's query, "This decision, will it be the decision that ultimately ends the war?" Obama gave another equivocal reply: "This decision will put us on a path towards ending the war" (Obama 2009aa).

Attempting to pin down the president on his decision about troop levels, Ed Henry of CNN asked whether most U.S. troops would be removed from Afghanistan by the end of his presidency. Once again, Obama refused to disclose any details, briefly answering that his "preference would be not to hand anything off to the next president." But Obama did take advantage of the opportunity to tell the network audience it was essential to ensure that al Qaeda could not again attack America nor use Afghanistan as a safe haven. "We have a vital interest in making sure that Afghanistan is sufficiently stable, that it can't infect the entire region with violent extremism," the president once more explained (Obama 2009bb).

In South Korea, on the final leg of his Asian trip, Obama spoke with Major Garrett of Fox News. Reflecting on the very differing advice he had been receiving about how to proceed in Afghanistan, the president noted that listening to "strong voices on both sides in a very complex issue"—even if some were opinions he did not want to hear—had allowed him to reach an optimum decision. And he indicated that it would involve a carefully-constructed centrist approach with some level of troop increase and continued aid to Afghanistan but not an ill-defined, open-ended commitment:

> There are voices who say this is a quagmire and we're wasting our resources and endangering our young men and women's lives and we should just focus on Pakistan and al Qaeda that's in Pakistan.
>
> There are those who say we have to go all in and commit and rebuild Afghanistan so it is a stable and just society.
>
> If I was just hearing one side, then I would probably not be getting the full reality of what's going on in Afghanistan, which is that, yes, we have a vital interest there, yes, we have to make sure that we don't get our mission creep and that we define our interests narrowly to make sure we're just going after extremists and preventing them from having safe havens. Yes, we have to have and effective Afghan government, and right now we don't have the kind of partner that we'd like; yes, we've got to have Pakistan cooperating; yes, we've to have more civilian cooperation, so all those variables then go into the decision-making process and, as I said, if I was just listening to hawks or doves on either side of the debate, then I probably wouldn't be making a very good decision. (Obama 2009cc)

But on his return to Washington, Obama still declined to speak in precise terms about his new Afghanistan strategy, using a news conference with the prime minister of India as an opportunity to reiterate America's general objectives in fighting the extremists rather than to answer reporters' specific questions about how many more troops he would send, how they would be paid for, and whether he would announce a timetable and/or exit strategy:

> It is in our strategic interest, in our national security interest to make sure that al Qaeda and its extremist allies cannot operate effectively in those areas. We are going to dismantle and degrade their capabilities and, ultimately, dismantle and destroy their networks. And Afghanistan's stability is important to that process ...
>
> It's important to the world, and ... the whole world, I think, has a core security interest in making sure that the kind of extremism and violence that you've seen emanating from this region is tackled, confronted in a serious way. (Obama 2009dd)

Obama also emphasized that it was his intention "to finish the job" and insure that the U.S. had both the resources and the strategy to "get the job done." But his brief comment that the plan was to dismantle and degrade the extremists' capabilities and destroy their networks seemed to presage a subtle but important shift to less ambitious and more circumscribed goals for the conflict than achieving a clear-cut military victory (Obama 2009dd).

A Defined and Focused Strategy

On December 1, 2009, in a televised, primetime address from the U.S. Military Academy at West Point, Obama at last revealed his widely-anticipated new strategy for Afghanistan. He announced that his extensive review was now complete and that after much consultation with top civilian and military advisors as well as America's key partners, he had determined it was in "our vital national interest" to send an additional 30,000 U.S. troops, the amount necessary "to seize the initiative" in the war (Obama 2009ee).

Although he did not mention the troop levels under consideration during the months of review, it was obvious from the president's remarks that he had settled on a middle path between what his military commander had requested and the far smaller number that some of his senior civilian advisors had recommended. Again shunning the label *surge,* Obama further explained that this increase in troops would allow the U.S. to achieve the three essential objectives he had laid out earlier in the year: denying al Qaeda a safe haven, reversing the Taliban's momentum and keeping it from overthrowing the regime, and strengthening the capacity of Afghanistan's security forces and government so that they could assume responsibility for the country's future (Obama 2009ee).

And because the extremists had taken refuge in Pakistan, that nation would be a major focus of U.S. anti-terrorism efforts as well. Although he clearly repeated that America's overarching goal was to disrupt, dismantle, and defeat al Qaeda, he had also inserted a narrower and more focused mission: *denying* the organization and its jihadist allies the means of accomplishing their stated terrorist ends by *degrading* their capabilities to plan and launch attacks. The goal of keeping America secure through whatever military measures were necessary, however, remained intact.

The troop increase would also take place within a specific time frame, Obama noted, a strategy that would allow a responsible transfer of military forces out of Afghanistan to commence by July of 2011. Eighteen months after the additional troops were in place, the president pledged, U.S. combat forces would "begin to come home," although the speed and specifics of the transition would have to take into account conditions on the ground. While he stressed that it was vital to U.S. national security to bring the conflict to a successful and responsible conclusion, Obama was equally adamant that America had no interest in fighting an "endless war in Afghanistan" (Obama 2009ee). The implication was obvious: The idea of open-ended nation-building through an all-out counterinsurgency campaign had been jettisoned. For Obama the missionary strand of exceptionalist belief was being supplanted by the exemplary strand that holds the U.S. should lead by example and an active program of foreign aid rather than open-ended military intervention in the affairs of another nation (see McCrisken 2001 and 2012).

The president also emphasized his reluctance to send more troops into harm's way. "I see firsthand the terrible wages of war," he stated. But sometimes, he acknowledged, there was simply no choice other than committing American forces to battle:

> If I did not think that the security of the United States and the safety of the American people were at stake in Afghanistan, I would gladly order every single one of our troops home tomorrow.
>
> So I do not make this decision lightly. I make this decision because I am convinced that our security is at stake in Afghanistan and Pakistan. This is the epicenter of violent extremism practiced by al Qaeda. It is from here that we were attacked on 9/11, and it is from here that new attacks are being plotted as I speak ... In the last few months alone, we have apprehended extremists within our borders who were sent here from the border region of Afghanistan and Pakistan to commit new acts of terror. (Obama 2009ee)

He hammered home the point that this was indeed a battle that warranted America's most heroic efforts and greatest sacrifices. Speaking directly to the West Point cadets assembled before him, Obama summed up his commitment to the troops in one definitive sentence: "I owe you a mission that is clearly defined, and worthy of your service" (Obama 2009ee).

To that end, Obama recapitulated his compelling—and remarkably consistent—narrative of why al Qaeda terrorists had attacked America on 9/11, why the U.S. had to respond with a declaration of war, why the war was both necessary and just, why Iraq had been a dangerous distraction from America's primary objective, why the terrorist threat still loomed so large, and why the U.S. needed a comprehensive new approach to confronting the terrorist foes. The final piece of the storyline—why America had to increase its military presence in Afghanistan and do so under a specified time frame and with a particular troop level—was given pride of place as he addressed the corps of cadets, many of whom, he carefully noted, had either already served in combat in the region or were likely soon to deploy there.

"Afghanistan is not lost," the president explained, "but for several years it has moved backwards." While the U.S. had made progress recently, huge challenges remained, and General McChrystal, the new commander in Afghanistan, had reported a more serious security situation than he had anticipated. The Taliban had gained momentum, al Qaeda retained their safe havens along the border with Pakistan, and U.S. forces lacked the full support they needed to effectively train and partner with Afghan security forces and secure the population. "This is no idle danger; no hypothetical threat," Obama declared; in short, "The situation in Afghanistan has deteriorated ... The status quo is not sustainable" (Obama 2009ee). Immediate action was essential.

To justify his call for a troop surge delimited by a specific date for U.S. withdrawal to commence, Obama reviewed—and in turn rejected—the major arguments against his proposal. This rhetorical technique allowed him both to summarize the wide range of options he had considered and defend the position he ultimately selected. But it also provided the opportunity for Obama to recapitulate the dire threat that terrorism posed while rejecting the option of unending military engagement. The president was going to some lengths to explain why, given the problematic situation America confronted in the Afghanistan and Pakistan region and the grave economic problems the nation faced at home, his decision to seek a balanced approach had been the most appropriate.

He first addressed those who equated Afghanistan with the quagmire of Vietnam and had argued that because it could not be stabilized America was better off cutting its losses and rapidly withdrawing. These critics, he maintained, had engaged in a "false reading of history." Unlike Vietnam, Obama pointed out, the U.S. was now joined by a broad coalition of nations, it was not facing a broad-based popular insurgency, and—most importantly—the American homeland had been "viciously attacked from Afghanistan" and remained a target for those same extremists "who are plotting along its border." Inviting though this critique of his proposed policy might be to some, he concluded, it simply ignored the ugly facts of America's struggle against terrorist extremism (Obama 2009ee). The necessity to fight the terrorists was a given, he argued; he would not countenance a basic challenge to the idea that a military response had been necessary.

To those critics who recognized that the U.S. could not leave Afghanistan in its current state but believed it could proceed with the troops already in place, Obama presented two rebuttals. First, this approach would simply "maintain a status quo in which we muddle through, and permit a slow deterioration of conditions there," and secondly, it would ultimately prove more costly and prolong America's stay, because "we would never be able to generate the conditions needed to train Afghan security forces and give them the space to take over." Like the first critique of his policy, the president argued, this one also naively called for a solution contradicted by harsh realities on the ground (Obama 2009ee).

And to those who rejected the idea of a time frame and even called for a "more dramatic and open-ended escalation of the U.S. war effort—one that would commit America to a nation-building project of up to a decade," the president had a straightforward message: He would never agree to a course of action with goals that went beyond "our responsibility, our means, or our interests." By the time he took office, Obama explained, the cost of America's two wars approached a trillion dollars, and his new strategy in Afghanistan would likely add $30 billion for the military in 2009 alone. At the same time it was attempting a responsible transition from two wars, America was facing an economic crisis and a growing deficit. To "rebuild our strength here at home," the U.S. needed to maintain a balance among its competing priorities. The nation simply could not afford a solution so blatantly at odds with current economic realities. As Obama dramatically proclaimed, "That's why our troop commitment in Afghanistan cannot be open-ended—because the nation that I'm most interested in building is our own" (Obama 2009ee).

Obama concluded his narrative of Afghanistan with an impassioned reminder of everything the conflict represented. Since the days of Franklin Roosevelt, he noted, America had "borne a special burden in global affairs." His exceptional nation had never sought world domination or other nations' resources: "What we have fought for—what we continue to fight for—is a better future for our children and grandchildren. And we believe that their lives will be better if other peoples' children and grandchildren can live in freedom and access opportunity." He pointed out that America had lost nearly 3,000 civilian and 700 military lives in the battle against terrorist extremism, a war it did not enter by choice. But because of the peace, security, justice, and opportunity that America stands for, history had called it to that struggle. The U.S. had answered that call, and the new way forward in Afghanistan, Obama declared, would help to ensure a "world that is more secure, and a future that represents not the deepest of fears but the highest of hopes" (Obama 2009ee).

While the president had utilized lofty and stirring rhetoric to rally the public to his plan, his senior national security and diplomatic advisors and top military commander in Afghanistan turned to the more prosaic task of selling the mission to a skeptical Congress. While offering some more specifics, they too tended to fall back on generic warnings about the many threats still lurking in the region now increasingly known as "Af/Pak." But they were united in their praise for the revised strategy, clearly intent on insuring that their messages dovetailed with Obama's.

In prepared remarks to the Senate Armed Services Committee on December 2, Secretary of Defense Gates dutifully reiterated the core goal of disrupting, dismantling, and defeating al Qaeda in both Afghanistan and Pakistan, and he placed particular emphasis on the problematic status of the nuclear-armed ally where terrorists had found safe haven. Defeating al Qaeda and enhancing Afghan security were "mutually reinforcing" missions, Gates insisted, as the Taliban and al Qaeda had become symbiotic, "each benefiting from the success and mythology of the other." Both were operating out of the lawless border area between the two nations. The U.S. therefore could not separate the security situation in Afghanistan from the stability of Pakistan (Gates 2009c).

Echoing his commander-in-chief, Gates maintained that this approach was far from open-ended nation-building. But neither did it involve a repudiation of the martial response to terrorism. It entailed instead a "narrower focus" tied tightly to America's core goal and measured by "observable progress" on six primary objectives—reversing Taliban momentum through sustained military action; denying the Taliban access to and control of key population and production centers and lines of communication; disrupting the Taliban outside secured areas and preventing al Qaeda from regaining sanctuary in Afghanistan; degrading the Taliban to levels manageable by the Afghan national security forces; increasing the size and capability of those security forces; and selectively building the capacity of the Afghan government (Gates 2009c). This revised approach would take "more patience, perseverance, and sacrifice by the United States and our allies," Gates admitted, but he quickly added that the new way forward had a critical advantage: It was achievable with the proposed troop level and within the specified time frame (Gates 2009c).

Admiral Mullen, Chairman of the Joint Chiefs of Staff, also went to bat for the president's plan in testimony before the Senate Armed Services Committee. Calling Obama's new strategy a "balanced and sustainable approach" that he supported "fully, and without hesitation," Mullen noted that U.S. military objectives had been appropriately narrowed and refined to focus on achieving the security of key population areas, training and mentoring Afghan military and police, and establishing the conditions necessary for the Afghans to assume their own security (Mullen 2009).

Mullen similarly sought to assure the assembled senators that the commitment to a rapid, coalition-wide buildup of additional combat forces should allow the U.S. to make sufficient progress in the war to begin a troop drawdown within the stated time frame. And following the president's lead, he highlighted the need to concentrate on Pakistan, contending that South Asia was the epicenter of global Islamic extremism, a region that had not only nurtured those who struck America on 9/11 but was also home to jihadists who continued to plot against the U.S. While progress in the region would be "gradual, and sometimes halting," Mullen concluded, the president's announced surge strategy and the accompanying force flow decision "give us the best possible chance for success" (Mullen 2009). But he also emphasized that July 2011 would merely be the start of the U.S. drawdown and that the precise withdrawal timeframe would be contingent on conditions in the region.

General Stanley McChrystal, the top U.S. and NATO commander in Afghanistan who had originally requested an increase of 40,000 combat troops, also supported his commander-in-chief's new strategic approach in testimony before both the House and Senate Armed Services committees. America's core goal, he carefully stated, was to defeat al Qaeda and prevent its return to Afghanistan. Doing so meant that the U.S. must also "disrupt and degrade the Taliban's capacity, deny their access to the Afghan population, and strengthen the Afghan security forces." And he too insisted that appropriate changes on the ground would have to occur before U.S. troops were fully removed. When asked directly by the chair of the House Armed Services Committee about whether his mission would succeed, the general unhesitatingly effused, "I believe we will be absolutely successful" (McChrystal 2009).

The U.S. Ambassador to Afghanistan, Karl Eikenberry, who had previously expressed strong reservations about what a troop surge in Karzai's Afghanistan might accomplish, now testified in favor of Obama's new, more focused approach. "The mission was refined, the ways forward were clarified, and the resources have been committed to allow us to achieve the refined mission," and therefore, he declared, "I am unequivocally in support of this mission." But unlike his military colleague, the ambassador was decidedly more guarded about the prospects for achieving U.S. goals in the region. "Afghanistan is a daunting challenge," he cautioned. "Success is not guaranteed, but it is possible" (Eikenberry 2009; Jaffe and Kessler 2009).

Stating that "the fog of another war" had led America to ignore for far too long the growing extremist threats in Afghanistan and Pakistan, Secretary of State Hillary Rodham Clinton gave an equally ringing endorsement of Obama's new strategy, especially its call for a "long-term, sustainable relationship" with the leaders and people of the region. She emphasized that while U.S. military presence would be time limited, its "significant" political, economic, and diplomatic commitment would "continue long after our combat forces leave." These civilian efforts were already bearing fruit, she told the Senate Armed Services Committee, and even though there were important lingering concerns about political corruption in Afghanistan, President Karzai had now pledged to address these problems, a promise for which he would definitely be held accountable (Clinton 2009b).

But the secretary of state's highlighting of the non-military side of the Afghanistan mission raised a thorny question that had haunted Obama's policy since he first addressed the war in March: How did this comprehensive new way forward really differ from nation-building? As Clinton extolled the accomplishments of the growing legion of U.S. civilian officials in Afghanistan and spoke in glowing terms of the potential for a better future for the people of the region, she did not address that issue and was no more able than her national security colleagues to provide a hint of when America's extended relationship might end and "mission accomplished" could be declared.

Redefining Victory

It was obvious that on one essential point Obama and his senior national security team were presenting a completely united public front: The U.S. military commitment in Afghanistan would not be open-ended; America's combat forces would start to leave the Af/Pak region within the near future. But they were less in lock-step over when the U.S. might accomplish its goals and whether the mission's success would be assured. That aspect of the war narrative involved a more nuanced storyline and a revision of the conventional conception of military victory.

In a July interview on ABC's *Nightline*, Obama had directly broached the difficulty with defining victory in the post-9/11 world. The term *victory*, he stated, traditionally invoked the notion of "Emperor Hirohito coming down and signing a surrender to MacArthur." But a war against a non-state actor—"a shadowy operation like al Qaeda"—would not end with such a formal declaration of peace; the closure that had always been taken for granted was, quite simply, no longer attainable (Obama 2009r). The U.S. therefore had to recalibrate what success meant in this new kind of war and be satisfied with less than a decisive, surgical end point. The most realistic goal, the president concluded, would be to keep al Qaeda and its jihadist allies from attacking the United States, ensuring that they could not set up permanent bases for training recruits and launching terrorist strikes (Obama 2009r).

Success would thus entail a lengthy, complex process that required constant monitoring and vigilance, as well as an on-going commitment to assist the Afghan people in improving their security situation, stabilizing their government, and achieving economic development. This was the only way, Obama stated, to "continue to contract the ability of al Qaeda to operate" (Obama 2009r), and he implied that in this new approach to victory, the U.S. must not allow the quest for the perfect to become the enemy of the good it could actually attain.

Anyone seeking a traditional definition of winning in Obama's West Point address would therefore have been disappointed as the president once more outlined only the broad goals America sought to achieve—preventing Afghanistan from again becoming an al Qaeda safe-haven and increasing the capacity of the new Afghan government to hold that dreadful possibility at bay. Obama again enumerated the role that U.S. civilian and military forces would need to continue to play in training Afghan troops and providing economic and political support as well as legal expertise for the fledgling new government. He also repeated his call for more military, diplomatic, and economic engagement on the part of U.S. allies, countries around the world, and the United Nations (Obama 2007ee). But nowhere did the president spell out how Americans might know when victory could be declared, at what point the troops might be fully redeployed, and how long U.S. civilian trainers and advisors would remain in the region.

In a *60 Minutes* interview that was taped before he left for Norway to accept the Nobel Peace Prize, Obama responded to correspondent Steve Kroft's contention that he had seemed very analytical, detached, and unemotional in his December 1 address. The president immediately took issue, claiming that his Afghanistan speech had in fact been the most emotional one he had delivered since becoming president. First of all, Obama replied, he was addressing a group of cadets, some of whom would shortly be deployed to Afghanistan. That not all would return from this mission was an intensely personal reminder of the enormity of the decision that he had reached (Obama 2009gg).

The speech also "hit me in the gut," Obama asserted, because it brought to mind the very unfortunate "triumphalist sense about war" that U.S. leaders had displayed throughout much of the time since the 9/11 attacks. Under the previous administration, there had been a tendency to say, "We can go in, we can kick some tail, this is some glorious exercise, when in fact this is a tough business." Obama emphasized that he had embarked on a different rhetorical course, consistently arguing that even when war is necessary and justified, it is always ugly and tragic, and must never be undertaken lightly (Obama 2009gg).

But when pressed about his plans for a surge of 30,000 troops to be followed by a transitional drawdown phase of uncertain duration, Obama leapt to the defense of his military strategy for Afghanistan. He adamantly denied that the policy he had presented was confusing or contradictory. The U.S. had to stabilize Afghanistan, establish a functioning Afghan military, and enhance the government's capacity to provide for its own security before America could withdraw. All of this would initially require an infusion of U.S. troops, Obama patiently explained. And he again emphasized that the borders between Afghanistan and Pakistan were "the epicenter of violent extremism directed against the West and directed against the United States. This is the heart of it. This is where bin Laden is" (Obama 2009gg). The president remained unwavering in his defense of his way forward in the conflict as he highlighted the master narrative of why America had gone to war.

Conceding, however, that a majority of the American public and most of the people in his own party no longer believed that Afghanistan was a conflict worth fighting, Obama said he had gone ahead with the troop increase strategy "because I think it's the right thing to do, and that's my job ... As commander-in-chief, obviously I reserve the option to do what I think is going to be the best for the American people ... and our national security" (Obama 2009gg). The president also injected this note of somber realism into the discussion: "I don't have the luxury of choosing between the ideal and what exists on the ground. I have to make decisions based on how, given where we are right now, how do we get to the best possible place" (Obama 2009gg). And that best place would not entail a specific moment when he could proclaim the terrorists had been defeated and thus formally declare the U.S. was victorious.

The Omnipresent Terrorist Threat

The year would end with news of yet another terrorist attempt, this one on a Christmas day Northwest Airlines flight en route to Detroit from Amsterdam. Although the would-be attacker was quickly subdued and the plane landed safely, the episode demonstrated just how difficult it would be to achieve true closure in the battle against terrorist extremism. As Obama stated in remarks from vacation in Hawaii, this was "a serious reminder of the dangers that we face and the nature of those who threaten our homeland" (Obama 2009ii).

For a final time in 2009, the president put on alert anyone who sought to do his nation harm. Warning that the terrorist threat was no longer confined merely to Afghanistan or Pakistan, Obama used this occasion to recommit to the three goals he had previously set for his anti-terrorism efforts. He would not be content merely to disable al Qaeda and its extremist allies across the globe; it was also essential to vanquish them:

> ... those who would slaughter innocent men, women, and children must know that the United States will ... do more than simply strengthen our defenses; we will continue to use every element of our national power to *disrupt, to dismantle, and defeat* the violent extremists who threaten us, whether they are from Afghanistan or Pakistan, Yemen or Somalia, or anywhere they are plotting attacks against the U.S. homeland. (Obama 2009ii, emphasis added)

And as he had since first commenting on the 9/11 attacks more than seven years earlier, Obama declared that the cherished values and ideals the terrorists sought to destroy would remain undiminished as an exceptional nation stood united and unafraid:

> As Americans, we will never give in to fear or division; we will be guided by our hopes, our unity, and our deeply held values. That's who we are as Americans. That's what our brave men and women in uniform are standing up for as they spend the holidays in harm's way. And we will continue to do everything that we can do to keep America safe in the new year and beyond. (Obama 2009ii)

* * *

President Obama had unleashed his most potent rhetorical weapons in arguing the case for a new approach to combating America's terrorist foes. For more than seven years he had publicly argued that the U.S. needed to pursue and confront al Qaeda and its jihadist supporters through a combination of military force and diplomatic and economic engagement. From his days as a state senator through his time as a member of the U.S. Senate and candidate for president, Obama had painted terrorist extremism as an overarching threat and consistently called for a smarter, more integrated and comprehensive approach to battling this twenty-first-century menace.

Following Bush's lead, Obama had with equal constancy framed America's conflict with the terrorists as the defining ideological conflict of this generation—a titanic contest of competing world views, a struggle between an open, democratic, and individualistic society and its polar opposite that would require the application of military might. And even as he sought to bring the war to a conclusion and struggled to define victory in this complex and dangerous new battleground, Obama was insistent that the U.S. recommit to the fight against those who struck on 9/11 and who, along with their affiliated terrorist networks, continued to seek America's destruction. He consistently reiterated that American security, and the ideals the nation embodies, hung in the balance.

International relations scholars Richard Jackson (2012) and Trevor McCrisken (2011) have argued that in spite of re-casting Bush's war-on-terror language and repudiating the previous administration's harsh interrogation policies, Obama never rejected his predecessor's worldview that America was locked in a monumental struggle because of the fundamental principles the nation held most dear. As my analysis has similarly demonstrated, both commanders-in-chief embraced the exceptionalist notion of America as a global model and vigorous promoter of the values of liberty, individual dignity, and opportunity. Obama's most important departure from the Bush frame reflected his belief that the U.S. had failed meet the standards of an exemplary nation in its prosecution of the war. The two presidents thus differed in the war's implementation, not its necessity and what it represented. And by the time he announced his surge-then-exit policy from Afghanistan, Obama could tout success in reconciling his war-related actions with core American values. Hence the assumptions underlying Bush's global war on terror—that in a battle between good and evil nothing less than a military response would suffice—remained ascendant as Obama constructed his own endgame narrative of why America had been forced to fight and what it had achieved in that lengthy conflict.

But powerful though the presidential megaphone might be, other important political players, especially members of Congress, seek the spotlight to express their often competing perspectives. The words the commander-in-chief utters also reach the public through a myriad of media outlets, each staffed by reporters and commentators only too eager to highlight political controversy and add their own interpretations to whatever topic the president is addressing. I now turn to an examination of how leading national U.S. media outlets portrayed Obama's Afghanistan surge strategy and the rationale for war, an analysis that indicates some of the difficulties even the most rhetorically adept president faces in controlling the nation's political discourse, particularly when it involves a seemingly endless conflict. It will thus illustrate both the powers and the limits of the contemporary presidential bully pulpit on the most pressing topics of war and peace and keeping America secure.

Chapter 3
War's Surge-then-Exit through a Skeptical Media Lens

By the time President Obama took the oath of office, Afghanistan had been America's forgotten war for some six years, reduced to a minor supporting role as national attention focused first on the conflict in Iraq and the intense political controversy it engendered and then on the economic crisis that engulfed the United States in the fall of 2008. As we have seen, Obama had constructed a very consistent message on combating the extremists who attacked on September 11, arguing since the fall of 2002 that Afghanistan was the central front in the battle against militant jihadists and that American national security depended on disrupting, dismantling, and defeating an enemy still plotting to do harm. But even his compelling narrative of why the U.S. had to maintain the fight in Afghanistan had been muted on the campaign trail as the spillover effects from the financial collapse on Wall Street forced both presidential candidates to recalibrate their campaign messages.

As reporter Michael Abramowitz (2008) wrote in the *Washington Post* on the seventh anniversary of 9/11, that day's commemoration ceremony would mark a rare moment in the campaign when Obama and McCain would both focus on terrorism, "an issue that has lost prominence for American voters as the deadly attacks recede in the public memory." Arguing that terrorism had often seemed "the forgotten issue of 2008," Abramowitz noted that a mere 4 percent of those surveyed in an August Gallup poll deemed national security the nation's most pressing concern. It was therefore no surprise that the candidates' general election discourse reflected a turn away from the war-related topics that had helped each man gain his respective party's presidential nod. And even when they did debate foreign policy, Obama and McCain highlighted their disagreements on how to move forward in Iraq rather than the policy they essentially agreed upon—that the U.S. should send more troops to Afghanistan and beef up America's commitment to winning there (King and Wells 2009: 201–204).

Nor should it come as any wonder that from the lead-up to war in Iraq through the 2008 presidential campaign, America's national media outlets also averted their collective gaze from the fight against al Qaeda. Even a mounting death toll for U.S. forces in Afghanistan did not lead to heightened media interest: As 2008 became the deadliest year for American troops fighting al Qaeda and the Taliban, the Pew Research Center's Project for Excellence in Journalism (PEJ) found that the war accounted for only 1 percent of total news coverage (Project for Excellence in Journalism 2009c).

But as the new president declared his major foreign policy initiative to be a revised strategy for Afghanistan, media attention began to rise, and in late March, when Obama formally announced his disrupt and dismantle approach, the war in Afghanistan registered as one of the media's top five stories for the first time since the invasion of Iraq. The summer of 2009 was also when coverage of Afghanistan surpassed that of Iraq, as the wars switched places in the race for another dubious honor—the conflict America would most ignore. Even at this critical policy juncture, however, reports on the war in Afghanistan accounted for less than 5 percent of the total newshole in the 55 news outlets PEJ examined, trailing far behind the still dominant economic crisis storyline (Project for Excellence in Journalism 2009a, 2009b).

Throughout the spring and summer of 2009, as Obama continued to highlight the fight against al Qaeda and Afghan presidential and provincial council elections drew closer, media coverage continued to climb, reaching a high of 10 percent of total news stories in the week surrounding the August 20 vote (Project for Excellence in Journalism 2009b). For the next two months, Afghanistan would become the third-biggest story, comprising 9 percent of the newshole and trailing behind only the health care debate and the economic crisis. The week of October 5–11 would mark the first time that Afghanistan, at 20 percent of total news reports, topped the weekly news agenda, a phenomenon that would be repeated the week of Obama's West Point speech on his new surge and exit strategy, as stories on Afghanistan spiked to yet another high of 27 percent of overall media coverage (Project for Excellence in Journalism 2009c, 2009f).

The Tyndall Report, which monitors nightly network broadcast news coverage of domestic and foreign issues and events, uncovered a similar pattern of rising attention to Afghanistan during Obama's first year in office. NBC, CBS, and ABC devoted a total of 556 minutes to the war itself in 2009 and an additional 179 minutes to such related topics as the political, security, and economic situation in the region, almost five times as much air time as they had spent in any year since 2003 and one and a half times the coverage in 2002, the year prior to the U.S. declaration of war in Iraq. Afghanistan was the number three network news story of 2009 and the year's top war and foreign policy story. Iraq, in contrast, did not even make the top 20 broadcast news stories, receiving only about one-seventh of the coverage devoted to Afghanistan (Tyndall 2010).

While the president was able to prime journalists' attention to his new strategy for Afghanistan, he was less successful in controlling the substance and tone of their storylines. As media coverage of the war began to increase, so did the amount of negative news about the deteriorating conditions in Afghanistan. Amid an uptick in violence throughout the country, lax (or non-existent) security at the polls, low voter turnout, charges of widespread electoral fraud, a less than decisive outcome in the presidential contest, and calls for a runoff vote, there was little positive information coming from the August 20 elections (Project for Excellence in Journalism 2009b).

General McChrystal's confidential assessment that absent a significant infusion of combat troops the Afghanistan mission would likely end in failure was leaked to the *Washington Post* in late September, and the ensuing controversy drove the media storyline. Mounting U.S. troop casualties and civil unrest in Afghanistan lent a dramatic backdrop to this coverage. And divisions within the Obama administration about the appropriate troop levels for the war—accompanied by yet more leaks to the media—as well as concerns about the pace of the president's deliberations also led to less than glowing news reports and commentary throughout the fall. Escalating violence in the region and growing doubts about Afghanistan's presidential runoff election were cause for further critical stories in November (Project for Excellence in Journalism 2009d, 2009e).

The November shooting massacre at Fort Hood also injected the issue of domestic terrorism into the war narrative, as did the administration's decision to bring alleged 9/11 mastermind Khalid Sheikh Mohammed and four other terrorism suspects to trial in civilian court in New York City. As expected, both these incidents elicited much impassioned media commentary. And skeptical members of Congress from both sides of the aisle had ramped up their criticisms of the process and substance of Obama's decision-making on the war as the weeks wore on. No matter how one cared to slice it, bad news was simply outpacing the positive in the weeks prior to the president's December West Point address on his Afghanistan strategy.

To make matters even more difficult for Obama, the public's initial response to his plans for a troop buildup in Afghanistan was more tepid than enthusiastic, especially among members of his own party. While a majority of respondents had expressed support for the war against al Qaeda since the fall of 2001, favorable reactions had declined steadily throughout Bush's second term. And even though the conflict in Afghanistan never generated the crisis of legitimacy that continued to hound Iraq, there was definite public ambivalence about the best way to proceed in the war. More worrisome for a president wrestling with what strategy to pursue were polls that indicated the number of Americans who deemed the war not worth fighting passed the 50 percent mark for the first time in August 2009 (Holsti 2011: 68).

The cautious public optimism that greeted Obama's spring deployment announcement gave way over the course of the summer of 2009 to greater pessimism about what the surge in troops might accomplish. By mid-October, U.S. respondents were essentially evenly split on whether Obama would "do the right thing in Afghanistan" as well as on the question of whether he should send the 40,000 additional troops McChrystal had requested for the conflict. And throughout the fall, as the Af/Pak region became increasingly chaotic, the number who said that the war was going somewhat or very badly climbed past 60 percent (Pew Research Center 2009c; Holsti 2011: 67–72). The sharp partisan and ideological divide over Afghanistan also continued unabated, as Republicans and conservatives, by a two-to-one margin, continued to be more supportive than Democrats and liberals of the war in general and keeping U.S. troops in Afghanistan (Pew Research Center 2009c; Holsti 2011: 67–72).

As of the fall of 2009, however, a majority of the U.S. public was not prepared to pull the plug on America's engagement in Afghanistan. Most continued to see a rationale for the use of military force, concurring in a series of public opinion polls that the Taliban posed a major threat to U.S. interests and that failure in Afghanistan would result in dire consequences for the United States, particularly its ability to fight terrorism. Further complicating the already conflicted public perspective on the war was the rather high level of disinterest in the conflict, as a majority in a mid-October Pew Research poll said the news about Afghanistan always seemed the same and that they often lacked the background information to properly follow stories about the war (Pew Research Center 2009b).

Both U.S. public and media interest in Afghanistan began to build in early November as the Obama administration signaled that the president would shortly deliver a major announcement about his strategy for the war. While only 27 percent of the public claimed to have closely followed his February decision to send 17,000 more combat troops to Afghanistan, that number rose to 43 percent in the wake of his December announcement to deploy an additional 30,000 (Pew Research Center 2009d). And as just noted, there was also a comparable spike in media reports in the weeks leading up to Obama's primetime speech. As he worked to focus the spotlight on his policy proposals, the president could rightfully claim success in generating attention for his new way forward in Afghanistan.

But presidents not only seek to alert the media about what to cover; they attempt to influence the substance of media reportage. The presidential goal is to seize the public megaphone and deliver a carefully-constructed message that journalists deem sufficiently compelling to transmit essentially verbatim. Contemporary media norms, as we have seen, can dictate a far less passive approach, potentially setting the stage for contests between competing representations of important issues and events (see Althaus 2003; Entman 2003, 2004; Bennett et al. 2007; Baum and Groeling 2010; Esbaugh-Soha and Peake 2011; Edwards 2003 and 2012).

As the new commander-in-chief announced his strategy to bring closure to the war in Afghanistan, journalists responded with their own storylines about the status of the conflict and the president's strategy for pursuing it. In the following case study, I uncover the major themes U.S. reporters and commentators developed and then compare the media's narrative to Obama's official frame of the war. I look for evidence of media independence on Afghanistan as Obama unleashed the bully pulpit's powers of a primetime speech and numerous public statements to promote his vision of why America fought and how it might extricate itself from the conflict.

To assess the media's depiction of Afghanistan, I performed a qualitative content analysis of war-related news and commentary in five leading mainstream U.S. media outlets—the *New York Times*, *Washington Post*, Associated Press, NBC News, and Fox News—during the 60 days surrounding President Obama's December 1, 2009 address on his revised strategy for Afghanistan. Using the Lexis-Nexis Academic database and the keyword "Afghanistan," I located all the news reports and commentaries that dealt with the conflict during the specified time frame. I eliminated any story unrelated to the war, such as reviews of works of fiction.

As I searched for the primary media themes, I sought to answer several central research questions: Was the president successful in dominating the media discourse about his policy proposals for Afghanistan and the rationale for why America fought? Did the news outlets privilege the official Obama war frame or highlight alternative points of view, especially those on Capitol Hill? To what extent did policy disagreements among the Obama team drive the media narrative? Did event-based reporting from Afghanistan and Pakistan trump accounts of the Washington controversy over the war? And finally, did the media converge on a common war narrative, or did divergent storylines appear across the five media outlets?

One facet of Afghanistan coverage was glaringly apparent: the high level of attention devoted to the conflict and Obama's war-related policy proposals. During the two-month time frame, the *Times* included a total of 574 news and op-ed pieces that specifically mentioned the president's war strategy and deliberations, the political and security situation in the region, American political discourse about the war, and/or incidents involving domestic terrorism potentially linked to al Qaeda. the *Post* contained 506 such news reports and commentaries, and the AP had 835. NBC News broadcast 271 reports on the general topic of the war and Fox News presented 212. This information was delivered through a mix of news reports and analyses bearing the datelines Afghanistan, Pakistan, and Washington, DC; human interest stories, particularly about U.S. troops, from both the war front and home front; brief announcements and news digests (such as lists of war casualties); interviews with both political leaders and average citizens; and opinion pieces, commentaries, and editorials.

Journalists definitely had their own take on the war, and my analysis revealed four major themes that ran throughout the news reports and commentaries: 1) the rampant corruption and chaos in the Af/Pak region; 2) the president's protracted deliberations on the way forward in the war; 3) the disturbing specter of terrorism on U.S. soil; and 4) the strategic calculus behind Obama's surge-then-exit policy. As I discuss in detail below, while the media outlets followed the president's lead in their renewed emphasis on the war, they veered—sometimes rather dramatically—from Obama's frame of the strategy for Afghanistan, the prospects for success, and why America had to continue the fight. But as predicted, the elite U.S. media refrained from questioning the underlying Bush–Obama rationale of why an open-ended military response to terrorism was essential.

Af/Pak: Where Chaos and Corruption Reign

Engulfed in Violence

On November 1, in a news story filed from Kabul, the *Washington Post* reported that Afghanistan's presidential runoff election was very much in doubt as Dr Abdullah

Abdullah, the top challenger to President Hamid Karzai, was threatening to withdraw from the race amid continuing charges that the contest would once more be rigged. "This is a capital on hold," wrote correspondent Pamela Constable (2009), a place where daily life and future plans and dreams were being "held hostage to a messy and uncertain presidential election process." While residents were increasingly fearful of the political chaos and ethnic violence that might tear the capital apart if the challenger pulled out, Afghan and U.S. diplomats were growing more concerned that the electorate would refuse to accept a non-contested Karzai victory as legitimate.

And to make matters even worse, the article continued, Taliban insurgents were again targeting election participants, unleashing suicide squads as the city braced for "an escalation of urban warfare." The U.S. counterinsurgency strategy to weaken the Taliban by fostering a viable political alternative seemed in doubt. Economic projects were being canceled or postponed, wealthy Afghans were sending their families and their capital overseas, and ordinary citizens were trying as best they could to find some semblance of normalcy. As Constable (2009) completed her sketch of life in the paralyzed city, she left her readers with this unsettling image: "On the pink-streaked urban horizon stood the steel skeletons of several half-built offices—begun months ago at a time of promise for democracy and development, but now, like the hopes of the nation, suspended in midair."

A portrait of a society teetering on the security precipice appeared in news reports across all the outlets during the first week of this study. News reports of roadside bombs and attacks on shoppers in markets, mosques, government buildings, and police and military outposts would also continue throughout the months of November and December. On NBC's November 1 edition of *Meet the Press*, moderator David Gregory (2009a) began the segment on the war by noting that it had "been a very difficult week in Afghanistan, been a very difficult month and in fact it is a grim milestone for Afghanistan: October, 55 deaths compared to August, 51 deaths. These have been the worst since the war started back in 2001." NBC's chief Pentagon correspondent Jim Miklaszewski (2009a) added that the Taliban currently exerted more control over Afghanistan than they had before the war. Not only were they able to set up shadow governments and invoke their "own brutal brand of justice," but the "most compelling number is they're able to conduct terror attacks at will over 80 percent of the country."

Fox News correspondent Dana Lewis (2009) reported from Kabul that the Afghan army had now been deployed at key checkpoints once manned by local police, a "more muscular" security presence made necessary because Afghanistan was "on edge" due to uncertainty about who was in charge in the days before the runoff election. According to the *Post*, Kabul residents were particularly concerned that violence could erupt in cities across the country if Abdullah publicly denounced the outcome. One article warned that some of his powerful supporters who commanded regional or private militias had vowed not to recognize or obey a new Karzai administration (Constable and Wilson 2009), and when Abdullah angrily removed himself from contention a day later, a second *Post* story noted the lingering fears that his supporters might still cause violent unrest (Constable and Partlow 2009).

Yet another *Post* news story contained the grim news that the U.N. Afghanistan mission was relocating hundreds of staff members in the wake of a late October suicide attack on a U.N. guesthouse in Kabul that killed five international staff members (Partlow 2009a). Writing of the same lethal incident, *New York Times* correspondent Alissa Rubin (2009a) stated that "The relocation of its workers here, while temporary, is one more signal of mounting pressure on United Nations operations as security deteriorates around the region."

The Afghan public's growing sense of doubt and frustration in the face of mounting violence was another major focus of media stories in early November. Correspondents stationed in Kabul reported that even as al Qaeda's numbers diminished, perhaps to fewer than 100 in Afghanistan and 300 in Pakistan, they had formed an alliance with Taliban insurgent groups whose members numbered in the thousands. Relying on the "emboldened" Taliban for "protection and the manpower to carry out deadly attacks," the *Post*'s Joshua Partlow (2009b) wrote, al Qaeda was able to retain its "premier terrorist brand" and remain a "potent international force." "In bazaars and university across the country," Rubin (2009b) wrote from Charikar, Afghanistan, "eight years of war have left people exhausted and impatient. They are increasingly skeptical that the Taliban can be defeated." The mood on the street had become darker and more wary in recent months, and it was accompanied by a growing mythology of Taliban power. So precarious was daily life, especially outside Kabul, and so seemingly invulnerable were the insurgents, that many of those Rubin interviewed had "come to believe that the United States must want the fighting to go on."

Nor was Afghanistan the only location for stories about the mounting chaos. A brief *Times* article contained the disturbing news from Pakistan that the deadly guesthouse attack had been directed jointly by Taliban and al Qaeda forces based in the North Waziristan tribal area, yet another indicator of the close ties between the two extremist groups (Filkins 2009a). According to a November 1 report in the *Post*, the South Waziristan region was also staring into the security abyss as "a stew of Pakistani and foreign militants" continued to use it as a base from which to attack targets within Pakistan as well as U.S. forces in Afghanistan. Under the Taliban's "iron grip," the region had become a refuge for militant Islamists who had orchestrated a string of recent high-profile strikes across the country. While many of the local residents desperately wanted the Taliban to depart, it was a "deeply entrenched and organized group that has had years to force locals into submission," and the hundreds of thousands of civilians who had fled the latest ground offensive were fearful even to speak about the havoc they had endured (Khan and Brulliard 2009).

The Associated Press similarly reported that an "onslaught of militant violence" had transformed Pakistan's capital Islamabad from "a sleepy oasis to something of a city under siege, with its tree-lined streets barricaded, schools shuttered and jittery residents wondering when the next attack will come." Despite a nationwide security clampdown, suicide bombers and other militants had managed to attack a university and a U.N. office in Islamabad, a nearby army headquarters, a residential section of Lahore, and markets in the northwest. More than 300 people, mostly Pakistani civilians, had been killed, and no one expected the attacks to abate anytime soon (Brummitt 2009).

Additional reports of Taliban and sectarian violence across Pakistan, from IED and other suicide attacks to bombings in mosques, police stations, and military outposts, would also bring a steady stream of bad news throughout November. Particularly worrisome for the American effort in the region, the AP noted, was the Pakistani public's belief that the violence would stop if the U.S. pulled out of Afghanistan (Brummitt 2009). Drawing on more than a dozen interviews with ordinary Pakistani citizens, AP correspondent Chris Brummitt reported that public anger directed at his country was running high: "We want to see a normal life, so for God's sake, listen to what the (militants) are saying. They are against American forces in Afghanistan," an Islamabad carpet dealer complained. "What America is doing is illegal, and that is the root cause of all evils" (Brummitt 2009).

Media reports of violence across the Af/Pak region in no way ended in the wake of Obama's address on the surge in U.S. forces. A quick review of December *Times* news headlines about on-going attacks indicates that, if anything, their pace and scope were escalating: "36 Killed at Mosque for Officers in Pakistan"; "Pakistan: Attack on Intelligence Office"; "Market Attack in Eastern Pakistan Kills at Least 30"; "Twin Attacks in Pakistan Kill Dozens"; "Pakistan Police Say 5 Detained Americans Intended to Fight U.S. in Afghanistan"; "Militants Kill 16 Afghan Police Officers"; "Suicide Bomber Kills 8 at Hotel in Afghanistan's Capital"; "Pakistani Army's Victories Fail to Halt Taliban's Blows"; "9 Wounded in Suicide Bombing"; "Long Firefight with Militants Immobilizes Afghan City"; "Bomber Uses Cart to Kill 8 in Kandahar"; "Pakistan is Rocked by a Spate of Attacks"; and "Militants in Pakistan Strike Shiites Again, Prompting Fears of Sectarian Violence."

On December 31, the year's final *Times* headline carried this disturbing news: "8 Americans, Most with C.I.A., Reported Killed in Afghan Blast." As NBC correspondent Jim Maceda reported from Kabul to *Today Show* anchor Lester Holt,

> The loss is enormous, Lester, first for the CIA. The single biggest loss of life since the U.S. Embassy bombing back in 1983 in Beirut, and it's a blow to U.S. counterterrorism efforts along that Pakistan-Afghanistan border as well, especially those safe havens that are in there. The Taliban has claimed responsibility ... for the attack, which also wounded six other Americans and killed an Afghan civilian. Now, according to the Taliban, the suicide bomber was a uniformed Afghan soldier working for them ... and it raised all kinds of troubling questions about how that soldier breached a usually highly guarded gate and whether there was a letdown or complacency on the part of the Americans at this time of year. (Maceda 2009)

The AP's end-of-year story from Kabul contained the even more sobering report that 2009 had witnessed a record number of U.S. troop deaths, surpassing 500 for the first time in the war. The toll for Afghan civilians had also risen in the first 10 months of the year. And for both groups, improvised explosive devices were the number one cause of death (Heintz 2009).

Evidence of the prevalence of event-driven news was thus abundant in reports posted from Afghanistan and Pakistan in the weeks surrounding Obama's announcement of his new strategy for the region. As Bennett and his colleagues (2007) had found in on-the-ground reports as the Iraq conflict wore on, elite U.S. media outlets seemed less and less content to cover the Af/Pak region from the corridors of power in Washington, DC and ever more interested in eyewitness reports from where the action was occurring. Since unrelenting violence was the major story during the timeframe under study, the tone of news reports and commentaries echoed the negativity of the events themselves. In line with Baum and Groeling's (2010) and Glazier and Boydstun's (2012) hypotheses, as the gap between presidential and media frames widened, the favorability of media reports followed an ever more downward trajectory.

A Problematic Ally

The media storyline of escalating violence in the Af/Pak region underscored Obama's message that the rapidly deteriorating security situation demanded an immediate and sustained U.S. military response. But the more pervasive media tale of Afghanistan's dysfunctional and corrupt government and the fraudulent electoral process that allowed President Karzai to remain in power stepped all over the administration's narrative that the U.S. could forge some sort of viable political partnership with a functioning, legitimately-elected government and together combat America's terrorist foes.

Every news or opinion piece on Karzai invariably depicted him as a stumbling block to the Obama administration's strategy to successfully conclude the war. On November 1, for example, *Times* correspondents Dexter Filkins and Alissa Rubin (2009) noted that the two-month election deadlock that was supposed to be settled with a runoff had "highlighted the Afghan state's state of fragility" and "posed a worsening problem for American and other Western leaders, who have found themselves stuck with a leader who has lost the support of large numbers of Afghans, and whose government is widely regarded as corrupt." When asked how much Abdullah's withdrawal would complicate Obama's efforts to find a legitimate Afghan partner, Fox News commentator Brit Hume (2009) opined that "Karzai will now be tainted by this process" and a lot of people "will think that it was an illegitimate non-election really. So, yeah, it complicates the legitimate partner."

In an analysis titled "Buttressing a Tainted Ally," *Times* chief Washington correspondent David Sanger (2009a) similarly wrote of the White House's "reluctant embrace" of the leader it had sought desperately to replace. Published the day that Abdullah withdrew from the runoff, the article noted that President

Obama now faced a new complication: "enabling a badly tarnished partner to regain enough legitimacy to help the United States find the way out of an eight-year-old war." Achieving that goal, Sanger concluded, would be far from simple; a sentiment echoed in an editorial the *Times* published the following morning:

> Now that Mr Karzai has been re-elected by default, he is going to have to do everything in his power to persuade his people—and the rest of the world—that he is deserving of their trust. After the last seven years of mismanagement and corruption, that will be a hard sell.
>
> The Obama administration, which had to twist Mr Karzai's arm to agree to a runoff, is going to have to twist even harder to get him to build a viable government. President Obama's characterization Monday of the Afghan election process as 'messy' was, to say the least, an understatement. ('President Karzai's Second Term' 2009)

On NBC's *Nightly News*, anchor Lester Holt (2009a) charged that Obama had just "embraced a controversial decision" to leave Karzai as Afghanistan's president. Earlier that day, the network's chief foreign affairs correspondent Andrea Mitchell (2009) stated that the administration had gone to some lengths to persuade Abdullah not to call for a boycott of the runoff or endorse additional protests.

Chief NBC White House correspondent Chuck Todd (2009a) reported that Obama was "reluctantly" trying to project cautious optimism about a new relationship with the Afghan president, as demonstrated in Obama's description of the phone conversation he had just had with Karzai: "I emphasized that this has to be a point in time in which we begin to write a new chapter based on improved governance, a much more serious effort to eradicate corruption, joint efforts to accelerate the training of Afghan security forces so that the Afghan people can provide for their own security." In their description of that conversation, *Times* political correspondents Helene Cooper and Jeff Zeleny (2009) wrote that Obama had "admonished" the Afghan president, telling him that "he must take on what ... he avoided during his first term: the rampant corruption and drug trade that have fueled the resurgence of the Taliban." In an article titled "Obama warns Afghan president: Time for new chapter," the AP characterized Obama's message to Karzai as one of "stern solidarity," also reporting that the U.S. president had greeted Karzai's victory "with as much admonishment as praise" (Feller 2009).

Noting that Obama's words "appeared to be a sharp warning" that the American public would not support a military build-up unless it was satisfied that a "credible" Afghan government was fully committed to tackling "the problems of corruption and bad governance" that had swelled insurgent ranks, AP correspondents Heidi Vogt and Anne Gearan (2009) warned that support for the war was already dropping in the U.S. and other countries with troops in Afghanistan, and that "the image of a fraud-stained Afghan partner does little to reverse the slide."

Another AP story highlighted the extent to which corruption infused every aspect of Afghan life. Correspondents Robert Reid and Kathy Gannon (2009) wrote that while Karzai had promised to stamp out corruption, the image of his victory speech suggested otherwise as standing at his side were his two vice presidents, "both former warlords widely believed to have looted Afghanistan for years." "Reform is a tall order in a country awash in drug money," the article continued. "Afghans pay bribes for everything from driver's licenses to police protection, and the elite too often treat state property as their own." While White House spokesman Robert Gibbs was quoted to the effect that the U.S. embassy in Kabul was working with the Afghans on an anti-corruption compact, the journalists concluded that "Even with a good faith effort, corruption is so deeply entrenched in Afghan society that it could take decades to clean up" (Reid and Gannon 2009).

Media depictions of Hamid Karzai's character and behavior were particularly unfavorable; the adjectives used to describe the Afghan president were frequently as colorful as the multi-hued cape he wore, but far less flattering. AP correspondent Reid (2009a) was relatively restrained as he affixed the labels *weak* and *corrupt* to Karzai and wrote that he was "far from the strong and capable partner that Washington had hoped would emerge" from the electoral process that had made him, in the now-settled media storyline, the victor "by default" (Wilson and Chandrasekaran 2009; Vogt and Gearan 2009). Other news reports and commentaries were even less generous as journalists liberally applied the terms *tarnished*, *troubled*, *unsteady*, *vacillating*, *tainted*, *mercurial*, *embattled*, *erratic*, *unreliable*, *problem*, and *wild card* to the partner on whom the White House now had to pin its hopes in Afghanistan.

A leak from unnamed senior American officials that Ambassador to Afghanistan Karl Eikenberry had recently sent two classified cables to Obama expressing his deep concerns about Karzai's questionable behavior and his corrupt administration certainly served to feed the media storyline about America's flawed partner. AP correspondent Anne Gearan (2009a) noted that Eikenberry, a retired general who had previously served as the top military commander in Afghanistan, was the front line U.S. official dealing with Karzai and therefore knew only too well the bizarre but wily leader whose government was "stained by corruption and mismanagement." Using almost identical words to describe the Afghan regime, an article in the *Post* stated that the ambassador's communications had "highlighted the nagging undercurrent of the policy discussions: the U.S. dependence on a partnership with a Karzai government whose incompetence and corruption is a universal concern within the administration" (Jaffe, Wilson, DeYoung 2009).

Interviewed by David Gregory on *Meet the Press* following the revelation of Eikenberry's supposedly confidential missives, the best that Secretary Clinton (2009a) could muster when asked whether Karzai was an effective and reliable partner was the terse and tepid reply, "I believe that he has his strengths and he has his weaknesses." According to the AP, Obama offered the identical lukewarm assessment three days later during media interviews in Asia, and then went on to add that "I'm less concerned about any individual than I am with a government as a whole that is having difficulty providing basic services to its people" (Gearan 2009b).

Post national security correspondent Walter Pincus (2009a) perhaps best encapsulated the media's portrait of America's problematic ally in a late November article titled "Bad Karzai, Good Karzai." One of Obama's greatest problems as he wrestled with a new strategy for Afghanistan, Pincus stated, was "which Hamid Karzai he is dealing with: the leader who set out specific promising goals in his inaugural address last week, or the apparently bitter and defensive politician seen in a PBS interview broadcast 10 days earlier." Noting Karzai's frequent "mood swings," Pincus wrote that America and her allies could never predict the persona that would show up on any given day, an issue painfully illustrated when Karzai veered from promising in his November 19 inaugural speech that the Afghan army would assume full control of the country's security within five years to the startling pronouncement three weeks later that Afghanistan would not be able to pay for its own security until at least 2024 (Oppel and Bumiller 2009).

Needless to say, journalists were as quick to highlight the White House's tight-lipped response to Karzai's latest outburst as they had been throughout the fall to showcase the Obama administration's repeated—and increasingly exasperated—reassurances that things were going better in Afghanistan than events on the ground might seem to indicate. As *Times* White House correspondent Helene Cooper (2009) wrote, Obama faced "a stark conundrum": The U.S. really did not have any leverage over Karzai. America could "prod, cajole, or bully" all it wanted, but could not deliver on the obvious threat that Karzai must crack down on corruption "or else." And Karzai had already proven to be adept at calling the Americans' bluff as he repeatedly wiggled free of U.S. demands. An AP analysis also noted that the international community had no alternative to the Afghan government they were dealing with, and that Karzai was only too well aware America needed him to win the war against terrorist extremism and therefore had no recourse other than supporting his leadership. Correspondent Robert Reid concurred with his *Times* colleague that Karzai had "called our bluff and so he is in a very strong bargaining position" (Reid 2009b).

Media worries about Karzai's competence and integrity continued unabated in the aftermath of his November inauguration. A mid-December *Times* editorial perhaps said it most succinctly: "Whom Mr Karzai chooses for his new cabinet will be the first indicator, after his fraud-marred election, of whether he is truly determined to rein in epidemic levels of corruption and incompetence. His speech on Tuesday to an anti-corruption conference in Kabul suggested, ominously, that he still does not get it" ("A Test for President Karzai" 2009). The White House narrative that the U.S. had a viable political partnership was thus losing out to a consistent media drumbeat about political malfeasance and ineptitude and the growing likelihood that America might have enmeshed itself in yet another quagmire. Predictions that media independence—and media negativity—would increase as presidential assertions conflicted with realities on the ground were clearly supported.

Dithering or Deliberating?

In an October 2009 speech to the conservative Center for Security Policy, former Vice President Dick Cheney (2009a) declared that "The White House must stop dithering while America's armed forces are in danger. It's time for President Obama to do what it takes to win a war he has repeatedly and rightly called a war of necessity." Cheney's criticism of Obama's fall policy review immediately ricocheted across the media universe as the White House and its supporters issued sharp rejoinders to the man they held most responsible for the Bush policy of drift and neglect in Afghanistan. While the Obama administration ardently defended its actions as a serious and thoughtful deliberative process, concerns about the pace of the president's decision-making—already a matter of frustration and anxiety in some quarters—became a major media storyline and a prime example of journalistic obsession with political process and all its attendant emotion and excitement. Coverage of this theme provides support for Bennett's (2012: 42–44) assertion that the media are biased toward stories that can be personalized, dramatized, and easily distilled into short, accessible, and compelling segments.

Political figures on the conservative side of the political spectrum swiftly moved to add their own negative take on the dilatory nature of Obama's fall deliberations, and the media provided numerous forums for them to voice complaints. The two most prominent GOP leaders to take issue with Obama's slow decision-making were presidential candidate Mitt Romney, who groused in a widely-quoted CBS interview that "this Hamlet performance we're seeing out of the White House has been very disconcerting" ("Romney Prods Obama" 2009), and Senator John McCain, who stated in no uncertain terms that "I feel very strongly that we owe it to the men and women in the military and the national security of the United States of America to have that decision made and made as soon as possible" (McCain 2009).

On Fox's *Special Report*, correspondent Wendell Goler (2009a) also quoted House Minority Leader John Boehner (R-OH) to the effect that "The White House has no further pretext for delaying the decision on giving General McChrystal the resources he needs to achieve our goals in Afghanistan," and in a *Meet the Press* interview, Senator Kay Bailey Hutchison (R-TX) likewise urged the president to make a decision, arguing that "we need to make sure that the world knows we will not back away from Afghanistan. That it is in the American interest, it's in every freedom loving country's interest not to have al Qaeda build up and … export terrorism all over the world" (Hutchison 2009). A number of other GOP members of Congress repeated the same message in media reports and interviews in the weeks leading up to Obama's primetime speech, and the term *dithering* and a variety of related adjectives from *drawn out* to *protracted* appeared to have won the war of words in Washington as opponents went on offense and the Obama administration was forced time and time again to defend its lengthy review process.

Media columnists and commentators were just as eager to offer their analyses and assessments of what was rapidly becoming a major media-fueled controversy.

In a mid-November opinion piece titled "Enough Afghan Debate," veteran *Post* political reporter and columnist David Broder took Obama to task over what he caustically termed "all this dithering":

> The more President Obama examines our options in Afghanistan, the less he likes the choices he sees. But, as the old saying goes, to govern is to choose—and he has stretched the internal debate to the breaking point.
>
> It is evident from the length of this deliberative process and from the flood of leaks that have emerged from Kabul and Washington that the perfect course of action does not exist. Given that reality, the urgent necessity is to make a decision—whether or not it is right.
>
> The cost of indecision is growing every day. Americans, our allies who have contributed their own troops to the struggle against al-Qaeda and the Taliban, and the Afghans and their government are waiting impatiently, while the challenge is getting worse. (Broder 2009)

Post deputy editorial page editor Jackson Diehl (2009) also charged Obama with indecision, noting that the president's rhetoric on Afghanistan had been "noticeably wobbly" even in the face of Pentagon, congressional, and NATO agreement that Afghanistan could not be abandoned anytime soon and that the U.S. must redouble its efforts to build up the Afghan army and strengthen both national and local governance. "Obama's prolonged deliberations would be understandable," Diehl complained, "if he were choosing between escalating or ending the war, as Bush was. Yet he narrowed his options many weeks ago—and still has been unable to come to closure." In another *Post* op-ed piece, columnist and former Bush speech writer Michael Gerson (2009a) echoed his colleagues' critiques, decrying a "dysfunctional Afghan decision-making process in which chaos has preceded choice, complicating every possible outcome."

In a column bearing the title "Unicorns in Kabul; Karzai is making 'dithering' look like wisdom," conservative *Post* columnist George Will (2009a) advanced the argument that no matter how hard or long it tried, the U.S. could never transform Karzai into a legitimate leader or his government into an honest, competent administration. Assuming political legitimacy would descend on Karzai simply because he agreed to another election "controlled by his operatives" was at best an exercise in naïveté, Will wrote. Already the annual cost of America's "errand in Afghanistan" was larger than that country's GDP. And Americans, led by a commander-in-chief whose heart was not in it, would "not sustain the years of casualties and other costs necessary to create self-sufficient Afghan security forces beneath a corrupt regime." It was probably far better that Obama deliberate at length than latch onto an action plan doomed to fail. "If he is looking for a strategy that depends on legitimacy in Kabul," Will (2009a) sarcastically concluded, "he is looking for a unicorn."

A tongue-in-cheek piece in the *Post*'s *Outlook* section titled "94 Days: Was Obama dithering or decisive?" presented other historical decisions, big and small, and compared them to the length of Obama's Afghanistan assessment to determine if the president "rated as a slowpoke or a speed demon." At a mere two days stood the selection of Pope Benedict XVI in 2005; at the other end of the spectrum, at 269 days, was Elizabeth Taylor's shortest marriage. Obama's review was positioned between the time it took the Washington Nationals to sign the top pick in the 2009 draft and the duration of the 1787 Constitutional Convention in Philadelphia, which resulted in the creation of the American Constitution ("94 Days" 2009).

News reports and analyses also covered Cheney's charge of dithering as well as the White House response. An early November AP story stated flatly that Obama's next move on Afghanistan "is growing more difficult by the day" as the president continued to brush off criticism that he was taking too long to decide about McChrystal's troop increase request. "The longer the decision hangs fire," correspondents Anne Gearan and Lara Jakes (2009) wrote, "the more complications mount. The latest violence against foreign civilians and soldiers was unprecedented in scope. And that was on top of Afghanistan's perilous politics, an ongoing headache for the White House." While press secretary Robert Gibbs repeated the administration's talking points about carefully assessing the political and security situation, the article emphasized that the White House was neglecting other related problems such as delays in troop drawdowns in Iraq and increasingly restive coalition allies (Gearan and Jakes 2009).

Not all news reports were critical, however. The following week, *Times* national political correspondent Jeff Zeleny presented the White House's energetic defense of its deliberative process, writing that the Obama administration was "happy" to say the president had not yet reached a decision about his new military strategy for Afghanistan and that they had "purposely made no apologies for the extended timetable":

> The White House has been eager to show that Mr Obama is engaged in extensive deliberations before making what is likely to be one of the most debated decisions of his presidency. Drawing on studies of how decisions were made to escalate the war in Vietnam, Mr Obama and his aides seem intent on showing the nation and the world that he is not being rushed by the military, nor making a judgment without considering the long-term implications. (Zeleny 2009)

An AP article (Gearan 2009c) likewise noted that even though Republican critics had been pressing him for months to decide on a next step in Afghanistan, Obama had repeatedly said that he was "concerned with making a decision that was right rather than quick." But Zeleny's (2009) story contained this cautionary note: In the three plus weeks since the former vice president accused the current incumbent of dithering, the charge had gained public traction as a just-released CNN/Opinion Research poll found that the American public was split on the wisdom of his deliberative process, with 49 percent of those surveyed saying the president was taking too long to decide about troop levels.

Post staff writer Joel Achenbach (2009) described Obama's handling of Afghanistan as a "spectacle of deliberation" unlike anything seen in the White House in recent years—"almost defiantly deliberative, methodical and measured, even when critics accuse him of dithering." This unemotional, "Spock mode" approach to decision-making suggested weakness rather than wisdom to conservatives, while to liberals it indicated an over willingness to compromise. And given the "conundrum" he faced in Afghanistan, Achenbach concluded, it was not yet clear how well Obama's slow decision-making had served him.

AP writers Robert Burns and Ben Fuller (2009) presented a similar assessment of the pluses and minuses of Obama's deliberative process. The president's "drawn-out decision-making on Afghanistan is sending messages," they wrote: "To the Afghan government: Clean up your act. To the Pentagon: I'm no rubber stamp. To the American public: More troops can't be the sole answer." They noted that the slow process had allowed Republicans to accuse him of dithering on a situation that he had months earlier labeled "increasingly perilous." But in making it clear he would not be rushed, Obama was signaling his resolve and seriousness about finding a sustainable solution to the conflict. The AP article also allowed the president's own voice to be heard as he defended his "methodical approach" to wartime decision-making: "I've been asking not only General McChrystal, but all of our commanders who are familiar with the situation, as well as our civilian folks on the ground, a lot of questions. I want to make sure that we have tested all the assumptions we're making before we send young men and women into harm's way" (Burns and Fuller 2009).

On *The Today Show* shortly before Thanksgiving, NBC White House correspondent Savannah Guthrie (2009) reported that Obama was likely to make his decision on the war any day now, and that the president and his war council had extended their discussions late into the previous night. Host Matt Lauer offered the comment that "the deliberation process has been a long one," a perspective more dramatically underscored on that evening's *Nightly News* when former Vice President Cheney's latest broadside against the president's decision-making process was aired: "It's not one of those deals where you can just sit there and delay and delay and delay and think you're going to make a better decision," Cheney (2009b) again declared. The clip of Cheney was rebroadcast the following morning on *Today*, with chief Pentagon correspondent Jim Miklaszewski adding the far more neutral observation that the president's "intensive review" was still being fine-tuned (2009c).

Two days prior to Obama's primetime address, the host of NBC's *Chris Matthews Show* asked his guests to address the following question: "It took three months to make this decision. Will he look smart and deliberative for having taken all this time, or [is] the dithering shot still being cast at him by people like former Vice President Dick Cheney ... still going to hurt?" (Matthews 2009). The media panelists were uncertain. While *Post* correspondent Anne Kornblut replied that "the gamble they're making is that he'll look smart and he'll look like the anti-Bush for having thought about it for so long," her colleague David Ignatius cautioned that "the long period of analysis, very deliberative, robs this of passion … Too much college professor" (Kornblut and Ignatius 2009).

Commentaries on Fox News rendered particularly harsh verdicts on Obama's protracted policy review. In a November 1 interview on *Fox News Sunday*, radio talk show host Rush Limbaugh (2009) gleefully repeated Cheney's charge of dithering, as did the guests and host on *Fox Hannity* the following day (although co-host Judith Miller (2009) did interject that "the man who ignored Afghanistan to the point where it's gotten this bad has no right to criticize President Obama on this matter"). Employing his own verb of choice, commentator Bill O'Reilly (2009a) declared that Obama had been "*paralyzed* on Afghanistan for two months, maybe more." And in an interview with Greta van Susteren, former U.N. Ambassador John Bolton savaged the president for his indecisiveness and the deleterious impact it was having at home and abroad:

> This is like a slow-motion train wreck, watching this decision-making process, and it is really having a debilitating effect, I think, on troop morale in Afghanistan. And globally, it's having a debilitating effect on America's reputation. It's not just the president's indecisiveness in Afghanistan, but his weakness and indecisiveness in other areas, as well, that gives the reputation that he's got a problem making hard decisions. (Bolton 2009)

Fox News commentator Charles Krauthammer labeled Obama's deliberative process *agonizing* and argued that Obama had been dragging his feet not because he was concerned about the composition of the government in Afghanistan,

> but because he was worried about the composition of the government in the United States, meaning whether his popularity would suffer if he went with the generals, whether the Democrats are going to lose seats in the House and the Senate next year, whether or not he will be able to pass his cherished domestic agenda if he alienates his left by accepting an escalation of the war. (Krauthammer 2009b)

Krauthammer also voiced his strong suspicion that the president was not really committed to the fight against terrorism: "He said it is a war of necessity. Does he believe it? And that's the real issue. If you're going to go into war and escalate a war, you have to have a commander-in-chief who believes in the war. And the way he has acted it looks as if even if he decided he would go into it he will be half-hearted" (Krauthammer 2009b). The theme that Obama did not care about winning the war would be repeated on Fox in the weeks prior to the president's West Point address, as exemplified by panelist Stuart Varney's (2009) late November statement on *Fox Hannity* that "My perception is that his heart is not in it. Hence, the dithering and delay over Afghanistan. And the half-hearted idea of what we're going to do there," and Krauthammer's (2009d) complaint that same evening that Obama had been "all over the map during this deliberative period" and had yet to define his objective.

By mid-November, even editorially liberal outlets had begun to press President Obama to bring closure to the deliberative process on Afghanistan. Thus while it applauded the president's "sober, systematic review of his options," the *Times*'s editorial board ("Mr Obama's Task" 2009) warned that "the political reality is that the longer Mr Obama waits, the more indecisive he seems and the more constrained his options appear." *Post* associate editor and columnist David Ignatius (2009b) described Obama's policy review as "agonizingly slow" and wrote that his "slow-motion process of deliberation" had come at a cost in public support as his concern for finding "an early off-ramp" had led many to wonder whether he really wanted to engage the war at all. And restating Krauthammer's and Ignatius's earlier concerns, an editorial in the *Post* fretted that the president's "prolonged deliberations" as well as some of his public comments cast doubt on his commitment to pursue the war to a successful conclusion:

> As Mr Obama has deliberated, much of what has been said or leaked by his administration has concerned why the war might be unwinnable. Mr Karzai's failings have been thoroughly aired, along with Afghanistan's long history of swallowing foreign armies; there have been discussions of the high cost of more troops and of doubts about whether the Taliban really threatens the United States. If he now is to propose going forward with a campaign to defeat the Taliban and stabilize the country, Mr Obama needs to make the case strongly for why it is needed and how it can work. Both Americans and Afghans wonder whether the president believes in the war and has the will to win it. ('The Afghan Decision' 2009)

Since the fall of 2002, Obama had consistently highlighted his strong support for the fight against al Qaeda, and as president he regularly used the powers of bully pulpit to champion a muscular anti-terrorism policy, but his protracted strategic review had given his political opponents and journalists the opportunity not only to question the slow pace of his deliberations but to level the far more damaging charge that he did not really want to win the war against America's extremist foes. Against this backdrop of controversy, Obama would deliver an address on what NBC's Savannah Guthrie (2009) called "the most important national security decision the president will make, one aides here know could be the lasting legacy of this presidency." But an unanticipated, tragic event in early November—a shooting rampage on a U.S. Army base—would also form part of the context for Obama's primetime speech, and it too would help shape the media storyline about the U.S. fight against extremism in ways the White House could neither have anticipated nor welcomed.

Terrorism Again Hits Home

On November 6, the morning after the shootings at the Texas military base, the AP began a story titled "Troubling portrait emerges of Fort Hood suspect" with the following observation:

> His name appears on radical Internet postings. A fellow officer says he fought his deployment to Iraq and argued with soldiers who supported U.S. wars. He required counseling as a medical student because of problems with patients.
>
> There are many unknowns about Nidal Malik Hasan, the man authorities say is responsible for the worst mass killing on a U.S. military base. Most of all, his motive. But details of his life and mindset, emerging from official sources and personal acquaintances, are troubling. (Blackledge 2009)

Over the next few days, as all five news outlets I examined devoted extensive news reports and commentaries to the incident, a more complex media narrative would emerge. It became a tale not only of a deeply disturbed individual but of the often overwhelming stress facing U.S. troops in a time of two wars, the ambiguous status of U.S. Muslim troops in the post-9/11 era, the continuing threat of Islamic terrorism on American soil, and the many difficulties of keeping America secure. Once again, event-driven news had shifted the content of media reports away from the president's desired narrative.

When Minds Snap

In its initial story on the shooting, the *Post* employed a mental-health frame, emphasizing the psychological toll that repeated deployments were taking on today's all-volunteer force and implying that emotional problems could have been the precipitating factor for this horrific episode. The military personnel at Fort Hood, correspondent Ann Tyson (2009b) noted, had the highest number of suicides among Army installations since the U.S. invasion of Iraq, and while it was not yet clear why the Army psychiatrist had opened fire on his fellow soldiers, it was known that he had worked in settings where "the effects of combat stress were pervasive." And even though Hasan had not been deployed to the war zone, those who treated the mentally wounded, including doctors such as Hasan, were not "immune from the symptoms" of post-traumatic stress disorder.

Times columnist Bob Herbert also used the shooting incident as an opportunity to highlight the mental health problems of those currently fighting America's wars. Writing that the authorities would deal with Hasan, Herbert emphasized that the U.S. needed to look very closely at the "stress beyond belief" that was being endured by so many in the armed forces:

> Simply stated, we cannot continue sending service members into combat for three tours, four tours, five tours and more without paying a horrendous price in terms of the psychological well-being of the troops and their families, and the overall readiness of the armed forces to protect the nation.
>
> The breakdowns are already occurring and will only get worse as the months and years pass and we remain engaged in the conflicts in Afghanistan and Iraq … This small sliver of the overall U.S. population has carried the burden of the wars …, mostly without complaint, for years. It's time to reassess what we're doing to them. (Herbert 2009a)

A second *Post* article focused on the strains in the military health-care bureaucracy, highlighting the "tensions, frustrations and problems" as thousands of returning troops with psychiatric problems overwhelmed VA hospitals around the country. In the meantime, the article went on to add, more than two years after top military and political leaders had pledged to improve mental-health care, the top health-policy positions in the Pentagon were still unfilled, providing further evidence of an "undermanned, overworked health-care system" that ill-served all those in need (Hull and Priest 2009). NBC chief foreign correspondent Richard Engel (2009) reported from Bagram Air Base in Afghanistan that the combat stress center on the base was extremely active, performing up to 1500 counseling sessions every month. And he too emphasized that the mental-health professionals bore the stress of war: "Even though they're trained to keep perspective, listing to so many traumatic stories can take a toll on the caregivers."

A news report in the *Times* (Carey et al. 2009) similarly noted that the rampage had "put a spotlight" on the strains experienced both by the military's mental-health professionals and the patients they treated. "Major Hasan was one of a thin line of military therapists trying to hold off a rising tide of need," the article stated, and in a system stretched to the breaking point, some of those hired to heal others ended up needing help themselves. Another article in the *Times*'s *News of the Week in Review* stated that even in the absence of certainty about Hasan's motives, the U.S. needed to examine whether his "own psyche" was "undone by the kind of stress he treated." America's current wars, correspondent Erica Goode (2009) wrote under the headline "When Minds Snap," "have claimed more than their share of stress victims, with a rising number of suicides surging among soldiers and high rates of post-traumatic stress disorder. Such casualties often occur not on the battlefield but after it—or, sometimes, merely in its proximity."

AP writer Kimberly Hefling (2009) also advanced the snapped-under-stress storyline, stating that the rampage raised questions of whether there was "enough help for the helpers" in a system that a 2007 military mental health task force deemed problematic even for non-deployed mental health personnel. Noting that Hasan was shortly to be sent to the war zone, she wrote that with the U.S. fighting two wars, "an acute shortage of trained personnel has left these therapists emotionally drained and overworked, with limited time to prepare for their own war deployments."

Descriptions of the bravery and fortitude of America's fighting forces, a mainstay of presidential war framing, were given short shrift in media accounts as the mental health problems of countless military personnel took center stage.

A Jihadist Connection

As journalists sought to uncover the motivations for Hasan's attack, a second media storyline took root: the military psychiatrist's alleged connections to militant jihadism. Were his actions driven by stress related to his upcoming deployment to Afghanistan or did they stem instead from an Islamist political ideology? The media tale tended to intertwine these two contributing factors, emphasizing that an individual under mounting psychological duress had indeed been following an increasingly rigid ideological and religious path. And it served to mute the presidential narrative that America was winning the battle for Islamic hearts and minds.

An article in the *Post* two days after the massacre (Wilson, Johnson, Hsu 2009) noted a number of possible warning signs that the killings were a result of Hasan's extremist political sympathies, but stated that his acute emotional distress was also apparent as friends and acquaintances said Hasan had been increasingly agitated over the U.S. wars in Iraq and Afghanistan and reportedly claimed the U.S. "war on terror" was a "war on Muslims." An AP story revealed a similar disturbing pattern: "There was the classroom presentation that justified suicide bombings. Comments to colleagues about a climate of persecution faced by Muslims in the military. Conversations with a mosque leader that became incoherent" (Brown and Breed 2009). The *Times* reported that investigators believed Hasan's counseling activities fueled his anger and "hardened his increasingly militant views as he was seeming to move toward more extreme religious beliefs—all of which boiled over as he faced being shipped overseas, an assignment he bitterly opposed" (Johnston and Schmitt 2009). But despite his increasingly angry and outspoken opposition to American policies in the wars, there was still no evidence, the article concluded, that he was directed or steered into violence or ever traveled overseas to meet with extremist groups.

A *Times* editorial titled "The Horror at Fort Hood" (2009) suggested that harassment by fellow soldiers because he was a Muslim might have been one motivation for Hasan's shocking actions; other possible reasons included his opposition to America's military involvement in Afghanistan and Iraq and his desire for a discharge from the Army. While the editorial board also briefly mentioned eyewitness reports that Hasan shouted "God is Great" in Arabic before he began shooting, they did not pursue that more ideological line of speculation, concluding instead that no one might ever understand what led him to his "appalling rampage."

A *Times* news report published the same day (Krauss and Dao 2009) noted that officials were still unprepared to say whether the attack was the act of a "lone and troubled man" or was connected to foreign or domestic terrorist groups, and it cited Obama's request that the nation avoid jumping to conclusions while the investigations were in process. But the article also painted a mixed portrait of an introverted person with few friends who had limited his contacts with coworkers to debating the wars in Iraq and Afghanistan and making clear his strong opposition to both. Family members cited in the report mentioned anti-Muslim harassment in the Army, his desire to leave the service, and his increasing turn to religion but not extremism.

Another *Times* story emphasized the "struggles and frustrations," from name-calling and taunts to simple lack of understanding, that Hasan and his fellow Muslims in the service frequently experienced (Elliott 2009). But correspondent Andrea Elliott also noted that all the Muslim leaders, advocates, and military service members she interviewed went to great pains to denounce the shooting and distance themselves from Hasan. *Times* correspondents James McKinley and James Dao (2009) reported that Hasan had been growing more and more vocal about his opposition to the wars, increasingly disgruntled about the Army and the anti-Muslim harassment he was facing, and had sought legal advice about getting a discharge. They also detailed his turn to religion and his growing struggles with the idea of having to fight fellow Muslims if he were deployed.

The day after the shootings, NBC Pentagon correspondent Jim Miklaszewski (2009b) reported that Army officials agreed there were many missed warning signs that Hasan's commanders should have recognized as a potential threat and that some military experts claimed he should never been sent to Fort Hood or tapped for a combat deployment. On *Meet the Press*, host David Gregory asked Army Chief of Staff General George Casey whether Hasan had hardened political or religious views against the U.S. or its two wars. Casey (2009) said that the evidence was not yet clear, and when queried about whether warning signs of Hasan's growing disaffection had been missed, the general confessed that "all those things could add up to a conclusion by the investigators that ... we should have seen something."

Post columnist Eugene Robinson (2009a) scolded the military for failing to intervene before Hasan exploded into violence. "There's a difference between sensitivity and stupidity," he wrote. "If there were indeed signs that Maj. Nidal Hasan ... was becoming radicalized ... the Army had a duty to act—before he did." Although General Casey was right to worry about bigotry against Muslims, it "only feeds such paranoia to ignore alarm bells than an unstable individual, Muslim or not, is about to blow." If Hasan's superiors had investigated, they might have pieced together the story that seemed to be emerging: "that Hasan was behaving erratically, that his faith apparently had become increasingly political, that he desperately wanted out of the military and that he was distraught about being ordered to the war zone" (Robinson 2009a).

The *Post*'s editorial board concurred, writing that hints of potential trouble had been "there for all to see" for at least a year ("In Plain Sight?" 2009). From his "troubling" presentations at Walter Reed on Islam and the U.S. military to the email correspondence with a known radical Muslim cleric that caught the attention of the FBI, the damaging trail was obvious. And when two joint terrorism task forces became aware in December that Hasan had sent 10 to 20 emails to Anwar al-Awlaki, a radical imam in Yemen who had used his personal website to encourage Muslims to engage in jihad against America, "red flags should have become red alerts."

The *Times* also reported (Johnston and Shane 2009; Shane and Johnston 2009) that intelligence agencies had intercepted email communications the previous year between Hasan and al-Awlaki, but that federal authorities had dropped their inquiry after deciding Hasan's messages were consistent with research he was conducting and did not suggest any threat of violence. Another article contained the breaking news that additional clues to Hasan's radicalization had just been uncovered in the form of his personal business cards bearing the cryptic abbreviation "SoA," apparently referring to "Servant of Allah" or "Soldier of Allah" (Shane and Dao 2009). Was Hasan a terrorist driven by religious extremism or a troubled loner and misfit who cracked? *Times* correspondents Scott Shane and James Dao (2009) concluded that the current trail of evidence suggested both "emotional problems and nascent extremism" spurred his behavior. Thus the prevailing official theory remained intact—that Hasan acted by himself, "lashing out as a result of a combination of factors, including his outspoken opposition to American policy in Iraq and Afghanistan and his deepening religious fervor as a Muslim."

Some conservative commentators, particularly *Post* columnist Charles Krauthammer, were infuriated with the rush to "medicalize" this instance of mass murder rather than to frame it as a politically-motivated event (2009c). "What a surprise," he sarcastically wrote, "that someone who shouts 'Allahu Akbar' (the 'God is great' jihadist battle cry) as he is shooting up a room of American soldiers might have Islamist motives. It certainly was a surprise to the mainstream media, which spend the weekend after the Fort Hood massacre playing down Nidal Hasan's religious beliefs." Applying a psychological label of PTSD to a cold-blooded, ideologically-inspired massacre not only exonerated the perpetrator but turned a murderer into a victim, "indeed a sympathetic one." Military author and former Reagan Assistant Secretary of Defense Bing West (2009a) heartily concurred, writing in a *Post* op-ed column that Hasan was "a rational, evil murderer" who had chosen to betray his two sacred oaths as a doctor and a soldier not because he was "disturbed" but because he was part of a "tiny, evil minority" of Muslims who had hijacked their faith for their own twisted ends.

In its news coverage of the shootings, Fox News also highlighted the Hasan-as-terrorist storyline. The network's initial story featured a telephone interview between Fox anchor Shepard Smith (2009) and a retired colonel from Fort Hood who had heard Hasan make a series of comments to the effect that the U.S. should not be in Iraq and Afghanistan and that Muslims should fight the American aggressor. Fox News reports and commentaries then ran with this interpretation of events, decrying the missed warning signs and essentially dismissing any explanation other than that this was an act of terrorism.

As Fox strategic analyst Lt. Col. Ralph Peters stated on the *O'Reilly Factor* the following evening:

> What happened yesterday at Fort Hood was the worst terror attack on American soil since 9/11. It was committed by a Muslim fanatic, who shouted 'Allah is great' and gunned down 44 unarmed innocent soldiers and civilians. And our president tells us not to rush to judgment to wait until all the facts are in.
>
> What facts are we waiting for? This was an Islamist terrorist act. And I'm sorry if it's inconvenient for Washington to face the facts. But there is no question about it. It was a terrorist act. It was committed by an Islamist. We knew he was an Islamist. The military did nothing about it out of political correctness. (Peters 2009)

Host Bill O' Reilly (2009b) did present the alternative explanation that "while this guy was a rabid Muslim, and obviously sympathetic to the Muslim cause ... there is a possibility that this guy was so troubled personally that he just snapped, and that the Muslim thing wasn't the primary motivator for his killing of all those people." But Peters countered that this was a planned attack since Hasan had taken a couple of days to acquire the weapons, give away his possessions, and basically close down his apartment. "It was a cold-blooded act," Peters concluded. "It wasn't a crime of passion ... This was something very, very different. It was a terrorist act." O'Reilly quickly assented.

Two days later, on *Fox News Sunday*, Senator Joseph Lieberman (I-CT), chair of the Senate Homeland Security Committee, also broached the issue of Islamic terrorism. While cautioning that not all the evidence had been examined, Lieberman categorically stated that if the reports about Hasan's statements and actions turned out to be valid, "the murder of these 13 people was a terrorist act and, in fact, it was the most destructive terrorist act to be committed on American soil since 9/11" (Lieberman 2009). He also announced that his committee would shortly begin an investigation both of Hasan's motives and why the Army missed warning signs that should have led to his discharge. With the revelation that Hasan had an email correspondence with al-Awlaki, the terrorism narrative gained further traction on Fox. Former senior Bush advisor Karl Rove (2009) declared that this was a "cold-blooded murder" by somebody who was not simply a "misunderstood tragic figure" but was motivated by a "jihadist philosophy ... an alien ideology that hates our freedoms and hates what is at the core of being an American."

Representative Pete Hoekstra (R-MI), chair of the House Intelligence Committee, stated on *Fox Hannity* that the shooting "looks a whole like terrorism" and that even though Hasan acted on his own, he was motivated by "radical jihadism." And he and other commentators roundly criticized Obama for refusing to link Hasan to Islamic terrorism. As Hoekstra noted,

You need to remember the orientation of this administration. It was a few months ago that they said we don't want to use the word terrorism ... It is a political correctness that is making it unable for us to identify the real threat of homegrown terrorism. And if you can't define the threat ... you won't be able to put in place strategies to contain it and to defeat it. This puts us at greater risk. (Hoekstra 2009)

The White House would also find little support from voices on the left about the links between the killings and the larger issue of the war. While *Times* columnist Frank Rich (2009) vehemently disagreed with the conservative frame of Hasan as a terrorist aided and abetted by the so-called politically-correct liberal media, the inept national security bureaucracy, and the dithering Obama administration, his perspective on Afghanistan would be even more scathing than that of his conservative brethren. Critics on the right, Rich insisted, had failed to connect two crucial dots: "How our failing war against terrorists in Afghanistan might relate to our failure to stop a supposed terrorist attack at home." Perhaps the right wing was correct about Hasan, Rich sarcastically wrote, "and he is just one cog in an apocalyptic jihadist plot that has infiltrated our armed forces." But if that were true, they then had an obligation to explain how pouring more troops into Afghanistan would have stopped Hasan. "Don't hold your breath," Rich concluded. "If we have learned anything concrete so far from the massacre at Fort Hood, it's that our hawks, for all their certitude, are as utterly confused as the rest of us about who it is we're fighting in Afghanistan and to what end" (Rich 2009).

Times op-ed contributor and senior fellow at the New American Foundation Robert Wright (2009) took the liberal critique one step further, arguing that the shootings were "an example of Islamic terrorism being spread partly by the war on terrorism." America's "nearly obsessive focus on al Qaeda—the deployment of whole armies to uproot the organization and to finally harpoon America's white whale, Osama bin Laden," had merely spurred on other angry Muslims around the globe. If you were a Muslim "teetering toward radicalism and you have a modem," Write continued, "it doesn't take Mr bin Laden to push you over the edge. All it takes is selected battlefield footage and a little ad hoc encouragement: a jihadist chat group here, a radical imam there—whether in your local mosque or on a website in your local computer." This would stand as the only overt media challenge to the war-on-terror narrative in the five media outlets during the time period under study, testimony to a hegemonic frame's ability to control both political and media discourse (see Krebs and Lobasz 2007; Krebs and Jackson 2007).

The Ever-Looming Terrorist Threat

With the mid-November news that alleged 9/11 terrorist mastermind Khalid Sheikh Mohammed and his co-conspirators would be tried in civilian court near Ground Zero in New York city, the issue of terrorism and Obama's approach to dealing with it would also become entwined with the media narrative of his plans to fight extremism in Afghanistan. And once again conservatives voiced their criticism that the president was failing to pursue America's most important security battle. Former New York City mayor Rudolph Giuliani stated in the *Times* (Berger 2009) that treating the 2001 terrorist attacks "like an ordinary murder" was an enormous mistake and another example of Obama "deciding that we're not at war with terrorists anymore." And he had this to add about the Fort Hood shootings: "The administration has been slow to come to the conclusion that Hasan is an Islamic terrorist. These are acts of war."

Panelist Liz Cheney declared on *Fox News Sunday* (2009) that the decision to hold civilian trials was taking America back to a "pre-9/11 treatment of terrorism" and that it was "absolutely unconscionable" that the president was simultaneously denying U.S. troops in Afghanistan the resources they needed to prevail while providing terrorists "a public platform where they can spew venom, where they can preach jihad, where they can reach out and recruit other terrorists." And Fox senior correspondent Eric Shawn (2009) confirmed the suspects' intentions to exploit their federal civilian trial "as a platform to push al Qaeda propaganda," reporting that the lawyer for one of the suspects said all five had agreed to plead not guilty and would use the proceedings to "publicly criticize American foreign policy and explain why 9/11, in their view, was justified."

Reports of the thwarted airliner terror attack on Christmas Day also contributed to the twin media storylines that terrorism remained America's most intractable national security issue and that the White House was having difficulty confronting it at home. As the *Times* reported (Schmitt 2009), the plot, which apparently originated in Yemen, demonstrated the growing ability of al Qaeda affiliates to stage attacks; as a consequence, the administration now had to defend the U.S. from strikes conceived in "multiple havens abroad." Noting that "the last thing the world needs is another haven for al Qaeda," the *Times*'s editorial board wrote that if there was any good news here, it was that the administration—"which shockingly missed a series of warnings about the plot"—had recently been paying close attention to Yemen and had stepped up covert operations against al Qaeda forces there ("Now Yemen" 2009).

On *Meet the Press*, Secretary of Homeland Security Janet Napolitano (2009) struggled to explain why the bureaucracy she headed was caught so off guard and, walking back her earlier comment that "the system worked," why the U.S. intelligence system seemed to have been enmeshed in such a massive security failure. On *The Today Show*, Representative Peter King (R-NY), ranking Republican on the Homeland Security Committee, chastised the vacationing commander-in-chief for failing to address the incident for 72 hours. King noted his disagreement with Obama's contention that this was an isolated extremist, declaring that "He's an Islamic terrorist, who's part of an international movement, whether or not he's an actual member of al-Qaeda" (P. King 2009). And he added that the administration's decision to treat the suspect as a common criminal to be tried in the civilian justice system was a major error that would come back to haunt America's anti-terrorism efforts.

For Fox News, the Christmas airline bomber incident was yet another instance of the current administration's failure to grasp the gravity and true nature of the on-going terrorist threat. As commentator Stephen Hayes (2009) asserted on *Fox Special Report*, it was "stunningly foolish" of the president to claim that the suspect was an isolated extremist when all evidence was pointing to the terrorist group al Qaeda in the Arabian Peninsula. And anchor Jim Angle remarked that even though Obama said this was a serious reminder of the nature of those who threatened America, he continued to deny their real nature: "He calls them violent extremists. A guy who shoots an abortion doctor is a violent extremist. The nature of the threat that we're facing is jihadism …; that's the threat. It is a word he dare not use" (Angle 2009). The AP also highlighted the dangerous terrorist network inside Yemen, citing the warning of a terrorism expert: "The ultimate achievement for these folks is being able to replicate something that previously only al Qaeda central could achieve. If you can be sophisticated enough to hit a target in the continental United States, that's a tremendous achievement" (Abu-Nasr 2009).

According to a *Post* editorial, the thwarted airplane bombing raised three causes for alarm: America's porous airport screening system, a clumsy terrorism bureaucracy, and the emergence of Yemen as a terrorist training ground. To that list, the editorial board added a fourth concern: the "disturbingly defensive reaction" of the Obama administration. The system did not work, as Secretary Napolitano originally claimed; the attack had been averted only through the luck of a faulty detonator and the quick response of alert passengers ("Unconnected Dots, Again" 2009). The editorial also noted that the episode served as "another sobering reminder that eliminating Afghanistan as a haven for terrorist planning is necessary but not sufficient." A successful U.S. counterterrorism strategy would also have to devote attention to states such as Yemen and Somalia to assure they did not become the next Afghanistan. As a second editorial concluded: "Does the trouble in Yemen mean that the United States is wasting its resources on Afghanistan? Of course not. Al-Qaeda's central base remains the Afghanistan-Pakistan borderlands. The hard truth is that the fight against Islamic extremism will have to be waged on multiple fronts" ("The Trouble with Yemen" 2009).

This aspect of the media storyline dovetailed perfectly with Obama's consistent message that terrorism remained a grave threat to America and that confronting it continued to be the nation's greatest challenge. Unfortunately for the White House, the media take on this latest security failure did little to advance the narrative that the current administration was well positioned to do the actual job of keeping America safe.

Assessing Obama's Strategic Gamble

As Obama's announcement of the course he would follow in the war drew closer, the media focused also on the substance of the president's deliberations. On November 1, the AP reported that the administration had been grappling for months with whether to continue targeting the Taliban with more U.S. forces in an "increasingly deadly war" in Afghanistan or focus on eliminating al Qaeda and other terrorists with unmanned spy planes in Pakistan. The story noted that about 68,000 American troops had already been ordered to deploy to Afghanistan by the end of the year, and that General McChrystal wanted at least an additional 40,000 (Jakes 2009). Correspondent Lara Jakes wrote that the White House had signaled it would probably send more forces, but fewer than what McChrystal desired. A high-level source stated that the national security team was trying to define a "sufficiency standard"—the number of U.S. troops sufficient to stabilize Afghanistan militarily, politically, and economically over the next three to five years (Jakes 2009). A week and a half later, the AP reported that Obama was nearing a decision to add tens of thousands more forces, but likely not quite the number his top general sought, a strategy officials had dubbed "McChrystal Light" (Gearan and Hurst 2009).

Other media reports added further analysis, interpretation, and speculation to this basic information. *Post* associate editor and columnist David Ignatius wrote that the strategy Obama was formulating would combine elements of broad counterinsurgency with a narrower counterterrorism approach, a "complicated and ambitious" plan that was not without its dangers:

> A strategy that combines stroking your friends and pounding your enemies runs the risk of sending mixed messages. The public, here and around the world, may conclude that for all their new talk about drinking tea, the Americans are ruthless killers. Meanwhile, the enemy may conclude that whatever its firepower, the United States is impatient and will eventually go away. The wires may get crossed, in other words, with people getting the opposite message from the one intended. (Ignatius 2009a)

Post correspondents Scott Wilson and Rajiv Chandrasekaran (2009) emphasized the complications President Karzai posed to the troop-intensive counterinsurgency effort favored by McChrystal, noting that several of Obama's senior civilian advisors, led by Vice President Biden, had used Karzai's weakness and corruption to argue that the U.S. should instead adopt a narrower counterterrorism campaign focused on defeating al Qaeda in Pakistan primarily through drone strikes. So the basic question still remained: Whose approach would prevail? For America's leading media outlets, this strategic question was far more intriguing than a more substantive, policy-based analysis of the merits of the various approaches to fighting terrorism.

The *Times* began its November coverage by searching for clues to the answer. Political writer for the *New York Times Magazine*, Matt Bai (2009), looked to the president's basic character, stating that "despite the Republican hype about his radical nature, Obama is a leader who instinctively seeks the center lane of American politics." His colleague David Sanger (2009a) focused on the president's words, noting that early in his term Obama had dropped the grandiose Bush-era talk of turning Afghanistan into a Western-style democracy and had recently narrowed U.S. military objectives to destroying al Qaeda in Pakistan while subverting the Taliban's ability to re-take Afghanistan. A middle-of-the-road approach thus seemed likely.

Times correspondents Peter Baker and Helene Cooper (2009) reported the following week that officials had confirmed Obama was considering a 30,000-troop plan predicated on the belief that the Taliban could not be completely eradicated in Afghanistan and that al Qaeda was the real threat—a hybrid approach combining elements of both counterinsurgency and counterterrorism. Their colleagues Elisabeth Bumiller and David Sanger (2009) also wrote that three top advisors—the secretary of defense, secretary of state, and the chair of the Joint Chiefs of Staff—were leaning toward that option, but that the president remained unconvinced America had an adequately viable political partner in President Karzai to allow this strategy to succeed.

The media predilection for conflict, controversy, and palace intrigue came to the fore with the leak of Ambassador Eikenberry's reservations about a major troop increase, as the prospect of a dramatic power struggle within the upper echelons of the Obama administration formed the backdrop for additional stories about the content of the strategic review. The *Post* (Jaffe, Wilson, de Young 2009) reported that the secretaries of state and defense had backed a major increase in U.S. forces, arguing that only a large-scale counterinsurgency could produce an Afghan government able to prevent the country from again becoming an al Qaeda haven. On the other side of the policy divide stood the Biden supporters, now allied with Eikenberry, who were pushing for a far more modest troop increase and a focus on non-troop incursions in Pakistan.

In an article titled "Ambassador's Views Show Sharp Afghanistan Divide," *Times* reporters Mark Landler and Jeff Zeleny (2009) wrote that the administration's "behind-the-scenes tug-of-war over policy has become increasingly bitter" as Eikenberry and McChrystal pointedly disagreed over the ability of the Karzai regime to create the stand-alone Afghan army envisioned in the general's counterinsurgency approach. The AP reported (Fuller and Gearan 2009) that Obama's unwillingness to accept any of his war council's recommendations in large part reflected the "forceful reservations" Eikenberry had voiced about the credibility of the Afghan government, and that as a consequence Obama was reevaluating McChrystal's troop requests. According to the wire service, the sense that he was being "rush and railroaded" had "stiffened the president's resolve" to seek further information and options, although unnamed officials said a "substantial troop increase" was still likely.

For Fox News, the storyline of dissensus within the Obama administration took a back seat to an overriding concern that the president was refusing to follow the recommendations of the general whom he had just put in command. Bing West (2009b) epitomized this perspective when he stated on *Fox Hannity* that if this country wanted to win the war in Afghanistan, it could: "It just has to have the resolve to do it." Given that Obama had now spent a couple of months openly questioning his own military, he was sending the signal that he did not want to be a wartime president. And that, West declared, "is deadly."

Obama's Tough Sell

By late November, media speculation about Obama's pending decision had become intense and journalists had honed in on the idea that he would indeed select some sort of middle path. Journalists continued to focus on strategy and controversy to the detriment of less emotionally-engaging, substantive analysis. As *Post* columnist E.J. Dionne (2009a) wrote, "When there is no good solution to a problem, a president has three options: to avoid the problem, to pick the least bad of the available options, or to mix and match among the proposed solutions and minimize the long-term damage any decision will cause." Given domestic economic and political realities, especially the war weariness that permeated the U.S., Dionne concluded Obama was likely to go with option C, a decision, he added, that would probably please no one.

The AP (Gearan and Loven 2009) reported that military officials and others expected the president to settle on a middle-ground option, but one that would also involve an exit strategy that clarified when U.S. troops would turn responsibility over to the Afghan government and under what conditions. Noting that the White House was bracing for "a tough sell," a second AP article (Gearan and Flaherty 2009) stated that Obama would shortly be speaking to a "war-weary American public" whose support for the conflict had dropped significantly over the past nine months, with a majority now saying both that they opposed the war and that it was not worth fighting. The report added that the president also had to sell his plan to foreign allies as well as to congressional Democrats, who were already indicating they might be the toughest audience of all.

Speaker Pelosi's comment that there was "serious unrest" in her caucus over the prospect of another vote to finance an expanded war elicited much media interest, and a story in the *Post* (Shear and Kane 2009) contained the reminder that back in June the speaker had "strong-armed" anti-war Democrats into voting for a $100 billion measure to fund the wars in Iraq and Afghanistan and had no intention of doing so again. News articles also reported that Democrats had introduced legislation to impose a surtax to cover the costs of the two wars, and even though it stood little chance of enactment, it underscored the high level of frustration among Democratic lawmakers (Schmitt and Cooper 2009; Pincus 2009b). A major media storyline thus became what steps the president might take to quell these anxieties, and whether he could do so without alienating the congressional Republicans whose support he needed.

Times correspondent David Sanger (2009b) wrote that the policy Obama was about to adopt involved a troop surge and an exit strategy, an approach with something for both sides. But he also wrote that speeding the U.S. toward an exit by adding troops was a "tricky message" for Obama to deliver given the multiple audiences he had to convince both at home and abroad. Assuring Democrats, especially the antiwar base, that in sending more troops he was not escalating the war LBJ-style could negate the arguments to Republicans that he was giving the military what it needed to beat back the Taliban and keep al Qaeda at bay. And calibrating his message so that it signaled resolve to U.S. allies and the enemy but not open-ended commitment to the American people was also a "potential minefield" for the president.

In late November, *NBC Nightly News* anchor Lester Holt (2009b) gave this sobering appraisal of the war: "What began eight years ago as a conventional war to deny al Qaeda sanctuary in Afghanistan has devolved into a bloody hit-and-run guerrilla conflict without a well-defined endgame and at a growing cost in American lives." Savannah Guthrie reported that the additional troops would focus on protecting population centers and building up Afghan security forces, and she also quoted Obama's just-delivered remark that "it is my intention to finish the job." With that statement, Jim Miklaszewski (2009c) pronounced the next morning on *Today*, Obama had "officially declared Afghanistan his war."

Also zeroing in on Obama's statement about finishing the job in Afghanistan, Fox commentator Charles Krauthammer (2009d) said the president still needed to address the real issue—"How does he define the objective?" Only when he clearly explained what the job actually was could anyone determine whether the troop level was appropriate. If, as it appeared the week before the speech, Obama had decided to go with close to the number McChrystal had requested, that would imply White House concurrence with a counterinsurgency approach. But, Krauthammer warned, if Obama bought the general's troop level but announced a narrower strategy, it would be hard to understand what he really hoped to achieve.

On the evening of Obama's West Point address, NBC correspondent Chuck Todd (2009b) stated that the core of the president's strategy was speed, as the new U.S. troops were expected to be in place by the summer of 2010 and an ambitious timetable for withdrawal was set to begin 12 months beyond that date. It now seemed to be all about America's exit, a strategy that raised as many questions as it answered. Just minutes before Obama began his speech, David Gregory (2009b) posed this basic query: "He said this is a war of necessity, not of choice, that he's going to finish the job. What if the job is not done in that time frame? And the history in Afghanistan shows that's distinctly possible."

Can the U.S. Really Escalate and Exit?

The day after Obama's West Point address, the national media were filled with analyses and assessments of his proposed strategy for the war. Journalists quickly honed in on two major points: the "escalate-then-exit" plan's feasibility and the public and political response it was likely to receive. *Post* senior political correspondent Dan Balz's post-mortem of the speech merged these two issues into an overarching strategic and political calculation frame, and this rapidly became the predominant media storyline:

> President Obama assumed full ownership of the war in Afghanistan on Tuesday night with a speech arguing that the fastest way out of the conflict is a rapid and significant escalation of it. But the muted response from key Democratic congressional leaders and the skepticism from Republicans about an exit strategy signaled that the president faces a stiff fight to sell the policy.

> Obama adopted the risky approach of both calling for a sizable troop surge—bigger in terms of percentage than the Iraq surge ordered by then-President George W. Bush—and outlining an exit strategy in the same speech. That was a clear acknowledgment of the fragile state of public opinion after eight years of conflict in Afghanistan, as well as the political divisions. (Balz 2009)

Post senior national correspondent Karen DeYoung (2009) wrote that the president was "attempting to change the metabolism of a war that has sputtered along for more than eight years." She noted that Obama's carefully-constructed middle path contained narrower and more explicit objectives and a clearer timeline for achieving results than the broad counterinsurgency approach of his top military commander. DeYoung also stated that if the strategy were successful, control in Afghanistan would begin to be turned over to local officials as early as the following year and that insurgent sanctuaries along the mountainous Af/Pak border region would be destroyed. But if the strategy were a failure, she cautioned, "it could come just as the 2012 election cycle gets underway."

Times correspondents Peter Baker and Adam Nagourney (2009) commended Obama for his political and rhetorical deftness in crafting an approach that fit the context of a polarized nation. As they wrote, "President Obama went before the nation Tuesday night to announce that he would escalate the war in Afghanistan. And Mr Obama went before the nation to announce that he had a plan to end the war in Afghanistan." Playing to two audiences, he had told those who still supported the war that he was sending more troops. But for those against it, he had offered "the assurance of the exit ramp." The president's mastery of the difficult political landscape also elicited this favorable assessment from AP White House correspondent Jennifer Loven (2009): "His is a very Obama-like approach, threading the needle between an unapologetically muscular attack on the deteriorating Afghanistan situation and a politically aware nod to the dangers of escalating a war increasingly disliked by the public and, especially, Obama's fellow Democrats."

Political pundits employed a similar strategic frame to assess the president's plan, but even among ideological soul mates there was a mixed reaction to the wisdom of the surge-then-exit decision. On Fox's *Special Report* Charles Krauthammer (2009e) faulted Obama's commitment to the war and his emphasis on an exit: "On the one hand, he sends in the troops, and on the other hand, he says we are leaving in 18 months ... He spoke about unwavering resolve, and yet he talks about exit ... That is not a clarion call. It's an uncertain trumpet." In a *Post* column two days later, Krauthammer (2009f) complained that the president had delivered "a call to arms so ambivalent, so tentative, so defensive," a speech not of a commander-in-chief but of a politician, "perfectly splitting the difference. Two messages for two audiences. Placate the right—you get the troops; placate the left—we are on our way out." His *Post* colleague George Will (2009b) unleashed an equally withering indictment: "George Orwell said that the quickest way to end a war is to lose it. But Obama's halfhearted embrace of a half-baked nonstrategy— briefly feinting toward the Taliban (or al Qaeda or a 'syndicate of terror') while hugging the exit ramp—makes a protracted loss predictable."

But other conservative commentators such as Fred Kagan (2009) of the American Enterprise Institute signaled cautious approval in light of official assurances that July 2011 merely marked the possible beginning of a U.S. exit. This was also good enough for conservative columnist William Kristol (2009) who wrote in the *Post*'s opinion blog that the "pseudo-deadline" for beginning to transition out was "thankfully modified" by pledges that it would be based on conditions on the ground. And Bush speechwriter turned *Post* columnist, Michael Gerson, commended Obama for a "courageous" decision that, in contrast to the expectation he would settle on a "timid half-measure," amounted to more of a "seven-eighths measure" (Gerson 2009b).

In a column titled "The Analytic Mode," right-of-center *Times* columnist David Brooks (2009) wrote admiringly that the Obama White House revolved around "a culture of debate" in which long, analytic discussions brought competing arguments to the fore, with the president presiding over them "like a judge settling a lawsuit." The result was policies that were often a balance as he tried to accommodate different points of view. It was, in short, a style "biased toward complexity," as shown in Obama's decision to expand the war while at the same time presenting a plan for the withdrawal of American troops.

Liberal columnists and commentators were equally mixed in their assessments of Obama's strategic calculations. Among those expressing grave concerns were *Times* columnist Bob Herbert and *Post* columnist Eugene Robinson. On the eve of Obama's address, Herbert (2009b) lamented that "After going through an extended period of highly ritualized consultations and deliberations, the president has arrived at a decision that never was much in doubt, and that will prove to be a tragic mistake. It was also, for the president, the easier option." Four days later, Robinson (2009b) declared that Obama's "escalation of the war may achieve its goals, but at too great a cost—and without making our nation meaningfully safer from the threat of terrorist attacks." *Post* columnist David Ignatius also intertwined national security strategy and political calculation but offered a far more neutral analysis:

> Politically it's an Afghanistan strategy with something to make everyone unhappy. Democrats will be angry that the president is escalating a costly war at a time when the struggling economy should be his top priority. Republicans will protest that by setting a short, 18-month deadline to begin withdrawing those forces, he's signaling to the Taliban that they can win if they just are patient …
>
> The most important question about Obama's strategy isn't political but pragmatic. Will it succeed? He has defined success downward, by focusing on the ability to transfer control to the Afghans. He shows little interest in the big ideas of counterinsurgency and insists he will avoid 'a nation-building commitment in Afghanistan.' That will make it easier to declare a 'good enough' outcome in July 2011, if not victory. (Ignatius 2009c)

And the liberal editorial boards of both newspapers gave generally favorable evaluations of Obama's surge-and-exit decision. Noting the strategic and political pitfalls the president had avoided, the *Post*'s editorial board wrote approvingly that his troop decision was "both correct and courageous": "correct because it is the only way to prevent a defeat that would endanger this country and its vital interests; and courageous because he is embarking on a difficult and costly mission that is opposed by a large part of his own party" ("An Afghan Strategy" 2009). The *Times* also gave a nod to the president's "considerable political courage" in addressing why America could not walk away from the war and outlining "an ambitious and high-risk strategy for driving back the Taliban and bolstering the Afghan government so American troops can eventually go home." The editorial did, however, go on to warn that the Afghan government on which this plan depended was "barely legitimate and barely hanging on in the face of an increasingly powerful Taliban insurgency," and therefore cautioned that success remained far from certain ("The Afghanistan Speech" 2009).

Some news reports framed Obama's surge decision as evidence of his willingness to take a military risk that held no guarantee of victory. The AP (Reid and Brumitt 2009) wrote that he was "holding an uncertain hand in his high-stakes gamble in the fight against Islamic extremism" as "weak partners in both countries, doubts about the speed of building up Afghan security forces and allies reluctant to commit themselves wholeheartedly to the battle all raise questions about the strategy." *Times* correspondent Dexter Filkins (2009b) stated that in "laying down the gauntlet" for the Afghans, the president was setting criteria for success that he and his field commanders might be able to influence, but ultimately would "not be able to control." His colleague Peter Baker (2009) noted the adroit strategic calculation Obama employed in making clear that America had to balance what he had previously called America's war of necessity against what he now warned was its cost to this country in blood and treasure. The implication of this and other news reports was that clever strategic calculations did not necessarily translate into military success, a problem highlighted by the *Post*'s Chandrasekaran (2009) as he observed that the White House had carefully eschewed terms such as "winning" and "victory."

News articles also detailed the political risk Obama was taking as restive Democrats in Congress, many of whom opposed his troop increase policy, clashed with Republicans who worried about a withdrawal timeline and demanded that the U.S. find a funding source other than a tax increase. The *Times* summarized the GOP perspective with a quote from Senator John Cornyn (R-TX): "Setting a draw-down date before this surge has even begun is a mistake, and it sends a mixed message to both our friends and our enemies regarding our long-term commitment to success" (Stolberg and Cooper 2009). And from the other side of the aisle came this statement from Representative Louise Slaughter (D-NY): "I see no good reason for us to send another 30,000 or more troops to Afghanistan when we have so many pressing issues—like our economy—to deal with in this country" (Stolberg and Cooper 2009). The *Post* also noted that Speaker Pelosi was finished asking colleagues to back wars they did not support, and quoted her retort that "the president's going to have to make his case" (Kane 2009).

Correspondent Kelly O'Donnell (2009) of NBC's *Nightly News* highlighted the resistance of many congressional Democrats, among them two outspoken skeptics in the House. "My fear, as the fear of so many others, is that we could easily get bogged down in an endless war. What happens if this doesn't work? Do we ... leave in three years as the president stated, or do we stay longer?" Representative Eliot Engel (D-NY) asked the day after Obama's address, and his colleague Bill Delahunt (D-MA) posed the equally thorny question, "We've been there eight years now and we're still talking about turning it around. Is 18 months going to be sufficient?"

But as the AP reported (Flaherty and Gearan 2009), even a "deeply skeptical" Congress had seemingly resigned itself—at least in the short run—to the president's plan, with leading Democrats saying that their serious misgivings about the troop deployment and its cost would not mean they would try to block it, and Republicans giving their assent to the force increase in spite of concerns about the specific exit date and how to fund the war. No other news reports disputed this conclusion; the media had rapidly reached consensus that Obama would get his way even in the face of substantial congressional grousing.

Post columnist E.J. Dionne (2009b) summed up Obama's decision on the war as both "gutsy and politically risky," arguing that by identifying a neither too hawkish nor too dovish "Goldilocks strategy," he was employing a careful political calculation that even if each side in Congress found much to dislike in his plan for Afghanistan, neither camp could disagree with everything. As a consequence, Dionne maintained, Obama would likely succeed in his short-term goal of gathering sufficient support to give his policy a chance: "If he's right that progress can be made quickly and that troops can begin to withdraw, political opposition will recede," but quickly went on to warn that "if the policy fails or stalls," the president "will have hell to pay."

In other words, even with his victory in the immediate political skirmish for congressional approval, Obama's ability to succeed in the vastly more consequential, long-term struggle to retain support for America's fight against terrorism remained in doubt, as did military success in America's longest conflict. Winning the political battle, journalists reminded their audiences, was definitely not the same as winning the war.

* * *

As President Obama worked assiduously to convince America that Afghanistan represented a just and necessary war and that his was the best path to bring closure to the conflict, the media storylines about the war and the president's strategy to pursue it represented anything but a simple recapitulation of the official narrative. One major point of divergence was the political and security situation in the Af/Pak region.

Even as the White House pressed the case for a viable political partnership with the Karzai regime, journalists had only to turn to their own or their colleagues' first-hand observations of the deepening morass to provide evidence for a competing storyline. So a powerful media narrative of seemingly unending violence and political corruption and malfeasance took hold. Not even constant official assurances of gradual progress and a better tomorrow could loosen the grip of this event-based reporting. As noted above, throughout all five media outlets the gap between the Obama narrative that things were improving in the Af/Pak region and the evidence from reports on the ground was widening quite dramatically. As Baum and Groeling (2010) and Glazier and Boydstun (2012) had predicted, when reality contradicts presidential assertions, the media will not supinely follow the official narrative. And if that divide between official rhetoric and reality increases with the passage of time, media reportage trends ever more negative despite, in this case study, all the promotional efforts of the commander-in-chief to paint a relatively glowing portrait of the possibilities for Afghanistan's future and American security.

There was, however, evidence for the staying power of the wider war-on-terror narrative first espoused by President Bush in the wake of the 9/11 attacks. During the period under study, none of the media outlets questioned the need to wage an extended war against America's terrorist enemies. But while members of the media offered little resistance to Obama's central argument that Afghanistan was a just and necessary war, neither did they highlight that essential component of his narrative. It remained at best part of the background context of their reportage. In fact, Obama's emphasis on the need to combat the continuing menace of terrorism got enmeshed in media stories of the administration's failure to address security risks such as the shooter at Fort Hood and the would-be airline bomber. And Obama's theme of American exceptionalism was also simply taken for granted—

never contested but also rarely emphasized in news reports or commentaries. Thus media acquiescence to the Bush–Obama terror frame did little to win journalists' acceptance of Obama's narrative that the war was winding to a successful conclusion under his stewardship.

Journalists instead focused on the themes of political conflict, strategic positioning, and inside-the-Beltway gamesmanship as they first presented the exciting storyline of Obama's protracted deliberations about Afghanistan and then the equally intriguing disagreements within the upper echelons of his national security team about the proper course to pursue. Congressional Democrats' visible distress at the very notion of a troop surge also fanned the media storyline of a war of words in Washington. And once the president announced the path he would follow, the media emphasized the wisdom (or lack thereof) of his choice, the political and security risks it entailed, and its rather dubious prospects for success. Substance was subsumed within a frame that privileged strategy and process, as reporters and commentators assessed the likelihood that his policy "gamble" would pay off. The tone of coverage was decidedly mixed, as there was no overall common ground on the repercussions of Obama's strategic calculations either for the war's outcome or for the president's political future.

Not surprisingly, therefore, the public's reaction to Obama's surge-then-exit decision was also one of ambivalence as polls taken in the aftermath of his West Point address indicated a moderate level of support but also a healthy dose of skepticism. The president's speech did have some impact on the public, as a *New York Times*/CBS News poll found a 10 percentage point bump in support for Obama's handling of the war over the previous month (Nagourney and Sussman 2009). But the bad news for Obama was that overall approval of his decision stood at only 48 percent, with 53 percent of Democrats opposed. Just under half of respondents thought the U.S. would succeed in what Obama said was a central mission: preventing terrorists from using Afghanistan as a base of support. And only 39 percent said that an increased effort in Afghanistan would make America safer from another terrorist attack, arguably Obama's central message (Nagourney and Sussman 2009).

Anyone seeking strong evidence of presidential ability to turn media sentiment to his side would be hard pressed to find it in the case of Afghanistan and the president's decision to surge then exit from the conflict there. I now turn to a second case study of how Obama framed the drawdown narrative for a war he had consistently opposed since the fall of 2002 and examine whether it provided any greater evidence of presidential ability to control the media and public discourse.

Chapter 4
Turning the Page on Operation Iraqi Freedom

In a July 2008 *New York Times* op-ed piece titled "My Plan for Iraq," presumptive Democratic presidential nominee Barack Obama recapitulated almost six years of withering criticism of the Iraq War. Declaring that "Iraq is not the central front in the war on terrorism, and it never has been," he characterized the conflict as a "grave mistake" and "the greatest strategic blunder in the recent history of American foreign policy." He thus pledged that on his first day in office he would "give the military a new mission: ending this war" and initiate a phased redeployment of U.S. combat troops. Obama emphasized that the drawdown would be undertaken thoughtfully and deliberately; as he memorably phrased it, "We must be as careful getting out of Iraq as we were careless getting in" (Obama 2008b).

Opposition to Iraq had been a constant rallying cry for Obama since the fall of 2002, when as a little-known Illinois state senator he had first characterized the proposed incursion against Saddam Hussein as "a dumb war ... a rash war," based "not on reason but on passion, not on principle but on politics" (Obama 2002). Upon assuming his U.S. Senate seat in 2005, Obama continued to condemn the war, but while his words remained highly critical his attention quickly turned to a more pragmatic issue: how best to overcome the harsh realities the U.S. now faced in the conflict. In every public statement on Iraq, the senator would roundly castigate the Bush administration for a litany of failures from the faulty intelligence used to make the case for war to the extraordinary mismanagement of the war itself. But his primary concern was focusing the national debate on the best outcome for a war in which there unfortunately were "no magic bullets" (Obama 2005).

"War is a serious business," Obama flatly declared in a speech to the Chicago Council on Foreign Relations in November 2005; America therefore needed to cease the Washington "political war" of "talking points and Sunday news shows and spin" and develop "a pragmatic solution to the real war we're facing in Iraq." Rather than retreating to the divisive and politically expedient "cut and run or stay the course" rhetoric, those responsible for U.S. national security had to get down to the critical task of devising a strategic approach that would allow the nation to "exit in a responsible way—with the hope of leaving a stable foundation for the future, but at the very least taking care not to plunge the country into an even deeper and, perhaps, irreparable crisis" (Obama 2005).

A New Strategy for a Misguided War

Claiming that he had neither "the expertise nor the inclination to micro-manage the war from Washington," Senator Obama nonetheless began to offer some suggestions as to the "broad elements" that should be included in the discussion of a new strategy for Iraq. First and foremost, he argued in his 2005 Chicago speech, the United States needed to concentrate on how to decrease its military footprint there. Drawing a critical distinction between *reducing* and *fully withdrawing* American troops, Obama emphasized the former as he argued that U.S. forces had to be part of the solution. An American military presence would be necessary to prevent Iraq "from exploding into civil war, ethnic cleansing, and a haven for terrorism," and U.S. strategic goals should therefore incorporate only a limited drawdown (Obama 2005).

Ever careful of his choice of words, Obama also called for a timeframe for a phased withdrawal rather than a precise date for U.S. troop pull-outs. "We must find the right balance," he explained, "offering enough security to serve as a buffer and carry out a targeted, effective counter-insurgency strategy, but not so much of a presence that we serve as an aggravation. It is this balance that will be critical to finding our way forward." Rounding out his ideas about how to achieve a solution for Iraq, Obama said the U.S. also should think about the sort of Iraqi government it wished to leave behind, improve its reconstruction record in Iraq, and launch a major diplomatic effort to get the international community and key regional players more involved (Obama 2005). It was becoming apparent that the junior senator from Illinois was working to situate himself as a leading voice of the sensible center on Iraq, seeking the still-elusive path to an exit that would not plunge that country into further chaos.

In remarks the following year to the Chicago Council on Foreign Affairs titled "A Way Forward in Iraq," Obama's feelings of dismay and frustration were evident as he presented the litany of problems that had only worsened over the previous 12 months. Characterizing the results of the 2006 midterm elections as a public vote of no confidence in Bush's Iraq strategy, he declared that Americans were now demanding "a feasible strategy with defined goals in Iraq—a strategy no longer driven by ideology and politics, but one that is based on a realistic assessment of the sobering facts on the ground and our interests in the region" (Obama 2006). Obama observed that this was precisely what he had already proposed, and that 74 U.S. senators had joined him in passing a resolution that 2006 mark a year of "significant transition" in Iraq. To America's great misfortune, it had instead witnessed "a year of significant deterioration ... in a country that is quickly spiraling out of control" (Obama 2006). But the senator pressed forward with the message that despite the sorry state of affairs in Iraq, it was still possible "to salvage an acceptable outcome to this long and misguided war." He cautioned, however, that this mission would be far from easy:

> For the fact is that there are no good options left in this war. There are no options that do not carry significant risks. And so the question is not whether there is

some magic formula for success, or guarantee against failure, in Iraq. Rather, the question is what strategies, imperfect though they may be, are most likely to achieve the best outcome in Iraq, one that will ultimately put us on a more effective course to deal with international terrorism, nuclear proliferation, and other critical threats to our security. (Obama 2006)

America needed to have "a serious conversation about the realistic objectives we can still achieve in Iraq," Obama insisted. Rather than focusing on "dreams and hopes" of democracy and a perfect government in Iraq, the U.S. had to turn to those "concrete objectives" it was actually possible to attain—"namely, preventing Iraq from becoming what Afghanistan once was, maintaining our influence in the Middle East, and forging a political settlement to stop the sectarian violence so that our troops can come home" (Obama 2006). In Obama's vision of the future of Iraq, pragmatism seemed clearly the order of the day.

Again Obama highlighted his strategy for the way forward in Iraq. The solution, he now maintained, must be political rather than purely military. The U.S. had to pressure the Iraqi government to reach an agreement among warring factions that could create some sense of stability in the country, and the most effective means of doing this was through a phased redeployment. Obama was particularly insistent that any sort of U.S. troop increase would merely put more soldiers "in the crossfire of a civil war." American fighting forces, Obama noted, had carried out their responsibilities with excellence and valor, but these same troops were well aware that there was no military solution to this war (Obama 2006). "Our troops can help suppress the violence, but they cannot solve its root causes," Obama concluded. "And all the troops in the world won't be able to force Shia, Sunni, and Kurd to sit down at a table, resolve their differences, and forge a lasting peace." He also called for some of these forces to be sent to Afghanistan, where "our lack of focus and commitment of resources has led to an increasing deterioration of the security situation there" (Obama 2006).

Once the phased troop redeployment was underway, Obama continued, the U.S. needed a plan that put Iraqi security forces in the lead, intensified American efforts to train those forces, and increased the number of U.S. personnel who could provide guidance in training and advisory roles. And the final elements of the revised strategy should be to link continued aid to Iraq with tangible political progress and to engage neighboring countries in the whole process of achieving success in Iraq (Obama 2006). Obama ended his 2006 Chicago speech with three strategic lessons the nation ought to have learned from the misbegotten conflict in Iraq. The first was that America "should be more modest in our belief that we can impose democracy on a country through military force." While it was always in America's interest to help foster democracy through diplomatic and economic means, the institutions of democracy "cannot be built overnight, and they cannot be built at the end of a barrel of a gun." The second lesson was that in any conflict, "it is not enough to simply plan for war; you must also plan for success." It was inexcusable, he declared, that the Bush administration had given no thought as to the political situation it would find after the fall of Baghdad and how this would affect the military mission (Obama 2006).

The final lesson the U.S. should have learned from Iraq was for Obama the most critical because it involved the original rationale for why the nation had to fight—to defeat the terrorists who had attacked it on 9/11 and continued to formulate destructive plots. Because of Iraq, America had been distracted from the broader threats that it still faced around the globe. The decision to go to war in Iraq "has had disastrous consequences for Afghanistan," he proclaimed. "We have seen a fierce Taliban offensive, a spike in terrorist attacks, and a narcotrafficking problem spiral out of control. Instead of consolidating the gains made by the Karzai government, we are backsliding toward chaos" (Obama 2006). Also of grave concern was that the war had created more terrorists in Iraq than were being defeated in Afghanistan and elsewhere. In addition, Iraq had alienated many nations that had previously joined with America in the battle against the violent extremists. And not least, the U.S. government had lost credibility with its own people as increasing numbers turned away from international engagement of any sort. "We cannot afford to be a country of isolationists right now," Obama warned:

> 9/11 showed us that try as we might to ignore the rest of the world, our enemies will no longer ignore us. And so we need to maintain a strong foreign policy, relentless in pursuing our enemies and hopeful in promoting our values around the world.
>
> But to guard against isolationist sentiments in this country, we must change conditions in Iraq and the policy that has characterized our time there—a policy based on blind hope and ideology instead of fact and reality ...
>
> The time for waiting in Iraq is over. It is time to change our policy. It is time to give the Iraqis their country back. And it is time to refocus America's efforts on the wider struggle yet to be won. (Obama 2006)

Throughout 2006, as conditions in Iraq continued to deteriorate, an intense policy debate had raged about how to proceed with the war, and Obama's November remarks reflected all the passions and disagreements that had been roiling Washington for months. As we have seen, the Bush administration had been considering a variety of strategic shifts, a policy review that culminated in the president's January 2007 announcement of the decision to increase the U.S. troop presence in Iraq. Obama's reaction to the surge was scathing. In a Senate floor statement the following week, he recapitulated his earlier critique of all that had gone wrong with both the war's premise and its management. Again and again, Obama declared, the American people had been given "promises and assurances about progress and victory that do not appear to be grounded in the reality of the facts." They had been told that the troops would be greeted as liberators and that the insurgency was in its last throes. The White House had also pledged that the Iraqis "would soon stand up so we could stand down and our brave sons and daughters could start coming home." The public had been asked to wait, to be patient, to give the Iraqi government six more months, and then six more after that, and then yet another six more (Obama 2007a).

"Now, after the loss of more than 3,000 American lives, after spending almost $400 billion, after Iraq has descended into civil war, we have been promised, once again," Obama charged, "that the President's plan to escalate the war in Iraq will, this time, be well planned, well-coordinated, and well supported by the Iraqi Government." There was simply no evidence, he continued, that the Iraqis wanted such a partnership, let alone any proof that it was actually even feasible (Obama 2007a). Stating that "we have tried this road before," Obama once more argued that "in the end, no amount of American forces can solve the political differences that lie at the heart of somebody else's civil war. As the President's own military commanders have said, escalation only prevents the Iraqis from taking more responsibility for their own future." And for good measure, Obama also noted that "it is even eroding our efforts in the wider war on terror as some of the extra soldiers will come directly from Afghanistan, where the Taliban has become resurgent" (Obama 2007a).

To emphasize just how thoroughly he opposed the idea of a troop surge, Obama employed the term of choice that had been so frequently and effectively used to criticize America's Vietnam strategy some 40 years earlier—*escalation.* Eight times in his brief floor speech, Obama made reference to Bush's new strategy as an escalation, and each time the negative echoes of Vietnam reverberated across the chamber. Having made the monumental error of giving Bush the open-ended authority to wage this war back in 2002, it was now up to the Senate, Obama bluntly informed his colleagues, not to repeat the same mistake. To that end, Obama announced that he would shortly introduce legislation to place a cap on the number of troops in Iraq and implement a responsible, phased drawdown. "The time for promises, for waiting and patience is over," he angrily concluded:

> Too many lives have been lost and too many billions have been spent for us to trust the President on another tried-and-failed policy, opposed by generals and experts, opposed by Democrats and Republicans, opposed by Americans and even the Iraqis themselves. It is time to change our policy. *It is time to give Iraqis their country back, and it is time to refocus America's effort on the wider struggle against terror yet to be won.* (Obama 2007a, emphasis added)

It is obvious that even as he vigorously contested Bush's surge narrative, Obama was careful not to depart from his predecessor's ascendant worldview of a martial response to terrorism.

Although the Iraq War De-Escalation Act failed to garner a filibuster-proof majority in the Senate, Obama continued to speak out against the war. In his February 2007 announcement of candidacy for the presidency, he made due note of Iraq as a "tragic mistake" (Obama 2007b), and the following month he again took to the Senate floor to mark the war's fourth anniversary. Once more he repeated his central argument against the conflict: "A war based not on reason but on passion, not on principle but on politics would lead to a U.S. occupation of undetermined length, at undetermined cost, with undetermined consequences" (Obama 2007c). It had not been a failure of resolve that had led us to "this chaos," Obama declared; "it has been a failure of strategy—and that strategy must change. It is time to bring a responsible end to this conflict now." No amount of additional military effort would end the bloody mess in which America found itself:

> There is no military solution to this war. No amount of U.S. soldiers—not 10,000 more, not 20,000 more, not the almost 30,000 more that we now know we are sending—can solve the grievances that lay at the heart of someone else's civil war.
>
> Our troops cannot serve as their diplomats, and we can no longer referee their civil war. (Obama 2007c)

In his public remarks and writings over the remainder of 2007, Obama continued to emphasize his earlier call for a political solution to the civil discord raging in Iraq. In an April address, he noted that his plan made clear that continued U.S. commitment to Iraq would depend on the Iraqi government meeting "a series of well-defined benchmarks necessary to reach a political settlement." That the Iraqis had thus far failed to do this was in no small measure due to President Bush's insistence that a purely military strategy would suffice (Obama 2007d). Because the U.S. was signaling that its forces might remain indefinitely, Obama argued, Iraqis had no incentive to reach an accord. The administration therefore had to make it perfectly evident that a phased drawdown of American troops would be completed in early 2008. While Bush's "escalation of U.S. forces" might bring a temporary reduction to the violence in Baghdad, Obama concluded, "It cannot change the political dynamic in Iraq. A phased withdrawal can" (Obama 2007d).

In a 2007 *Foreign Affairs* article, Obama repeated his call for a political solution and a phased redeployment of U.S. combat troops. Labeling the current situation in Iraq a *morass*, he wrote that it "is time for our civilian leaders to acknowledge a painful truth" about the limits of American power in Iraq:

> We cannot impose a military solution on a civil war between Sunni and Shiite factions. The best chance we have to leave Iraq a better place is to pressure these warring factions to find a lasting political solution. And the only effective way to apply this pressure is to begin a phased withdrawal of U.S. forces, with the goal of removing all combat brigades from Iraq by March 31, 2008—a date consistent with the goal set by the bipartisan Iraq Study Group. This redeployment could be temporarily suspended if the Iraqi government meets the security, political, and economic benchmarks to which it has committed. But we must recognize that, in the end, only Iraqi leaders can bring real peace and stability to their country. (Obama 2007e)

Speaking to the Council on Foreign Relations in August, Obama presented Iraq as a "catastrophic war" that should "never have been authorized and never have been waged." Of particular concern was that Iraq had become "a training ground for terror," and had, in fact, become the very war the terrorists wanted America to fight. "Bin Laden and his allies know they cannot defeat us on the field of battle or in a genuine battle of ideas," Obama declared,

> But they can provoke the reaction we've seen in Iraq: a misguided invasion of a Muslim country that sparks new insurgencies, ties down our military, busts our budgets, increases the pool of terrorist recruits, alienates America, gives democracy a bad name, and prompts the American people to question our engagement in the world.
>
> By refusing to end the war in Iraq, President Bush is giving the terrorists what they really want, and what the Congress voted to give them in 2002: a U.S. occupation of undetermined length, at undetermined cost, with undetermined consequences. (Obama 2007f)

Building upon this theme in an October foreign policy campaign speech at DePaul University in Chicago, Obama reminded his audience while he and a few brave souls in Washington had argued passionately in 2002 against pursuing a war in Iraq, their words had fallen on deaf ears in the corridors of power. As a result, the American public had been betrayed, mostly by a president "who didn't tell the whole truth to the American people; who disdained diplomacy and bullied allies; and who squandered our unity and the support of the world after 9/11" (Obama 2007g). But the fault did not lie with President Bush alone, Obama insisted. The American people "were failed by much of Washington. By a media that too often reported spin instead of facts. By a foreign policy elite that largely boarded the bandwagon for war. And most of all by the majority of a Congress … that voted to give the President the open-ended authority to wage war …" (Obama 2007g).

"Even today's debate is divorced from reality," Obama continued. "We've got a surge that is somehow declared a success even though it has failed to enable to political reconciliation that was its stated purpose. The fact that violence today is only as horrific as in 2006 is held up as progress." He argued that only a candidate who stood apart from conventional Washington thinking could challenge the entrenched, outdated assumptions that had led the U.S. down the path to the debacle of Iraq. It was time for new leadership that would shift America's attention from past mistakes to future possibilities. "This election is a turning point," Obama declared. "The American people get to decide: Are we going to turn back the clock, or turn the page?" And the first step in that new, more positive direction was to end the war in Iraq (Obama 2007g). The senator had carefully positioned himself as the counterweight both to Bush and to those Democratic challengers who had voted to support the invasion of Iraq.

More than a year prior to Election Day, Obama had completed his narrative of Iraq. It was primarily a dismal three-part tale of mistaken judgment and outmoded thinking; of misrepresentation, distortion, and outright falsehoods; and of gross miscalculation and mismanagement where errors continued to be compounded by ever more strategic and tactical missteps. But his Iraq storyline also contained a kernel of hope that the U.S. could salvage something by recalibrating its policy. A thoughtfully-planned and implemented drawdown of American troops held the possibility that Iraqi leaders might finally decide to take responsibility for their own governance and begin to overcome their sectarian differences. And disengagement from Iraq also meant that America could begin to refocus on the real threat—the terrorist extremists and jihadists responsible for the 9/11 attacks. Nowhere in his Iraq critique did Obama ever question the idea that the U.S. must wage a war against terrorist adversaries; his only concern was that the battle be fought on appropriate terrain. Thus even one of Iraq's harshest critics would not contest the reigning war-on-terror frame.

The Iraq narrative Obama adopted for the 2008 presidential primaries is well illustrated in a speech he made on the fifth anniversary of the Iraq invasion. Focusing on the crucial notion of presidential judgment, Obama declared that Bush—and, by extension, those Democratic and Republican members of Congress who had voted to support his plan for war—had failed to meet President Wilson's basic test that America must never go to war unless absolutely necessary. He insisted that no matter how well U.S. troops were performing under the new surge policy, one fundamental fact remained: "We still have the wrong strategy" (Obama 2008a). The U.S. troop surge merely entailed a tactical adjustment, not a plan for success, Obama stated, and as long as America remained anchored in Iraq, the Iraqis would not make the political progress necessary to end their civil war. Only with a responsible end to the conflict in Iraq, Obama maintained, could the U.S. focus on its true objective of defeating al Qaeda. Proclaiming that "The central front in the war against terror is not Iraq, and it never was," Obama presented himself as the only candidate on either side of the aisle with the wisdom to focus on America's real fight against global terror and violent extremism as well as the foresight to confront the looming twenty-first-century threats of nuclear proliferation, poverty, disease, and climate change (Obama 2008a).

On a July campaign visit to Iraq and Afghanistan, Obama again situated his Iraq critique in the context of a larger foreign policy vision. He began by equating the magnitude of the security threats now confronting America with what it faced in the aftermath of World War II. In both instances, he argued, the nation needed a "new overarching strategy to meet the challenges of a new and dangerous world." Although the U.S. had succeeded brilliantly in devising a viable security plan some 60 years earlier, it had failed to do so following the 2001 terrorist attacks. The reason was the misconceived engagement in Iraq (Obama 2008c). By "fighting a war for well over five years in a country that had absolutely nothing to do with the 9/11 attacks" and allowing that war to dominate its foreign policy, America had diminished "our security, our standing in the world, our military, our economy, and the resources that we need to confront the challenges of the twenty-first century" (Obama 2008c).

Stating once more that Iraq was not the central front in the fight against terrorism, Obama was adamant that the first step in shaping a new security strategy "for an ever-changing world" must therefore be the "responsible redeployment" of U.S. combat troops at a pace that would safely remove them from Iraq within 16 months of his assuming office (2008c). His Republican opponent John McCain emphatically disagreed, arguing throughout the fall campaign that the surge had paid off with a significant reduction in ethnic and sectarian violence in Iraq. These hard-won gains would be lost, McCain contended, if the U.S. were to withdraw most of its troops; the disastrous consequence would be a return to the chaos that had enveloped Iraq in 2006 (McCain 2008).

Although he did admit that the surge had reduced the level of civil violence in Iraq to early 2006 levels, Obama continued to argue on the campaign trail that the security and political progress it had brought was far from adequate. "Despite the improved security situation," the Obama–Biden campaign website read, "the Iraqi government had not stepped forward to lead the Iraqi people and to reach the genuine political accommodation that was the stated purpose of the surge" (Obama 2008e). And Obama consistently delivered this message throughout the fall campaign. Thus even as he was forced to defend both his criticism of the surge and a withdrawal timetable that a number of observers thought too precipitous, Obama was insistent that only a military withdrawal from Iraq would provide the resources and personnel to finish what should have been the U.S. goal all along—eliminating the threat of terrorist extremism in Afghanistan (see King and Wells 2009, ch. 7).

Once he assumed office, Obama faced the task of overseeing a strategy that would achieve a responsible exit from a conflict he had branded as unnecessary, ill-conceived, and tragically mishandled. But a progression in his thinking on Iraq was becoming ever more apparent. As the newly-minted commander-in-chief, he would increasingly extoll the accomplishments and sacrifices of U.S. military forces in Iraq and in so doing, begin to signal an important shift in his previously censorious narrative on Iraq and bring it more into line with Bush's war-on-terror frame. And even though he never agreed that Iraq was the appropriate battlefield for the struggle against America's terrorist adversaries, Obama's narrative of the war would begin to include a glimmer of hope that an appropriately-constituted post-Saddam regime could contribute to U.S. security, regional stability, and a world-wide march toward democracy.

A Responsible End to a War of Choice

Although foreign policy no longer held pride of place in Obama's 2009 inaugural address, the just sworn-in president reiterated his campaign promise that "we will begin to responsibly leave Iraq to its people" (2009a) and informed his global audience that he was directing his national security team to undertake a comprehensive review of how to achieve a long-term solution to the conflict. On February 27, in a major primetime speech on Iraq at the Camp Lejeune Marine base, Obama laid out the timeline for his withdrawal plans. "Let me say this as plainly as I can: By August 31, 2010, our combat mission in Iraq will end," he announced, also affirming that the U.S. would comply with the Status of Forces Agreement to remove all its troops from Iraq by the end of 2011 (Obama 2009g).

But what did a responsible exit strategy entail? As Obama explained to the assembled Marines, it would begin with a clearly-articulated, attainable goal: "An Iraq that is sovereign, stable, and self-reliant" (2009b). The long-term solution was thus political, not military, and the war would end through a transition to full Iraqi governing responsibility. Gone was any triumphalist rhetoric or hint of an artfully-staged "mission accomplished" moment as the president outlined a pragmatic and circumscribed endgame narrative. America must focus on the possible, he insisted, rather than the idealistic and overly-ambitious:

> What we will not do is let the pursuit of the perfect stand in the way of achievable goals. We cannot rid Iraq of all who oppose America or sympathize with our adversaries. We cannot police Iraq's streets until they are completely safe, nor stay until Iraq's union is perfected. We cannot sustain indefinitely a commitment that has put a strain on our military and cost the American people nearly a trillion dollars. (Obama 2009g)

A responsible drawdown also involved careful planning and an orderly, 18-month redeployment of combat troops that would ensure as much as possible the safety of both U.S. fighting forces and the Iraqi people. Obama noted that he had kept his promise to consult closely with military commanders and had followed their recommendation to extend his original withdrawal timeline by two months so as to better protect the troops and preserve the gains they had made. And once the combat troops were removed, the U.S. mission would shift to supporting the Iraqi government and its security forces. To that end, America would retain a transitional force of some 50,000 troops to train and advise the Iraqi forces, conduct targeted counterterrorism actions, and protect ongoing civilian and military efforts (Obama 2009g).

The president also assured the Iraqis that America would engage in a sustained diplomatic effort on their behalf as part of a comprehensive U.S. engagement that extended from Israel to Syria, Iran, Afghanistan, and Pakistan. America's intentions, he emphasized, were to "build a lasting relationship founded upon mutual interests and mutual respect as Iraq takes its rightful place in the community of nations." "The future of Iraq," he declared, "is inseparable from the future of the broader Middle East, so we must establish a new framework that advances Iraq's security and the region's" (Obama 2009g). As he noted the upcoming sixth anniversary of what had "already been a long war," the president reflected on what the U.S. had accomplished in Iraq. While his words to the Marines were filled with praise, they also hinted at the work the Iraqis still needed to undertake:

We sent our troops to Iraq to do away with Saddam Hussein—and you got the job done. We kept our troops in Iraq to help establish a sovereign government—and you got the job done. And we will leave the Iraqi people with a hard-earned opportunity to live a better life—that is your achievement; that is the prospect you have made possible. (Obama 2009g)

Warning that "Iraq is not yet secure, and there will be difficult days ahead," Obama was nonetheless cautiously optimistic about what the future could hold for that beleaguered nation. There was, he maintained, "a renewed cause for hope in Iraq" that rested on successful implementation of his new political and diplomatic strategy. But America could not do it all. While it could help lay the foundation for a more democratic, peaceful, and prosperous Iraq, only the Iraqi leaders and their people could ensure a positive outcome. "Iraq's future is now its own responsibility," Obama declared: "Iraq is a sovereign country with legitimate institutions; America cannot—and should not—take their place" (Obama 2009g). In a PBS *News Hour* interview on the evening of his Camp Lejeune speech, the president offered a carefully calibrated response to the query about whether the Iraq mission might now be viewed as a success. "Well, I think what we can say unequivocally is that our military succeeded in every mission that was given to them," he began, but quickly went on to add this important caveat: "I don't think that we can rightly say that the strategy cooked up by our civilian leadership, with respect to either going in in the first place or how the war was managed, was a success" (Obama 2009h).

Obama also repeated his earlier claims that Iraq had certainly been an "enormous diversion of resources and attention" but showed little further interest in revisiting the missteps of the previous administration. Stating to anchor Jim Lehrer that his intent was not to "look backwards" and that he in no way wished to "relitigate" the long debate about the wisdom of having gone into Iraq in the first place, Obama called for America to move forward. He also conceded that some good—especially the removal of Saddam Hussein and tentative steps toward democracy—had indeed come out of the conflict, but argued that the task at hand was to determine how to achieve the political, economic, and security progress that had thus far proved unattainable in Iraq (Obama 2009h).

In the months that followed, Obama adopted the term "war of choice" as a handy catchphrase that encapsulated his previous critique of Iraq as a tragic and costly distraction from America's real national security priorities. But a marked softening of his previously harsh rhetoric was becoming ever more apparent. On an unannounced visit to Baghdad in early April, the president pressed Prime Minister Maliki to do more to advance political reconciliation, improve governance and basic services, and enhance security. But he also noted that overall violence in Iraq continued to decline and that there was movement on important political questions. And to U.S. troops at Camp Victory, he uttered words of praise for what they had accomplished: "You have given Iraq the opportunity to stand on its own as a democratic country. That is an extraordinary achievement, and for that you have the thanks of the American people" (quoted in Myers and Cooper 2009).

In a discussion with Turkish students the day before, Obama was asked about the apparent similarity between his Iraq policies and those of his predecessor. In at least a partial acknowledgment, Obama replied, "Moving the ship of state is a slow process. States are like big tankers. They're not like speed boats." And in his meeting with Maliki, he emphasized that "I remain convinced that our shared resolve and commitment to progress is greater than the obstacles that stand in our way," a sentiment that George Bush most surely would have echoed (quoted in Myers and Cooper 2009). In his June Cairo address, Obama similarly expressed his hope that Iraq could—with U.S. assistance—forge a brighter tomorrow even as American combat forces began to withdraw. The angry, frustrated tone that had been the hallmark of his earlier remarks on Iraq was no longer in evidence as the president rhetorically pivoted to the future and the promises it held:

> Unlike Afghanistan, Iraq was a war of choice that provoked strong differences in my country and around the world. Although I believe that the Iraqi people are ultimately better off without the tyranny of Saddam Hussein, I also believe that events in Iraq have reminded America of the need to use diplomacy and build international consensus to resolve our problems whenever possible. Indeed, we can recall the words of Thomas Jefferson, who said: 'I hope that our wisdom will grow with our power, and teach us that the less we use our power the greater it will be.'
>
> Today, America has a dual responsibility: to help Iraq forge a better future—and to leave Iraq to Iraqis. I have made it clear to the Iraqi people that we pursue no bases, no claims on their territory or their resources. Iraq's sovereignty is its own. That is why I ordered the removal of our combat brigades by next August. That is why we will honor our agreement with Iraq's democratically-elected government to remove combat troops from Iraqi cities by next July, and to remove all our troops from Iraq by 2012. We will help Iraq train its Security Forces and develop its economy. But we will support a secure and united Iraq as a partner, and never as a patron. (Obama 2009q)

No longer would the president publicly enumerate America's past mistakes or even the many problems still facing Iraq, and as he turned to Afghanistan as the "right" target of the "struggle against extremism," the Iraq conflict started to assume a supporting role in his national security discourse. By the summer of 2009, Iraq had been relegated mostly to a rhetorical counterpoint to the "war of necessity" that America was now gearing up to fight. And in his December 1 primetime address on his new strategy for Afghanistan, Obama devoted only two short paragraphs to Iraq, an overview that once again allowed him to mention the problems with the conflict but, more importantly, to champion the possibilities of a successful conclusion:

> In early 2002, the decision was made to wage a second war, in Iraq. The wrenching debate over the Iraq war is well-known and need not be repeated

here. It's enough to say that for the next six years, the Iraq war drew the dominant share of our troops, our resources, our diplomacy, and our national attention—and that the decision to go into Iraq caused substantial rifts between America and much of the world.

Today, after extraordinary costs, we are bringing the Iraq war to a responsible end. We will remove our combat brigades from Iraq by the end of next summer, and all of our troops by the end of 2011. That we are doing so is a testament to the character of the men and women in uniform. Thanks to their courage, grit and perseverance, we have given Iraqis a chance to shape their future, and we are successfully leaving Iraq to its people. (Obama 2009ee)

But as the date for the drawdown of U.S. combat forces from Iraq drew closer, the subject of Iraq began to appear somewhat more frequently in Obama's public statements. Continuing his turn away from all that had previously gone awry, the president now looked more and more to the future as he sketched out a vision for post-war Iraq and the role America would play. In his 2010 State of the Union address, he tersely alluded to the problems that the war in Iraq had caused by fracturing America's post-9/11 unity of purpose. But he just as quickly closed the door on that chapter of U.S. history: "We can argue all we want about who's to blame for this," he stated, "but I'm not interested in re-litigating the past" (Obama 2010b).

In the one State of the Union paragraph devoted explicitly to his Iraq policy, Obama noted that by "responsibly leaving Iraq to its people" he was fulfilling his campaign promise to end the war. While promising that the U.S. would "support the Iraqi government as they hold elections" and "continue to partner with the Iraqi people to promote regional peace and prosperity," Obama was insistent on his bottom line: "This war is ending, and all of our troops are coming home" (2010b). Over the next six months, he would provide some details of America's new relationship with Iraq, but his public focus on George Bush's war would continue to pale in comparison to his attention to the fight now identified as his own.

In a foreign policy address at the U.S. Military Academy's May 2010 commencement, Obama again touched only briefly upon the conflict that had been the major foreign policy focus of his predecessor's two terms in office. Unwilling to put a positive spin on the war itself, but equally uninterested in re-engaging a policy debate, he chose instead to highlight all that American troops had achieved in Iraq under the most trying of circumstances. Praising the nation's fighting forces for enduring through great adversity and meeting "a set of challenges that were as daunting as they were complex," the president managed to interject one parting jab at the entire Iraq engagement: "A lesser army might have seen its spirit broken. But the American military is more resilient than that. Our troops adapted, they persisted, they partnered with coalition and Iraqi counterparts, and through their competence and creativity and courage, we are poised to end our combat mission in Iraq this summer" (Obama 2010d).

Obama's statement of what America still hoped to accomplish in Iraq remained notably short on details and explanation. First emphasizing that "our commitment to the Iraqi people endures," and then pledging that we would continue to "advise and assist" Iraq's security forces, he said that "A strong American civilian presence will help Iraqis forge political and economic progress." While admitting that this would be no simple task, he laid out his criteria for measuring success: "An Iraq that provides no haven to terrorists; a democratic Iraq that is stable and self-reliant" (Obama 2010d). Not the most precise metric, but one Obama hoped the war-weary nation could embrace.

In early August 2010, the Obama administration embarked on a campaign to highlight and promote the Iraq transition. Starting with an August 2 speech to the Disabled Veterans of America Conference in Atlanta, Georgia, and culminating with a September 23 address to the United Nations General Assembly, the president delivered six speeches and radio addresses on the subject of the drawdown and its aftermath and implications. He was ably assisted by Vice President Biden and Secretary of Defense Gates who each gave several speeches and media interviews related to the troop withdrawal and conditions in Iraq. As they fleshed out a more thorough interpretation of why America fought and what had been accomplished, these leaders adhered to a carefully scripted narrative about the war and what it represented. A close analysis of the content and tone of their public statements during this time frame illustrates the transformation of Obama's interpretation of Iraq from scathing campaign critique to a hope-filled vision infused with promise. It also underscores the triumph of the war-on-terrorism paradigm.

Reconstructing the Meaning of Iraq

The Iraq narrative the Obama administration unveiled at the time of the 2010 drawdown contained five interrelated themes that the president had been refining from the time he took the oath of office: 1) the U.S. fulfilled its responsibilities and met its commitments in Iraq; 2) U.S. troops served with honor and met success; 3) the war's benefits outweighed the costs; 4) America must refocus on the real security threat; and 5) Iraq could now achieve a democratic destiny. I shall examine each of these in turn and note how they were woven into a compelling and coherent storyline intended to elicit the support of the American public both for the conflict that was ending and the security challenges that lay ahead.

Promises Kept and Responsibilities Met

To the disabled veterans, Obama reaffirmed his commitment to withdrawing from Iraq and argued that the end of combat operations would mark the close of an important chapter of the American story. He also reminded his military audience that by concluding the war appropriately and expeditiously, he was fulfilling a central campaign promise. A few weeks later in his weekly radio address, Obama underscored the withdrawal as "an important step forward" in responsibly ending the conflict and meeting his pledge that he "would end this war" (Obama 2010e and f). And the president's August 31 primetime address to the nation, only his second from the Oval Office, bestowed additional gravity on this "milestone" and "historic moment," as he yet again stressed that "Through this remarkable chapter in the history of the United States and Iraq, we have met our responsibility" as well as his promise to the American people (2010h).

The president and vice president also emphasized that the drawdown had been set in motion by former President Bush and thus warranted full bipartisan support. For the most part there was partisan accord that the U.S. had met its responsibility in Iraq, even though Republican leaders did have their own script for this occasion. Both Senate Minority Leader Mitch McConnell (R-KY) and House Minority Leader John Boehner (R-OH) marked the end of combat operations in Iraq by praising the former commander-in-chief whose surge policy, in their judgment, made the American withdrawal possible. McConnell's office issued a press release titled "The Surge Worked" (McConnell 2010), and Boehner gave several speeches praising President Bush and General Petraeus for the success of the surge and highlighting the current president's and vice president's opposition to Bush's military gamble in 2007.

Asked about this point in an interview on PBS's *News Hour*, Biden brushed aside the GOP claim about the import of the surge. Treating it as an irrelevant issue, the vice president dismissively quipped, "I don't want to argue—look if—John Boehner or anyone else wants to say the surge did this, fine. Fine." He then reiterated the administration's position that success depended on political, not military, progress (Biden 2010a). While there may have been partisan differences on the impact of the surge, however, neither McConnell nor Boehner publicly objected to ending the American combat mission in Iraq and did not bring the subject up for formal congressional debate. Thus the squabbling over which president was entitled to the credit for the drawdown provided ample evidence that the opposition party viewed it as a positive event. There was no Republican counterframe to the narrative that America must exit from Iraq—and that it was possible to do so with both honor and some measure of success.

Democrats on Capitol Hill were also largely supportive of the decision to end the U.S. combat mission in Iraq. The only dissent came from some progressive members who expressed dismay that the administration was proceeding too slowly and that by delaying the date for the removal of all troops the president had failed to meet an important campaign promise. Obama had moved quickly to deflect that criticism in his February 2009 PBS interview with Jim Lehrer. Dryly remarking that these critics "maybe weren't paying attention to what I said during the campaign," he reviewed the pledges he had made as a candidate and outlined how he was now responsibly meeting each one (Obama 2009h).

The newly inaugurated president also emphasized that his withdrawal plans had been finalized through widespread consultation with commanders on the ground, the CENTCOM commander, the Joint Chiefs of Staff, the secretary of state, the national security advisor, and even "individuals who like me had opposed the idea of going into Iraq in the first place." As a result, he argued, a "very strong consensus" across the political spectrum had been reached that this was "the right way to go" (2009h). A few liberal Democratic members and their allies continued to grumble as the official drawdown date approached, but none introduced any congressional motions or debated the issue on the floor. Democrats were once again unable to marshal a viable rejoinder to the narrative that the U.S. would not simply head for the exits in Iraq, a rhetorical victory for the Bush frame that the surge had accomplished its goals of allowing the U.S. and its allies to establish a friendly regime that would further U.S. security and the cause of democracy.

President Obama also reaffirmed America's ongoing commitment to Iraq throughout 2009 and 2010, emphasizing that far from abandoning it, he was merely opening up a new phase in American–Iraqi relations. Iraq would assume lead responsibility for its own fate, but the U.S. would continue to provide noncombat advice and assistance. Once again he highlighted this topic in his August 2, 2010 remarks, reiterating that "Our commitment in Iraq is changing—from a military effort led by our troops to a civilian efforts led by our diplomats" (2010e). While Operation Iraqi Freedom was over, Operation New Dawn would begin. Returning to this theme in his national address on August 31, Obama characterized the relationship as follows: "This new approach reflects our long-term partnership with Iraq—one based upon mutual interest and mutual respect." While the combat phrase might be ending, "our commitment to Iraq's future is not," Obama declared, and he outlined a future of close cooperation with Iraq on such matters as political stability, national security, economic rebuilding, resettlement of refugees, and trade (2010g and h).

Ending the war responsibly also meant "meeting our responsibility to those who have fought it" (Obama 2010f), and the president devoted considerable space in his public statements to the issue of providing the best medical care possible for American veterans. In his remarks to the disabled veterans, Obama detailed the health problems of returning troops and the state of the art medical services and treatments now available to them. He also touted the new Post-9/11 GI Bill as a way to help veterans realize the American dream through achieving a college education, ending his speech on this lofty note: "These are the commitments my administration has made. These are the promises we have worked to keep. This is the sacred trust we have pledged to uphold—to you and all who serve" (Obama 2010e). In each presidential communication during this two-month time frame, there was at least one reference to America's obligation to its veterans.

In the lead-up to his drawdown announcement, the president continued his emphatic assertion that America's remaining 50,000 troops would be withdrawn on schedule by the end of 2011. As Obama succinctly stated on August 2, "We will remove all of our troops from Iraq by the end of next year" (Obama 2010e). The president repeated this pledge in his radio address: "But the bottom line is this: The war is ending. Like any sovereign, independent nation, Iraq is free to chart its own course. And by the end of next year, all of our troops will be home" (Obama

2010f). This statement was repeated almost verbatim in Obama's primetime address to the nation—"Consistent with our agreement with the Iraqi government, all U.S. troops with leave by the end of next year" (Obama 2010h)—and the same message was delivered by Vice President Biden in Baghdad the following day. Obama acknowledged that many uncertainties lay ahead for Iraq, but he stressed that "in the end, only Iraqis can resolve their differences and police their streets. Only Iraqis can build a democracy within their borders" (2010h). There was to be no turning back on ending the combat mission and the complete withdrawal of American troops. America was keeping her solemn promise. It was, in the words of the president, "time to turn the page."

Honoring Those Who Served

Even though the U.S. was closing the combat chapter in Iraq, Obama insisted that America would never turn its back on the thousands of military personnel who had so bravely served in one of the nation's longest wars. In each of his public comments in in the weeks surrounding the drawdown, he continued to thank the troops and their families for all they had sacrificed and to praise the military for its accomplishments and stellar performance in Iraq. To the disabled veterans, the president, not surprisingly, stressed the theme of the immense sacrifices of U.S. soldiers and their families: "For the past nine years, in Afghanistan and Iraq, they [American soldiers] have borne the burdens of war. They, and their families, have faced the greatest test in the history of our all-volunteer force, serving tour after tour, year after year … And we salute the families back home. They too have sacrificed in this war" (Obama 2010e). This was also the central message in the president's appropriately-titled weekly radio address, "As the Combat Mission in Iraq Ends, We Must Pay Tribute to Those Who Have Served" (Obama 2010f).

On the morning of August 31, President Obama spoke before a military audience in Fort Bliss, Texas. Most of his remarks were limited to expressions of appreciation to the fighting forces for their past and continuing service, as he once more acknowledged the hardships that the extended deployments and multiple tours of duty had extracted from military families. In his primetime address that evening, Obama noted that the greatest costs of war could be measured in the "enormous sacrifices" of our young men and women: "Thousands of Americans gave their lives; tens of thousands have been wounded" (Obama 2010g). At the official change of command ceremony in Baghdad the next day, the vice president echoed those sentiments. Observing that over one million American soldiers had served in Iraq, Biden said he was in awe of the sacrifices of the U.S. military, especially "for more than 30,000 troops wounded in action, and over 4,408 fallen angels who have made the ultimate sacrifice along with members of the international coalition" (Biden 2010b).

References to the military's exceptional performance and battlefield accomplishments in Iraq comprised the second thread in the administration's support-the-troops theme. It was also no coincidence that a military audience was often the setting for the administration's speeches. The imagery of men and women in uniform listening intently to their commander-in-chief is a visual backdrop presidents find hard to resist, and Obama and his senior lieutenants carefully selected military venues, both at home and in Iraq, for their events.

Much of Obama's and Biden's rhetoric about honoring those who served was also couched in the language and symbolism of American exceptionalism. No official public statement during this period neglected to overflow with admiration for the unparalleled accomplishments of the American military. A few examples should suffice. In his primetime address to the nation, Obama noted that "The Americans who have served in Iraq completed every mission they were given," a phrase that appeared in several of his speeches. Furthermore, "At every turn, America's men and women in uniform have served with courage and resolve. As commander-in-chief, I am incredibly proud of their service. And like all Americans, I'm awed by their sacrifice, and by the sacrifices of their families" (Obama 2010h).

Earlier in the day, the president had told the service personnel at Fort Bliss that "there has not been a single mission that has been assigned to all of you in which you have not performed with gallantry, with courage, with excellence." Through the troops' "extraordinary service" they had "written their own chapter in the American story. And by any measure, they have earned their place among the greatest of generations." He went on to note that although the U.S. had a history of political disagreements, including big debates about war and peace, "the one thing we don't argue about is the fact that we've got the finest fighting force in the history of the world" (Obama 2010g). Never one to be rhetorically upstaged, Vice President Biden offered these effusive comments about America's exceptional fighting forces the following afternoon to his audience in Baghdad:

> This change of mission, to state the obvious, would never have been possible without the resolve and tremendous sacrifice and competence of our military—the finest—if our Iraqi friends will forgive us, the finest fighting force in the world and I would argue the finest fighting force that ever has existed. And I don't believe that is hyperbole. (Biden 2010b)

The larger unstated significance of this ubiquitous praise for U.S. servicemen and women was to inoculate the military from any responsibility for the problems or failures in Iraq. Since, according to the Obama narrative, America's uniformed forces succeeded in every mission they were given, the blame for any failures had to lie elsewhere. An absolutely uncritical assessment of military performance is consistent with the exceptionalist assertion that the troops are heroes in time of war whether past or present. They also stand as a proud symbol of America's ideals and limitless potential, providing a gleam of hope in uncertain times that a brighter future awaits. In the stirring words of the president:

> Every American who serves joins an unbroken line of heroes that stretches from Lexington to Gettysburg; from Iwo Jima to Inchon; from Khe Sanh to Kandahar—

Americans who have fought to see that the lives of our children are better than our own. Our troops are the steel in our ship of state. And though our nation may be travelling through rough waters, they give us confidence that our course is true, and that beyond the predawn darkness, better days lie ahead. (2010h)

Iraq's Benefits Outweigh the Costs

The political costs of the war at home and abroad were also part of the official drawdown narrative, but they were couched as a problem that would now be resolved as the U.S. shifted from a combat role. Carefully employing a passive voice and speaking in the past tense, Obama briefly observed that due to America's engagement in Iraq, "Our relations abroad were strained. Our unity at home was tested." But the time had now come, the president urged in his primetime address, to put domestic disagreements aside and move on, as even fierce partisans and former political foes should join together in recognition of this important milestone:

> I'm mindful that the Iraq war has been a contentious issue at home. Here, too, it's time to turn the page. This afternoon, I spoke to former President George W. Bush. It's well known that he and I disagreed about the war from its outset. Yet no one can doubt President Bush's support for our troops, or his love of country and commitment to our security. As I've said, there were patriots who supported this war, and patriots who opposed it. And all of us are united in appreciation for our servicemen and women, and our hopes for Iraq's future. (Obama 2010h)

While both Obama and Biden briefly acknowledged the political divisiveness of the war on the home front, they made even less mention in the summer of 2010 of Iraq's cost to the international standing of the United States. Although this had previously been an issue of grave concern to Senator Obama, it was now framed as little more than a problem from the past, an issue worthy of only a fleeting reference to "strained relations."

The official drawdown narrative also entailed an important about-face on the issue of the war's impact on American security. Obama the candidate had always insisted that the war in Iraq was a distraction that made the U.S. less safe, whereas President Obama now concluded that Americans could sleep a little easier as a result of the conflict. The following statement to the troops at Fort Bliss on the day combat operations officially ended provides another indication of his evolving interpretation of the war: "Because of the extraordinary service that all of you have done, and so many people here at Fort Bliss have done, Iraq has the opportunity to create a better future for itself, and America is more secure" (Obama 2010g). Although Obama failed to specify in this speech just how the war had improved America's security situation, a careful reading of the evening's primetime address suggests what he believed the connection to be: A stable and democratic Iraq would be both partner and ally in a newly-energized battle against the greatest threat to U.S. national security—the forces of extremism still plotting in Afghanistan and beyond (Obama 2010h). Note that as he elaborated his drawdown narrative, his gaze shifted ever more squarely to the future and to the conflict that he had long indicated should be America's primary focus.

Obama also spoke in his Oval Office address of the economic toll Iraq had wrought on America, and his message on drawing down the troops morphed into something of an economic pep talk. Charging that the U.S. had spent more than a trillion dollars at war, a dangerous situation that had "shortchanged investments in our own people and contributed to record deficits," he claimed that "ending this war is not only in Iraq's interest—it's in our own" (Obama 2010h). Because America had failed to "shore up the foundations of our own prosperity," the president pledged that he would now focus on "our most urgent task"—restoring the U.S. economy. This must be, he declared, "our central mission as a people," and he exhorted the American public to "tackle those challenges at home with as much energy, and grit, and sense of common purpose as our men and women in uniform who have served abroad" (Obama 2010h).

Once more Obama turned from past and current problems to future possibilities, this time conflating what America could achieve on the economic home front with all that the troops had accomplished on the battlefield. He issued this clarion call: "Now it is our responsibility to honor them [our troops] by coming together, all of us and working to secure the dream that so many generations have fought for—the dream that a better life awaits anyone who is willing to work for it and reach for it" (Obama 2010h). It was no accident that the dream of which Obama so eloquently spoke is one of the bedrock values of American exceptionalism.

More than seven years of war had taken a severe political, economic, and security toll on Iraq, but this component of the drawdown narrative was decidedly downplayed. The president addressed it primarily through brief elliptical references to the Iraqis' "huge sacrifices of their own" as "terrorism and sectarian warfare threatened to tear Iraq apart" (Obama 2010h). It was left to the vice president and defense secretary to broach more fully the topic of Iraqi suffering, although their public comments were also notable for their brevity. In presiding over the change of command ceremony in Baghdad, Biden thus offered this short but moving tribute: "Today is also an important acknowledgment—it's important to acknowledge the magnitude … of the Iraqi losses in this conflict. Tens of thousands of security forces and innocent civilians have been killed. Many times that number have been wounded and displaced" (Biden 2010b). And in remarks before the American Legion, Secretary Gates similarly touched upon the "terrible cost" of this war in the "losses and trauma endured by the Iraqi people" (Gates 2010a).

But since the scale of civilian casualties and physical destruction of Iraq was among the major legacies of the war, it is noteworthy that the enormity of the costs and consequences for the Iraqi people was essentially an afterthought untethered from the president's wider narrative. And while the human toll in Iraq rated only passing mention, there was virtually no discussion of the many ongoing problems with Iraqi public services such as healthcare, education, water, sanitation, and electricity that rendered daily life such a struggle.

Rather than dwelling on Iraq's problematic past or present, President Obama now spoke of a nation that could construct a brighter future. The thorny issue of ongoing violence was thus contextualized with a positive spin that internal security was improving. The official narrative held that America had overthrown the biggest security threat to Iraq—a regime that terrorized its own people—and since that time, the U.S. and the Iraqis had been successfully confronting an insurgency. Much still remained to be done, the president conceded, but he was quick to offer these words of encouragement: "Even as Iraq continues to suffer terrorist attacks, security incidents have been near the lowest on record since the war began. And Iraqi forces have taken the fight to al Qaeda, removing much of its leadership in Iraqi-led operations" (Obama 2010g and h).

Iraq's inability to form a functioning government was similarly framed as a temporary setback, and the president urged her squabbling leaders to come together and establish "an inclusive government that is just, representative, and accountable to the Iraqi people" (Obama 2010h). Perhaps the best expressions of the administration's revamped take on the political impasse in Iraq came from Vice President Biden, first in a speech to the Veterans of Foreign Wars annual convention in Indianapolis and then at the official Baghdad ceremony inaugurating Operation New Dawn. To the VFW members, Biden proudly proclaimed that violence in Iraq had so decreased "you would not recognize the country today," and he offered the rather breezy characterization that "politics and not war has broken out in Iraq." One week later, standing at the podium in the rotunda of one of Saddam Hussein's opulent palaces to mark the official change of command in Baghdad, he uttered a condensed version of that rose-colored assessment: "politics is breaking out in Iraq" (Biden 2010b; quoted in Gordon and Bumiller 2010).

As Glazier and Boydstun (2012) note, presidential war rhetoric emphasizes a limited array of frames most favorable for the administration, and in the case of America's departure from Iraq, Obama consistently highlighted an optimistic storyline that future possibilities for politics and security in Iraq would outweigh all the past and current problems that had so bedeviled the nation. Progress in Iraq was apparently to be measured by the potential for greater stability and democracy, not the actual achievement of those goals, a perspective that dovetailed well with Bush's endgame narrative of what the war represented and how it would conclude.

Refocusing on America's Real Security Challenge

Less than half way through his primetime address to the nation, Obama began to wrap up his comments on Iraq and turn to a discussion of security in Afghanistan. The president used the phrase "time to turn the page" two times, suggestive of an effort to deflect further debate on the meaning of Iraq and to separate it from the larger discussion of national security issues. For Obama, the end of combat operations in Iraq was another useful moment to highlight his new way forward in Afghanistan, and he forcefully summarized the rationale for why the U.S.

must expand its efforts there and the reasons it was imperative to succeed. As the president made clear in his August 2 speech:

> Even as we end the war in Iraq, even as we welcome home so many of our troops, others are still deployed in Afghanistan. So I want to remind everyone, it was Afghanistan where al Qaeda plotted and trained to murder 3,000 innocent people on 9/11. It is Afghanistan and the tribal regions of Pakistan where terrorists have launched other attacks against us and our allies. And if Afghanistan were to be engulfed by an even wider insurgency, al Qaeda and its terrorist affiliates would have even more space to plan their next attack. And as President of the United States, I refuse to let that happen (Obama 2010e).

Throughout the first half of 2010, Obama had, in fact, devoted far more public rhetoric to Afghanistan and the problems of combating terrorism than he had to ending the war in Iraq. He began the year with a public statement on the failed 2009 Christmas airline attack, noting that his administration had already taken action to repair the intelligence and security failures that had permitted a "known terrorist" to board a plane bound for the U.S. He also used this opportunity to remind everyone of the existential battle America still fought: "We are at war. We are at war against al Qaeda, a far-reaching network of violence and hatred that attacked us on 9/11, that killed nearly 3,000 innocent people, and that is plotting to strike us again. And we will do whatever it takes to defeat them" (Obama 2010a).

Three weeks later, in a 2010 State of the Union address (Obama 2010b) that focused primarily on domestic economic issues, the president again emphasized that "we've renewed our focus on the terrorists who threaten our nation" and indicated that in the past year, hundreds of al Qaeda fighters and affiliates, including many senior leaders, had been captured or killed—far more, he hastened to add, than in the last year of the Bush administration. And in what would become a major theme of his 2010 Afghanistan narrative, Obama also stressed the progress the U.S. was making in this lengthy and difficult battle: increasing its troop presence, training Afghan security forces, providing the groundwork for good governance, reducing corruption, and supporting the rights of all the Afghan people (Obama 2010b). Results were already clearly evident. "Al Qaeda's leadership is hunkered down," he reported, "We have worked closely with partners, including Yemen, to inflict major blows against al Qaeda leaders. And we have disrupted plots at home and abroad, and saved American lives" (Obama 2010a).

In remarks during a surprise visit later that spring to the troops stationed at Bagram Airfield in Afghanistan, Obama again elevated the war against the terrorist extremists to the defining foreign policy battle of the new century, once more framing it as America's most pressing national security threat:

> We can't forget why we're here. We did not choose this war. This was not an act of America wanting to expand its influence, of us wanting to meddle in somebody else's business. We were attacked viciously on 9/11. Thousands of

our fellow countrymen and women were killed. And this is the region where the perpetrators of that crime, al Qaeda, still base their leadership. Plots against our homeland, plots against our allies, plots against the Afghan and Pakistani people are taking place as we speak right here. And if this region slides backwards, if the Taliban retakes the country and al Qaeda can operate with impunity, then more American lives will be at stake. The Afghan people will lose their chance at progress and prosperity. And the world will be significantly less secure. (Obama 2010c)

America's broad mission in Afghanistan is clear, Obama told the assembled troops: "disrupt and dismantle, defeat and destroy al Qaeda and its extremist allies." And he repeated the military and civilian objectives he had so frequently articulated over the past 12 months: deny al Qaeda a safe haven, reverse the Taliban's momentum, and strengthen the Afghan security forces and government "so that they can begin taking responsibility and gain confidence of the Afghan people" (Obama 2010c). While noting that there would be "some difficult days ahead," the president declared his complete confidence in his nation's success. The United States would eventually triumph because of "something essential about America" that separated its fighting forces—and all Americans—from those who sought the nation's destruction: "They've got no respect for human life. You see dignity in every human being. That's part of what we value as Americans. They want to drive races and regions and religions apart. You want to bring people together and see the world move forward together. They offer fear, and you offer hope" (Obama 2010c).

In a foreign policy commencement address at West Point in May, Obama spoke at greater length about the challenges that still remained in Afghanistan. While the U.S. had toppled the Taliban regime, a Taliban insurgency had achieved momentum; America had supported the election of a sovereign government, but still needed to strengthen its capacities. He also repeated his earlier assertions that the campaign to disrupt, dismantle, and defeat al Qaeda and its allies was "a different kind of war" that would involve "no simple moment of surrender to mark the journey's end—no armistice, no banner headline." And the terrorist extremists would "continue to recruit, and plot, and exploit our open society. We see that in bombs that go off in Kabul and Karachi. We see it in attempts to blow up an airliner over Detroit or an SUV in Times Square" (Obama 2010d).

But the commander-in-chief remained both confident and resolute. Despite the continuing threats, America would prevail in this conflict, he insisted, because "I see the strength and resilience of the American people." He also saw an exceptional nation founded upon the "different notion" that "all men are created equal, that they are endowed by their Creator with certain unalienable rights, that among these are life, liberty, and the pursuit of happiness" (Obama 2010d). The power of that idea, Obama declared, has bound the U.S. together as one people and has made it not only the greatest nation but the most resilient and optimistic: "From the birth of our existence, America has had a faith in the future—a belief that where we're going is better than where we've been, even when the path ahead is uncertain." And, he concluded, no clearer proof was needed than those young men and women assembled before him—the "Long Grey Line that has sacrificed for duty, for honor, for country" (Obama 2010d).

In the weeks leading up to the end of combat operations in Iraq, Obama continued to speak as much about Afghanistan as about the war he was about to draw down. Addressing the Disabled Veterans in early August, Obama employed a phrase almost identical to the one he had used to reassure the public about Iraq: "It's important that the American people know that we are making progress and we are focused on goals that are clear and achievable" (Obama 2010e). As he continued to highlight the theme of progress, the president noted that nearly all the additional forces he had ordered were now in place and the U.S. was mounting an offensive against the Taliban. His administration was also insisting on greater accountability from the Afghan government, and its leaders were taking "concrete steps" to foster development and combat corruption. And he reported that the Pakistani government had also make headway in its steps to fight violent extremists within its borders (Obama 2010e).

To the troops at Fort Bliss on the morning of August 31, Obama admitted that America obviously still had "a very tough fight" ahead in Afghanistan. "It is going to be a tough slog," he stated, "but what I know is that after 9/11, this country was unified in saying we are not going to let something like that happen again. And we are going to go after those who perpetrated that crime, and we are going to make sure that they do not have safe haven." Under the command of General Petraeus, the U.S. and its allies would start "taking the fight to the terrorists." While that would mean some casualties and heartbreak, the special nation would rise to the occasion because "the one thing that I know from all of you is that when we put our minds to it, we get things done" (Obama 2010g). In that evening's primetime address on the official end of combat operations in Iraq, Obama reiterated Afghanistan's importance to American security, insisting that "no challenge is more essential to our security than our fight against al Qaeda" and reminding everyone that, "Americans across the political spectrum supported the use of force against those who attacked us on 9/11" (Obama 2010h). Once more he invoked the memory of the terrorist attacks and thus the idea of a blameless America so unjustly targeted.

In Bush's and Obama's narratives of the 2001 terrorist attacks, the strikes on America had become the archetypical example of good under assault by evil. As we have seen, central to the Bush frame of Iraq was the disciplined effort to link Saddam Hussein to these horrendous deeds. Since the attacks stood as an indelible cultural marker for America as innocent victim, even the suggestion of a connection provided a useful tool for seeking retribution against vaguely defined adversaries (terrorists and the sponsors of terrorism). While the Bush storyline of direct ties between Saddam and al Qaeda unraveled over time, the political utility of recalling the horrors of 9/11 had not diminished. Even for the president who was in the forefront of uncoupling Iraq from the Bush war-on-terror narrative, September 11 was at times invoked broadly enough that it seemed still to encompass the war in Iraq. As Jackson (2011) argues, the language of terrorism had become so embedded in American discourse that Obama's endgame conflation of the two conflicts seemed both eminently reasonable and entirely appropriate.

President Obama did continue to clarify the differences between the 2001 terrorist attacks and the on-going insurgency in Iraq, mentioning in his August 2 speech, for instance, that "When terrorists and militias plunged Iraq into sectarian war, our troops adapted and adjusted—restoring order and effectively defeating al Qaeda in Iraq on the battlefield" and noting that the U.S. must remain vigilant "as terrorists try to derail Iraq's progress" (Obama 2010e). One wonders, however, if the president's differentiation between al Qaeda in Iraq and al Qaeda in Afghanistan was a distinction without a difference to most Americans. And his narrative of Iraq's conclusion certainly left no space for a critique of the surge policy he had originally so condemned, nor did it allow for any further interrogation of the global war against America's terrorist adversaries.

In remarks at the Pentagon on the ninth anniversary of 9/11, Obama provided evidence of the depth of the exceptional grievance that is associated with the attacks and their imprint on American collective identity. "We gather to remember, at this sacred hour, on hallowed ground—at places where we feel such grief and our healing goes on," the president intoned. He continued, "And though it must seem some days that the world has moved on to other things, I say to you today that your loved ones endure in the heart of the nation, today and forever" (Obama 2010i). Posing the question of how best to remember the victims of 9/11, Obama replied in words that recapitulated his consistent anti-terrorism narrative:

> We need not look far for our answer. The perpetrators of this evil act didn't simply attack America; they attacked the very idea of America itself—all that we stand for and represent in the world. And so the highest honor we can pay those we lost, indeed our greatest weapon in this ongoing war, is to do what our adversaries fear the most—to stay true to who we are, as Americans; to renew our sense of common purpose; to say that we define the character of our country, and we will not let the acts of some small band of murderers who slaughter the innocent and cower in caves distort who we are. (Obama 2010i)

As this passage illustrates, Obama's Pentagon remarks were replete with powerful signifiers to the idea of America as the paragon of democratic virtue, an indication that in his as in Bush's exceptionalist narrative, the only acceptable interpretation of 9/11 was that an innocent, freedom-loving nation was preyed upon that day by barbaric murderers who hated it not for its policies but for its ideals. Hence as the president again declared, in the battle against al Qaeda in Afghanistan "our cause is just" (Obama 2010h). Any reference to Iraq's role in impeding this epic struggle was conveniently omitted; no longer did Obama draw a clear moral line between the two conflicts. The closer the U.S. came to a formal exit from Iraq, the more Obama seemed to incorporate America's "bad" war of choice into what he had deemed America's "good" war of necessity.

Forging a New Iraqi Destiny

Mindful of his predecessor's disastrous 2003 declaration of victory aboard the aircraft carrier, Obama was careful to emphasize that his official announcement of the end of combat operations in Iraq was "not going to be a victory lap" (Obama 2010g). Secretary of Defense Gates was on the same rhetorical page as the president. While addressing the National Convention of the American Legion on August 31, Gates told his audience that "This is not the time for premature victory parades or self-congratulations ... We still have a job to do and responsibilities there" (Gates 2010a). According to the president, "In an age without surrender ceremonies, we must earn victory through the success of our partners and the strength of our own nation" (Obama 2010h). Thus it was too early to know with certainty whether to label Iraq a success; as of fall 2010 the U.S. could not yet claim an unfettered legacy of military or political victory.

But the president did not hesitate to trumpet the vast democratic *possibilities* that America had opened up for Iraq. In Obama's words, this entailed nothing less than "the opportunity to embrace a new destiny," and he called upon its leaders to "move forward with a sense of urgency" to establish a government worthy of all that the U.S. and the Iraqi people had sacrificed (Obama 2010h). In more subdued language, the vice president also encouraged the Iraqis to continue their progress toward an inclusive democratic regime and claimed that its formation would greatly improve the country's unsettled security situation (Biden 2010b).

Defense Secretary Gates struck a similar chord of tempered optimism as he spoke to reporters about Iraq's possible democratic legacy: "If Iraq ends up a democratic country, that is a constructive participant in international life, then I think looking back, although the cost of getting there would've been terrible, ... the potential for it being the core of significant change in this whole region as a democratic state, I think is hard to underestimate" (Gates 2010b). The prospect of a stable democratic regime thus trumped the war's dreadful toll, Gates reluctantly conceded. But when pressed on whether the war was worth it, Gates initially equivocated, stating that "it really requires an historian's perspective in terms of what happens here in the long term." And in what would become a widely-quoted comment, he went on candidly to acknowledge that the underlying rationale for the conflict would forever cast a dark shadow. Unlike the president and vice president, it seemed that the secretary of defense was not yet fully prepared to turn the page on Iraq:

> Well, the problem—the problem with this war for, I think, many Americans is that the premise on which we justified going to war proved not to be valid—that is, Saddam having weapons of mass destruction.
>
> So when you start from that standpoint, then figuring out in retrospect how you deal with the war, even if the outcome is a good one from the standpoint of the United States, *it will always be clouded by how it began*. And so I think that

this is one of the reasons why this war remains so controversial at home. (Gates 2010b, emphasis added)

Despite the administration's lingering concerns about the prospects for stability in Iraq and the defense secretary's admission that the war was initiated on a false premise, President Obama chose to accentuate the positive as he fashioned the tale of why America fought in Iraq, what the U.S. had accomplished, and what the conflict's legacy would be. The official narrative, grounded in core American values of freedom, democracy, and progress, was designed to be both familiar and comforting to the American public. And it should certainly have provided no small measure of satisfaction to members of the previous administration and their supporters.

Obama's closing argument on Iraq can be summarized as follows: By overthrowing a tyrant who had terrorized his own countrymen, America had liberated an oppressed people. By fighting to quell the resulting insurgency, the U.S. had protected the Iraqis and provided them with the security necessary to build a stable and functioning democracy. By continuing to advise and assist the new government, the U.S. would enable it to flourish and thereby contribute to the long-term peace and prosperity of the entire region. And by partnering with a new Middle Eastern ally in the fight against extremism, America would move forward in ensuring its own national security. There could be little doubt that Senator Obama's original, far more censorious depiction of America's mistaken entrance into war, the years of mismanagement that followed, and the tremendous costs incurred had undergone a substantially airbrushed makeover.

To his vast primetime audience, the president summed up his sanguine vision by proclaiming that America had persevered in Iraq "because of a belief we share with the Iraqi people—a belief that out of the ashes of war, a new beginning could be born in this cradle of civilization" (Obama 2010h). And to provide his storyline with a fittingly dramatic conclusion to the meaning of Iraq, Obama turned to the heroic sacrifices of U.S. troops:

> Those Americans gave their lives for the *values that have lived in the hearts of our people* for over two centuries. Along with nearly 1.5 million Americans who have served in Iraq, they fought in a faraway place for people they never knew. They stared into the darkest of human creations—war—and helped the Iraqi people *seek the light of peace*. (Obama 2010h, emphasis added)

The logic of the exceptionalist narrative, and the sense of mission embedded in it, requires U.S. foreign policy motives to rise above petty national interests because that is part of American identity as a nation firmly embedded on the right side of history. And as the president stressed in his Oval Office address, having provided Iraq with the framework for an improved and more secure democratic regime, the U.S. could now confidently turn the page on its military operations in Iraq and focus on other pressing needs. America had completed its combat mission in Iraq;

if the Iraqis now failed to step up and "seize the chance for a better future," the United States would not bear the blame (Obama 2010h).

Obama's last major address during the time period under study was filled with exceptionalist prose. In a September 23 speech before the United Nations, the president once more framed the shift from a combat mission in Iraq as part and parcel of the larger attempt to keep America secure by waging a more targeted and effective fight against al Qaeda extremism. Just as he had done in every other public statement on Iraq since assuming office, he assured the assembled diplomats that his administration was conducting a responsible drawdown and simultaneously building a lasting partnership with the people of Iraq (Obama 2010j).

But lingering only briefly on this conflict from the past, Obama quickly moved to a fuller exposition of what turning the page on the Iraq chapter of American foreign policy meant even beyond Afghanistan. First setting forth an ambitious international agenda that ranged from eliminating nuclear weapons to confronting climate change, holding Iran accountable, and pursuing peace in the Arab–Israeli conflict, the president then seamlessly shifted his substantive focus to a glimpse of "what kind of world we are trying to build" in the new century (Obama 2010j). Squarely framed in the exceptionalist notion of America as the embodiment of freedom's ideal, Obama tied the purpose of U.S. foreign policy to the universal cause of human rights: "The idea is a simple one—that freedom, justice and peace for the world must begin with freedom, justice, and peace in the lives of individual human beings. For the United States, this is a matter of moral and pragmatic necessity ... So we stand up for universal values because it is the right thing to do" (Obama 2010j).

Continuing to build upon this idealistic theme, the president proffered the belief that going hand-in-hand with human rights was America's commitment to promote a world in which each individual had the opportunity to reach his fullest potential, a goal that could be reached only when political and economic liberty were extended across the globe. In Obama's words:

> Yet experience shows us that history is on the side of liberty—that the strongest foundation for human progress lies in open economies, open societies, and open governments. To put it simply: Democracy, more than any other form of government, delivers for our citizens. And that truth will only grow stronger in a world where the borders between nations are blurred. America is working to shape a world that fosters this openness, for the rot of a closed or corrupt economy must never eclipse the energy and innovation of human beings. (Obama 2010j)

Linking U.S. foreign policy to a sense of exceptionalist mission, the president asserted that the "price of our own freedom is standing up for the freedom of others. That belief will guide America's leadership in this twenty-first century." To this end, he declared, America must embrace "unique responsibilities—that come with our power" (Obama 2010j). The U.N. address thus served as an opportunity for a restoration of moral purpose in the wake of America's problematic engagement in Iraq.

But Obama also sounded an important cautionary note hard learned from that conflict: In the future, American strategy in fighting to preserve its freedom and ideals would involve a "more targeted approach—one that strengthens our partners and dismantles terrorist networks without deploying large American armies" (Obama 2010j). There had to be, he implied, a smarter way to promote American security. Left unstated was that in the interim, thousands of U.S. troops would continue to fight the forces of extremism in the mountainous regions of Afghanistan and Pakistan while still others would engage in dangerous counterterrorism missions in America's new advise and assist role in Iraq. Also left unexplained was the technique his administration would employ in its more targeted approach to fighting terrorism—unmanned aerial vehicles, or drones—and the thorny moral and legal issues this new method of warfare would raise.

* * *

Obama's Iraq War narrative was more complex and nuanced than Bush's war-on-terror frame of why America had to fight Saddam Hussein or the progressive anti-war script that condemned any sort of post-9/11 military engagement. While arguing that Iraq had been the wrong response to the 2001 terrorist attacks, Senator Obama had consistently maintained that the U.S. was correct to engage in military combat against the forces of extremism. The previous administration had simply allowed itself to be distracted from the real battlefront. But even as he attempted to extricate America from the wrong war, President Obama did acknowledge that Iraq's legacy entailed some positive outcomes, especially when viewed through the rhetorical prism of American exceptionalism.

In the weeks surrounding Obama's 2010 announcement of the end of combat operations, there was neither official appetite to criticize the previous president for his failures in Iraq nor much desire to dwell on the darker or more troubling aspects of the war. In fact, except for honoring the troops, there did not seem to be much official interest in revisiting the war at all. An exceptionalist frame allowed the Obama administration to equate the heroism and sacrifice of America's fighting forces in Iraq with its national calling to preserve the peace and spread the cause of freedom and democracy across the globe—but this was possible only because scant attention was given to the actual course of the war and the deteriorating conditions Iraq still faced.

The withdrawal of U.S. combat forces from Iraq also provided another rhetorical pivot point for the president to refocus his security narrative on the "good" war against al Qaeda. Invoking the exceptional grievance of the 2001 terrorist attacks gave Obama a culturally powerful and resonant means to sustain his war of necessity in Afghanistan. As he had warned, the war against terrorist extremism would be a tough slog, but he continued to insist that Americans would remain as united and resolute as they had been in the immediate aftermath of 9/11. In an end-of-year review of his strategy for Afghanistan and Pakistan, Obama briefly acknowledged the importance of the Iraq drawdown for achieving America's "core goal" of disrupting, dismantling, and defeating al Qaeda:

> Indeed, for the first time in years, we've put in place the strategy and the resources that our efforts in Afghanistan demand. And because we've ended our combat mission in Iraq, and brought home nearly 100,000 of our troops from Iraq, we're in a better position to give our forces in Afghanistan the support and equipment they need to achieve their missions. And our drawdown in Iraq also means that today there are tens of thousands fewer Americans deployed in harm's way than when I took office. (Obama 2010k)

For Obama, Iraq was now a topic to be spoken of only in the past tense. Turning the page on Iraq meant that the U.S. could recommit to the real fight against those who continued to threaten it; rhetorically flipping the page also meant the presidential narrative could seek to restore an exceptionalist mission to the goals of U.S. foreign policy by defining an idealistic and optimistic future that framed a uniquely American moral purpose in the world. As McCrisken (2001) notes, America's national identity is deeply rooted in the vision of a society that seeks to perfect itself by learning from and correcting past errors. For Obama, ending the combat mission in Iraq provided that perfect opportunity to extract whatever good had come from America's engagement there, purge the many mistakes that had been made, and apply all that the nation had learned to confronting the other challenges of the new century, especially the still-looming threat of terrorist extremism.

As we shall see in the following chapter, Obama's August 31 announcement of the troop drawdown primed media organizations to increase attention to a conflict that they had largely ignored over the previous year and a half. But highlighting the troop withdrawal in no way meant that journalists would passively adopt the reassuring official frame of what the U.S. had accomplished in Iraq and the possibilities the future held for that troubled country. America's leading media outlets instead constructed their own, more foreboding narrative about what the conflict represented, what had actually been achieved, and the grim prospects for the beleaguered nation of Iraq.

Chapter 5
War's Drawdown through a Censorious Media Lens

The official end of U.S. combat operations in Iraq came at a time when America's attention was still riveted on the financial and economic crises that had plagued the country since the fall of 2008. The newly-elected president had also chosen to highlight his economic stimulus and healthcare plans, and as a consequence, the big Washington debates of Obama's first year and a half in office centered on these proposals rather than his national security initiatives. Even in the foreign policy realm, Obama's decision to increase the U.S. military footprint in Afghanistan drew far more notice than did his stated intention to withdraw its combat forces from Iraq. This stood in marked contrast to the policy battles of Bush's second term, a period in which Iraq had taken center stage. But as we have seen, by the time Obama was inaugurated, Congress had basically reached consensus that closure on Iraq was desirable and no longer a debatable issue.

A solid majority of the American public also appeared anxious to disengage from Iraq, as polls taken in the wake of the president's February 2009 announcement that combat operations would end by August of the following year indicated that around 75 percent approved of his plan (Holsti 2011: 66). While there was a significant partisan divide on the wisdom of the troop withdrawal, with Democrats and Independents far more approving than Republicans, even among the GOP ranks supporters of the drawdown outnumbered opponents by almost 10 percentage points. The fact that 40 percent of respondents sampled by the Pew Research Center (2009a) said they paid close attention to Obama's February statement on Iraq further suggests that the public was no less interested than the new commander-in-chief in turning the page on the conflict as expeditiously as possible.

The path that the public had traveled to reach that point had been lengthy and relatively convoluted. When the U.S.-led invasion of Iraq began in March 2003, around 60 percent were supportive, a number that rose to 74 percent shortly after President Bush's dramatic declaration at the beginning of May that the U.S. mission to overthrow Saddam Hussein had been accomplished (Pew Research Center 2003). But as any student of public opinion and Iraq knows only too well, the level of support headed steadily downward from that point on, declining slowly throughout 2004 and dipping below 50 percent approval by 2005 (see Holsti 2011: 38–42). As was the case for war in Afghanistan, however, the aggregate figures masked an enormous partisan split, with Republicans' approval for Iraq hovering around the 70 percent level through 2005, but Democrats' and Independents' support dipping below 20 percent and 40 percent, respectively, throughout the same time period (Holsti 2011: 88–89). And as the security situation in Iraq continued to deteriorate, so did public assessments of the war. According to an October 2006 Pew Research Center poll, only 35 percent agreed that the U.S. effort in Iraq was going well or very well, and while 58 percent of Republicans gave a positive assessment, a mere 18 percent of Democrats and 26 percent of Independents concurred (see Holsti 2011: 88–89).

With the implementation of Bush's surge policy came an uptick of support in late 2007 and early 2008, but once again the partisan gap was yawning, as a strong majority of Republicans saw progress in U.S. attempts to defeat Iraqi insurgents, provide a stabilizing force, and prevent a civil war while Democrats and Independents had the opposite reaction. By September 2008, however, a majority of Independents as well as Republicans thought the U.S. effort was going well or very well, and the number of concurring Democrats had increased to 40 percent (Holsti 2011: 89–91).

By 2008, the public had also become more favorably disposed to a timetable for withdrawal from Iraq, although once again there remained a significant partisan divide. In February, a Gallup/*U.S.A Today* poll found that only 35 percent wanted to keep a "significant number" of troops in Iraq until the situation improved, and in April, a CBS/*New York Times* poll reported that the number who said America should continue to fight as long as the president considered it necessary stood at a comparably low 34 percent. Even though two-thirds of Republicans remained opposed to setting a drawdown timetable regardless of the situation on the ground, they were distinctly in the minority (Holsti 2011: 92–95). Thus as the situation in Iraq appeared to improve, the public increasingly supported U.S. disengagement from the conflict.

While many experts had expected foreign policy to assume a significant role in the 2008 presidential election, the fall economic crisis pushed America's two wars aside. Even before the financial collapse on Wall Street, an August poll found that four in ten Americans were already claiming that the economy was their top issue, while only 15 percent named Iraq (Cooper and Sussman 2008). By Election Day, the number citing the economy as the most important issue had risen to 63 percent, and those declaring war in Iraq to be their primary voting issue had fallen to a mere 10 percent (Holsti 2011: 147).

Presidential campaign discourse on Iraq followed a similar downward trajectory as the date of the election approached. Even the first presidential debate, which was supposed to cover foreign policy, was devoted primarily to the economic crisis. And this was reflected elsewhere on the campaign trail as well. A *New York Times* analysis, for instance, found that Iraq comprised less than 5 percent of Obama's stump speech content at the end of October, and about the only reference he made to the conflict was the spending reduction that would result once the U.S. pulled out (Baker and Zeleny 2008). In a similar vein, a late October National Public Radio analysis of a typical McCain stump speech concluded that "there's almost no foreign policy in the speech, and very little about the war in Iraq" (Liasson 2008). And in an election eve column in the *Washington Post*,

Council on Foreign Relations member Robert McMahon (2008) also noted that by the end of the presidential contest, "the issues of terrorism and Iraq had faded to distant echoes amid the din of the financial crisis."

By the time of the 2008 presidential election, the mainstream U.S. media had also arrived at an assessment that America would achieve some sort of closure in Iraq in the near future. In fact, even before the campaign had ended, journalists were concluding that regardless of which candidate won, the war was essentially over and the U.S. would soon be making an exit. As a result, media attention to the conflict had already begun to plummet, as signaled by the closure in 2008 of many Baghdad news bureaus and the removal of a number of correspondents stationed in Iraq (King and Wells 2009: 201–204). An October 9 *Times* editorial bearing the title "Nearing the End" (2008) contained this declaration: "No matter who wins the presidential election, the United States is on its way out of Iraq. Senator Barack Obama offers the most specific and speediest withdrawal plan, but even Senator McCain will not be able to keep a large number of combat troops there for long." And a *Post* Election Day editorial titled "The War that Didn't Bark" (2008) echoed the same theme, noting that "by the time his [Obama's] general election competition with Mr McCain began, Iraq had faded as an issue."

The fact that Iraq constituted only 1 percent of the total campaign coverage during the latter stages of the general election campaign provided further striking evidence of the lack of importance both the candidates and the media placed on the war (Project for Excellence in Journalism 2008c). From 2007—when Iraq was the top overall news story comprising more than 15 percent of the total news hole—through the following year and a half, there was a clear downward trend in media coverage. The Project for Excellence in Journalism (2010d) found that Iraq accounted for only 4 percent of total news reports in 2008, 2 percent in 2009, and a mere 1 percent for the first half of 2010. So dramatic was this decline that even during the week Obama announced his withdrawal timeline in the spring of 2009, only 6 percent of media stories dealt with the topic of Iraq (Project for Excellence in Journalism 2009a).

Further evidence for the shifting of the media spotlight away from Iraq is provided by the Tyndall Report's track of nightly broadcast network news reports. In 2009, the total combined Iraq coverage of NBC, ABC, and CBS evening news was a mere 80 minutes, a drop of two-thirds from 2008. To place this in perspective, 2009 nightly network news attention to the economy totaled almost 2800 minutes, and the three networks' combined health care reportage for that year clocked in at just over 1880 minutes (Tyndall 2010). And even with the Obama administration's promotion of the end of combat operations in 2010, the year's total nightly network news coverage of Iraq stood at only 94 minutes (Tyndall 2011).

Facing widespread indifference toward what he heralded as an historic milestone, it is no wonder that Obama turned to the powers of the bully pulpit to draw attention to the military drawdown in late summer 2010. And the media did respond with an uptick in news reports about Iraq and the decision to remove U.S.

fighting forces. The two weeks from August 22 to September 5 marked the highest point of Iraq coverage since the fall of 2007 (Project for Excellence in Journalism 2010d), a likely indication of presidential ability to cue the media about important events and issues. But even at this critical juncture in winding down the war, Iraq accounted for less than 10 percent of the news hole in the 52 news outlets examined by PEJ, ranking behind the controversy over construction of a mosque at Ground Zero, Hurricane Earl, the economy, and the 2010 midterm elections (Project for Excellence in Journalism 2010d, 2010e).

As we have seen for Afghanistan, the amount of media attention gives little indication of either the substance or the tone of coverage. So I now turn to an analysis of how the five leading mainstream U.S. media outlets examined previously—the *New York Times*, *Washington Post*, Associated Press, NBC News, and Fox News—depicted the war in Iraq and Obama's proposal to end American combat operations during the 60 days surrounding Obama's Oval Office address to the nation on August 31, 2010, a time frame during which the president actively promoted the troop drawdown and the prospects for success in Iraq.

I again focus on several research questions about the content and process of media coverage: In portraying the withdrawal of U.S. combat troops and the status of the war did the news media act primarily as stenographers, carefully chronicling the administration's statements and parroting its storyline about the end of combat operations? Or did journalists follow a more independent path, developing their own interpretations and presenting narratives counter to the official tale of the drawdown and its meaning? Whose voices and perspectives did the media privilege given the absence of congressional debate? And was there a common media narrative about Iraq, or were there divergent storylines across media outlets?

In line with the method used to assess the media's portrayal of Afghanistan, I performed a qualitative content analysis of the war-related news and commentary in the five media outlets using the Lexis-Nexis Academic database and the keyword "Iraq" for the time frame under study. Any story unrelated to the war was eliminated from the analysis. I searched for the major themes in the media's representation of the conflict in Iraq and Obama's withdrawal plan and then compared the media's narrative to the official Obama frame of the troop drawdown and the wider meaning of the war.

Although the level of media attention paled in comparison to that lavished on the 2009 Afghanistan surge, all five news outlets increased their coverage of Iraq once the administration initiated its promotional activities about the drawdown. Between August 1 and September 30, 2010, the *Times* published a total of 105 news and op-ed pieces that specifically mentioned the end of combat operations, events and situations on the ground in Iraq, American war-related political discourse, or the wider implications of the Iraq conflict; the *Post* contained 113 such articles and the Associated Press had 195. NBC News broadcast 57 pieces on Iraq and Fox News presented 44. As was the case for Afghanistan, this information was delivered through a mix of news reports, news analyses, human interest stories, brief announcements and news digests (such as war casualty lists), interviews, opinion pieces and commentaries, and editorials.

As I discuss in detail below, while the media organizations all presented the end of combat operations as a welcome development and praised the efforts of America's fighting forces, there was less agreement with other aspects of the administration's drawdown frame. There is therefore substantial evidence for media independence as journalists for national print, broadcast, and cable outlets constructed competing storylines that undercut much of Obama's version of what America had accomplished in Iraq and what its future prospects might be. My analysis uncovered four major media themes: 1) the inadequacies of the official drawdown narrative; 2) the war's problematic aftermath in Iraq; 3) the war's detrimental impact on the U.S.; and 4) the war's dubious meaning and legacy. When taken as a whole, the media depictions of Iraq were significantly at odds with the president's portrayal. Thus even as he diligently promoted his narrative about what winding down the war meant, President Obama found himself unable to dominate this facet of U.S. national security discourse.

Inadequacies of the Official Drawdown Narrative

True to their mission to inform the public about important national and international events, the five media outlets made note early in August 2010 of Obama's intention to end the U.S. combat role in Iraq and the series of events the administration had planned to publicize the formal announcement at the end of the month. Throughout August and September, they also carefully described the content of the administration's public communications, highlighting through numerous quotes and summaries the main components of the official drawdown narrative. The news reports included such basics as the settings of the speeches and interviews (noting, for instance, the frequent military venues), the length of the addresses, and the audience response. But in many of these stories, the major reportorial focus was analytical and interpretive rather than descriptive, with media assessments only occasionally veering into positive territory. Although the various outlets highlighted some different problems with the drawdown and the trajectory of the war, their interpretations tended to reach the same sobering conclusion: The official U.S. narrative was overly optimistic, too simplistic, and did not adequately reflect the difficult political, security, or economic conditions still confronting Iraq.

Little Demonstrable Progress in Iraq

A news article from the beginning of August is illustrative of the media critiques that permeated the initial reporting on the drawdown. On the day after Obama's speech to the disabled veterans, the *Post*'s lead story on the event noted that while the White House had billed the president's remarks as a significant Iraq policy address, only a small portion was actually devoted to the issues the U.S. faced in Iraq. The journalists quoted the administration's assertions that America was indeed changing from a military to a diplomatic mission, that the departure timetable remained on schedule, and that Obama's management of the war represented an important foreign policy success (Wilson and Blake 2010). The story also included the president's warning that the nation had not seen the end of American sacrifice in Iraq, and it was this cautionary theme that the reporters chose to emphasize in drawing their own conclusions. "Iraq remains a fragile nation," reporters Scott Wilson and Aaron Blake (2010) warned, with a "potential power vacuum" and "periodic attacks against fledgling institutions remaining a threat to security." This was certainly not the primary message the administration would have preferred the media to deliver.

Writers for the Associated Press expressed similar concerns as they began their drawdown reporting. In an August 1 story titled "High Iraq deaths cast doubt on U.S. stability talk," correspondent Hamza Hendawi (2010a) wrote that while the Americans were anxious to show progress in Iraq and had "pronounced Iraq's security as stabilizing," new Iraqi government figures of rising civilian casualties told a different story. The article went on to state that the highest death toll since May 2008 underscored the country's "precarious security," and the success of the "resilient insurgency" showed the difficulties of achieving a political solution in a polarized society. In a similar vein, an AP article on Obama's speech to the disabled veterans the following day noted that the president's "celebratory rhetoric ... brushed past some of the more grim realities in today's Iraq." In what the reporters termed a display of "Iraq's fragility," two bombings and a drive-by shooting took place in Baghdad only hours before Obama spoke. The story also included the unpleasant reminder that such attacks were a daily occurrence, as was the failure of basic services such as electricity and drinking water (Pace and Loven 2010).

NBC elected to present its story of the drawdown and the situation confronting Iraq primarily through the eyes of its chief foreign correspondent, Richard Engel, who had returned to Baghdad on the day Obama addressed the disabled veterans. His first report for *NBC Nightly News* that evening painted a very different picture of Iraq than the theme of steady progress the president was promoting. In response to anchor Brian Williams' query about the state of life in Baghdad, Engel offered this downbeat perspective:

> Many people here don't share the same kind of optimism ... Life in Baghdad right now is very difficult. This is not what you could consider a normal or a stable city. Just coming in from the airport this morning and driving to our bureau, it's about a 12-mile journey along a short stretch of road, we had to pass through six different checkpoints. There is a curfew in place tonight as there is every single night. And that gives you an idea of how much stability there is here: not very—not very much at all. Also, Iraqis only have about three hours of power every single day. They had 24 hours of power here in Baghdad under Saddam Hussein. (Engel 2010a)

The final words of Engel's report were particularly disheartening: "So while the United States might want to close the door and turn off the lights on this conflict, many Iraqis are not even able to turn the lights on in their own homes. Many couldn't even watch the speech tonight because they didn't have power" (Engel 2010a).

In Fox News's initial coverage of the end of combat operations, commentators outlined a two-fold problem with Obama's Iraq narrative of continuing progress. The first was a politically-based critique, specifically his refusal to recognize the critical role Bush's surge policy played in laying the groundwork for the drawdown. On *Fox News Sunday*, Senate Minority Leader Mitch McConnell (R-KY) paid this backhanded compliment to Obama: "Well, I have to commend the president for basically ... ignoring his own campaign rhetoric in 2008 and adopting the program of the Bush administration to wind down the war ... So I commend the president for continuing the policies." But while acknowledging that the U.S. had made some progress in Iraq because of what the previous president had initiated, the senator also pointed out that insurgent violence remained a major unresolved issue (McConnell 2010a). Conservative commentator Charles Krauthammer (2010a) was more bluntly critical of Obama's failure to credit Bush's 2007 strategic shift, noting that "The surge was something Obama opposed, and that is the only reason, the success of the surge is the only reason we are now in a position that we can drawdown." He then proceeded to argue that the current administration had proved incapable of moving Iraq beyond the baseline of military success provided by the surge.

For Fox News commentators, the second problem with Obama's early August drawdown narrative was its failure to inject adequate substance into the discussion of how America would move forward in Iraq. As Stephen Hayes (2010) complained after Obama's address to the disabled veterans, too many important questions remained unanswered in a speech that was more politically driven than policy-oriented: "You have a government [that] isn't yet formed. You have real serious and potentially increasing security problems. You have a question of the U.S. long term strategic commitment to the people of Iraq. You have broader questions about liberty and democracy." Charles Krauthammer (2010a) concurred, adding that "what is really disturbing is in Obama's speech he spoke about ending the war four times. He did not use the word 'success' or anything of the sort ... The president has essentially washed his hands of the war. All he has ever spoken of is ending it and getting out." But as Krauthammer admitted, the problem lay also with the Iraqis themselves as they had repeatedly failed to get elections done and establish a stable government.

The day after Obama's August 2 speech, a news analysis by AP diplomatic writer Barry Schweid (2010) took up the related theme that the president's drawdown timing was motivated more by political considerations on the home front than the actual deteriorating conditions in Iraq. Arguing that Obama's decision to stick with the withdrawal date despite the increase in violence "gives more weight to domestic dismay at American losses than to countering political unrest in the U.S.-liberated country," Schweid offered this supporting quote from a former U.S. embassy official in Baghdad: "My sense is the administration needed a good-news story it could deliver, and the withdrawal of combat troops from Iraq was the best news they had." Former U.N. Ambassador John Bolton was also quoted to the effect that, "This is exactly the wrong moment to complete the withdrawal of combat forces ... I think it is related to Afghanistan ... He is looking to the dissatisfaction from the Democratic left on Afghanistan" (Schweid 2010).

Was America about to reach a true milestone, the actual turning point that the official narrative claimed? Journalists were highly skeptical. A critical *Times* news report on Obama's early August speech highlighted the president's "telling, if largely overlooked, caveat" that the nation had not seen the end of American sacrifice in Iraq. The official end of combat was actually "not the end of much," reporter Steven Myers (2010b) opined; it signified primarily a "period of uncertainty" in a context of political stalemate and festering violence. A news analysis written a few days later by *Times* Baghdad bureau chief Tim Arango similarly asserted that in direct contradiction to the official narrative, the unsettled political and security reality in Iraq might well defy America's ability to meet its withdrawal deadline or prevent Iraq from sliding into civil war (Arango 2010b). Yet another *Times* news analysis contained the observation that "the symbolism of the departing troops that played out on network television masked the more complex reality on the ground" (Baker 2010a).

Both Fox and NBC did rely on the compelling visual imagery of U.S. troops engaged in what was described as the monumental logistical challenge of moving an entire army, the biggest such operation since World War II. NBC's Richard Engel, embedded with the 4th Stryker Brigade, the last combat troops in Iraq, included brief comments by soldiers delighted to be leaving the field of combat and several commanders who sounded pleased with how the redeployment was progressing. Reports by Fox Middle East correspondent Dominic Di-Natale, also accompanying the Stryker brigade as it crossed into Kuwait, presented similarly positive images of the massive redeployment process as well as excited and relieved comments from the troops. But Di-Natale's own commentary injected elements of caution and concern:

> Fourth Stryker brigade is last in line to leave Iraq because it's been structured in such a way that's enabled the U.S. military to respond to any crisis, right up until the final days of the drawdown. There's a reason for that. Iraq has been in political paralysis for the past five months. Inconclusive elections left the country without a new government. And U.S. commanders have been concerned they may need to call on the Strykers to help contain any violence. (Di-Natale 2010b)

Throughout his reporting from the Stryker brigade, Engel similarly emphasized the many problems that would continue to confront Iraq now that combat troops had been withdrawn. Thus while televised images may have buttressed the official narrative's themes of American military competence and a drawdown proceeding according to plan, the accompanying commentary gave a far more mixed message about what the U.S. was leaving behind.

The administration's official narrative depicted post-drawdown Iraq as a country that would continue to make halting but steady progress on all fronts; the image of Iraq that emerged in media accounts was usually far gloomier, indicative of journalists' willingness to highlight the perceived gap between presidential rhetoric and reality that came from years of first-hand reporting from the region. *Times* correspondent Anthony Shadid, winner of the Pulitzer prize for his reporting in Iraq, for instance, reminded his readers that current U.S. attempts to bring closure collided with "a disconnect familiar since 2003: The charts and trend lines offered by American officials never seem to capture the intangible that has so often shaped the pivots in the war ..." and he offered this pointedly cautionary note: "The Iraq that American officials portray today—safer, more peaceful, with more of the trappings of a state—relies on 2006 as a baseline, when the country was on the verge of a nihilistic descent into carnage" (Shadid 2010h). Experienced reporters were thus more than willing to interpret and evaluate situations on the ground, not content merely to present descriptions of events or serve as official mouthpieces.

On the evening of Obama's address to the disabled veterans, Fox News's *Special Report* contained an interview with analyst Michael O'Hanlon of the Brookings Institution. Responding to O'Hanlon's assertion that the U.S. had "finally emerged with more or less an acceptable outcome in Iraq after huge mistakes and huge costs," correspondent Wendell Goler offered a far less optimistic appraisal:

> But aside from security, Iraq has a long way to go. Its five major political parties have yet to form a government, almost five months after the last election. Its infrastructure is woefully inadequate with power out more often than it's on. And the bigger question O'Hanlon says is whether Iraq will be ready at the end of next year when all U.S. troops are supposed to leave. (Goler 2010)

Post reporter Janine Zacharia (2010) warned that even as Washington policymakers sought to put the Iraq war behind them, "the American mission in Bagdad is becoming more complicated" and the longer-term vision beyond Operation New Dawn was "even blurrier." Her colleague Leila Fadel (2010a) similarly noted that even as the last U.S. combat brigade pulled out, "Iraqis remained embroiled in a battle for stability." And on the day of Obama's Oval Office address, *Post* White House correspondent Anne Kornblut (2010) worried that his "celebration of an arbitrary deadline—much like Bush's premature 'Mission Accomplished' declaration in 2003—could also come back to haunt him if U.S. troops continue to die and the Iraqi government remains unformed."

A U.S.–Iraqi Perceptual Disconnect

A second media critique involved the apparent gulf between U.S. and Iraqi perceptions of what the end of combat operations meant for Iraq. Writing in the *Times* on the day of Obama's speech to the disabled veterans, Arango (2010a) asserted that while America's official withdrawal storyline emphasized diminishing violence as the capabilities of Iraqi security forces improved, the Iraqi public had a far different take on their security situation, especially "the durability of the narrative of steady improvement." The "fog of war," Arango observed, still shrouded Iraq. *Times* correspondent Shadid (2010a) similarly emphasized the U.S.–Iraqi perceptual disconnect in a news piece published two days later. From America's first days in Iraq, he argued, the two countries "seemed divided by more than language; they never shared the same vocabulary." Noting that Obama had just likened the drawdown to "the closing of a chapter," Shadid contended that in light of the elusive security situation, "To an American audience, it might resonate that way. Less so to Iraqis."

In the opening sentence of an article on the drawdown as a turning point, *Post* correspondent Fadel (2010b) observed from Baghdad that "On the last day of the official U.S. combat mission in Iraq, there was no dancing in the streets, no celebratory gunfire and no sense that a milestone had been reached." Highlighting Biden's contention that it was now "much safer" in Iraq, the article noted that the vice president and the reporters accompanying him to Baghdad were closely guarded and had to wear body armor—and that all of Biden's meetings took place in the safety of the Green Zone. It then went on to quote several Iraqi citizens who took the opportunity to vent their fears and frustrations over the continuing violence. An AP report also pointed out that when Biden left the Green Zone, his entourage had to duck for cover three times upon hearing alerts for incoming rocket and mortar fire (Jakes and Santana 2010). And a *Times* quotation of the day revealed an unsettling divergence in perceptions about the impact of democracy from a shop owner in Baghdad: "Democracy didn't bring us anything. Democracy brought us a can of Coke and a beer" (Farhan 2010).

Other stories highlighted the Iraqis' hesitancy to believe that the U.S. would still remain engaged with Iraq and continue to assist it. The worry about being deserted and left to a frighteningly uncertain future was expressed throughout news reports in quotes from Iraqi officials and ordinary citizens as well as the reporters' own assertions. "The Americans are leaving and they didn't solve the problems. So far they've failed and left Iraq to other countries," one Sunni legislator complained in a *Post* news piece (Fadel 2010a); "Right now, if you ask any Iraqi: What do you think of democracy? They will say it's blood, stagnation, unemployment, refugees, cheating," former Prime Minister Allawi lamented in another *Post* article (Londono, 2010a). Patently inaccurate official statements would not go unchallenged by reporters only too well aware of the state of affairs in the region. And eyewitness accounts carried distinctly more weight in media reportage than the repeated reassurances of U.S. officials.

Between August 13 and 18, *NBC Nightly News* broadcast six news segments titled "Iraq: The Long Way Out." A major focus was also the gap between American and Iraqi perceptions about what the pullout really meant. While U.S. troops and their commanders offered predominantly positive comments on Iraq's readiness to stand up as America stood down, Iraqi citizens strongly disagreed. One Baghdad resident gave Richard Engel (2010b) this brief but pointed assessment of what the withdrawal meant for the members of the Awakening forces who had been integral to the success of the surge: "The Americans used us for a while and then left us"; another complained that "We had a common interest in fighting al Qaeda. Now the Americans have moved on." In the same news report, General Odierno offered the far more reassuring take that the new Iraqi government would care for those Iraqis who had aided the U.S. The all-too-obvious contrast between the two perspectives did little to buttress the official frame of cautious optimism.

Fox News's August 12 *Special Report* noted that Iraq's senior military officer would like to have U.S. troops stay in the country well beyond the 2011 final pull-out date, but that American officials were not prepared to talk about extending their military commitment. The network's news commentators offered their perspectives that Iraq was simply not ready for the Americans to depart. Charles Krauthammer (2010b) stated that even though America was "on the cusp of success" in Iraq, "we could lose it all if we drawdown too quickly," and he argued against what he termed a hard and arbitrary withdrawal date. Fellow commentator A.B. Stoddard (2010) added the warning that "we know that al Qaeda is not going to let go." Even champions of the war in Iraq were unable to refrain from expressing concerns about the implementation of the troop withdrawal, a storyline that also displaced the Obama theme of slow but steady endgame success.

In the *Post*, Fadel (2010a) quoted one young, educated Iraqi to the effect that the future was disturbingly unclear: "It's bad. I'm worried not just for myself, but for my country and my future." In a *Times* article published after Obama's August 2 speech, Shadid (2010a) wrote that another young Iraqi greeted the president's announcement of withdrawal "with the cynicism that colors virtually any pronouncement the United States makes here, itself a somewhat intangible but pervasive legacy of seven years of invasion, occupation, war and, now, something harder to define." And in a subsequent news analysis, Shadid (2010c) summed up the U.S.–Iraqi perceptual disconnect by explaining that American-ordered deadlines, timetables, and benchmarks merely "sought to create realities where realities never existed." Most unsettling of all, Shadid concluded, were the words of a proverb from the Egyptian Muslim Brotherhood that encapsulated the yawning gulf between Middle Eastern and Western time perspectives, an old saying that applied as much to the current situation in Iraq as it had across the decades to the West's many failures elsewhere in the region: "God is with the patient."

The Triumph of Hope over Reality

As the official drawdown date approached, op-ed pieces in both the *Times* and *Post* were generally unsympathetic to the administration's efforts to paint even a guardedly optimistic portrait of the troop withdrawal. *Times* columnist David Brooks (2010) came closest to reflecting the official narrative that there were signs of progress on the economic and security fronts, but even as he noted some accomplishments he cautioned about the lack of social and political trust: "Fear still pervades Iraq. Ethnic animosities are in abeyance, but they are not gone. Guns have been put in closets, but are not destroyed." And, he concluded, even America's somewhat limited progress "has been too hard won," and would fail to materialize unless "we shelve our plans to withdraw completely."

While *Post* columnist Eugene Robinson (2010a) applauded Obama for fulfilling the pledge to extricate America carefully from Iraq, he warned that "a messy, uncertain political situation" was being left behind. He also argued that only one thing was clear about the end of combat operations: "We didn't win," and contrary to the official narrative, wars "end in a fog of ambiguity, and it's easier to discern what's been sacrificed than what's been gained" (Robinson 2010b). Employing Obama's chosen metaphor about the drawdown, *Post* columnist E.J. Dionne (2010) charged that "turning a page is not the same as writing the next chapter," and that Obama must now "produce a narrative compelling enough to alter a story line that, on its current trajectory, does not end well for him." Many of the two papers' commentaries contained the implication—or outright assertion— that the president had failed to be adequately forthcoming about the problems the withdrawal would entail, and a majority were skeptical of the hopeful tone that the administration tried to sound about the future of Iraq. It was the *Times*'s Frank Rich (2010b) who best captured the thrust of the columnists' critiques of the official withdrawal narrative with the damning quip that Obama's Oval Office address was "about as persuasive as a hostage video."

Editorials in the *Times* and *Post* also took some issue with the implications of Obama's drawdown strategy and vision. The *Post*'s editorial board fretted that the president would fail to commit to the long-term engagement that the still-chaotic nation of Iraq needed ("In Iraq, A Long Engagement" 2010) and worried that Obama's insistence on withdrawal deadlines was "discordant" and potentially damaging to U.S. and Iraqi security interests ("Something For Everyone" 2010). Prior to his August 31 address, the *Times*'s editorial board ("Leaving Iraq" 2010) also warned the president that America could not afford "to walk away" from Iraq and that it was his obligation to explain more fully why that was the case.

An analysis by AP national security correspondent Robert Burns (2010b) on the evening of Obama's primetime address presented a particularly trenchant response to the question of what had gone wrong in Iraq. The title, "U.S. hopes for Iraq collided with reality," said it all. From the moment of the 2003 invasion, Burns argued, America misunderstood the political and social realities of Iraq, a disconnect that "played a powerful role in altering what initially looked like a U.S. rout into a long, maddening fight. The shadowy and resilient Iraqi insurgency refused to bend to a tidy American vision for Iraq's future." Burns (2010b) concluded that this triumph of hope-filled vision over experience continued to bedevil America more than seven years later, as it remained unclear whether Obama's hope that Iraq would not unravel as U.S. troops headed for the exits matched "the reality of a country still in political turmoil."

The War's Toll on Iraq

The final sentence of a *Times* editorial ("The War in Iraq" 2010) on the day following Obama's formal withdrawal address took note of some "grim numbers," including one "that most American politicians are loath to mention: at least 100,000 Iraqis dead." The toll that war had taken and continued to exact on Iraq and its people was a major focus of news reportage and commentary across the two month period surrounding the official drawdown announcement. The media tone rarely struck a positive note, and the general thrust of the outlets' stories gave lie to the official U.S. narrative of gradual political, economic, and security progress in Iraq.

On the day of Obama's speech to the disabled veterans, the *Times* published the first of a three-part series titled "What is Left Behind." Illustrative of the paper's focus on the economic and social service failures in Iraq, this article detailed the government's inability to provide one of a modern nation's most basic services—electricity—and the devastating impact this was having on the country's economic development and its citizens' quality of life. Journalist Steven Myers's (2010a) conclusions were grim as he noted that the chronic power shortages ultimately reflected "a dysfunctional government that remains deadlocked and unresponsive to popular will." Quotes from disgruntled and discouraged Iraqi citizens served to provide a backdrop for the wider media theme of a nation foundering politically as well as economically. The more upbeat assessments of a battery of American civilian and military officials on meeting economic benchmarks allowed the official narrative of slow but steady progress to be heard, but throughout the five outlets' news reports the U.S. perspective was contradicted by Iraqi citizens and the reporters' own assertions about substandard living conditions.

In a report titled "U.S. wasted billions in rebuilding Iraq," AP reporter Kim Gamel (2010) noted that the U.S. was leaving behind hundreds of abandoned or incomplete reconstruction projects, a waste of more than 10 percent of the some $50 billion America had spent attempting to rebuild the country. Even completed projects "for the most part fell short of original goals," and deteriorating remnants of good intentions gone awry littered the countryside. "Iraqis can see one of the most egregious examples of waste as they drive north from Baghdad to Khan Bani Saad," the report claimed. "A prison rises from the desert, complete with more than two dozen guard towers and surrounded by high concrete walls. But the only signs of life during a recent visit were a guard shack on the entry road and two farmers tending a nearby field."

Gamel also reported that a 2004 U.S. project to house some 3,600 inmates had started six months late and continued to fall behind schedule. Citing massive cost overruns from the company it had awarded the contract, U.S. officials first pulled the plug on that firm in 2006, then abandoned the whole project a year later and handed the unfinished facility over to the Iraqis—who promptly refused to complete or occupy it. "It will never hold a single Iraqi prisoner. Forty million dollars wasted in the desert," was the comment from U.S. Inspector General Stuart Bowen (Gamel 2010). Another unfortunate reconstruction example Gamel uncovered was the Fallujah waste water treatment system, originally scheduled to open in 2006. Finally reaching completion, it would open at a cost overrun of more than three times the original estimate and had been scaled back to serve just a third of the intended population. "Desperate residents, meanwhile, have begun dumping their sewage in the tanks," a local Fallujah official complained (Gamel 2010).

And one of the reconstruction crown jewels, a state-of-the-art children's hospital in Basra that had been scheduled to open in late 2005, had still not been completed due to poor subcontractor performance and oversight, unrealistic timeframes, poor soil conditions, and security problems at the site, including the murder of 24 workers. Yes, there were some reconstruction success stories, Gamel concluded, but even in these cases "the verdict is still out on whether the program reached its goal of generating Iraqi good will toward the United States" (Gamel 2010).

As we have seen, NBC correspondent Engel began his reports from Iraq with personal observations about the sorry state of basic services in Baghdad, and he returned to the theme of dismal economic conditions throughout the weeks surrounding the drawdown. In one story of a particularly deadly attack at a Baghdad army recruiting station, Engel (2010c) noted that the recruiting center was exceptionally crowded because people were desperately seeking work. "Unemployment is high in this country," Engel observed. "There aren't that many jobs available." An AP report on the same incident also stressed the dire economic straits of many Iraqi citizens, as highlighted in the following quote from a father who returned to the bloody street after taking a friend to the hospital: "I have to get this job at any cost in order to feed my family. I have no option but to come back to the line. If there were other job opportunities, I would not be here in the first place" (Jakes 2010a).

A second component of the Iraq-in-turmoil theme was the country's disturbingly unsettled political condition, particularly the failure to create a governing coalition almost six months after national elections. News reports and commentaries routinely employed terms such as *impasse*, *stalemate*, *gridlock*, *deadlock*, *political vacuum*, *failed*, and *paralysis* to depict Iraq's current political situation, and these were frequently accompanied by descriptions of the country's uncertain political future such as *perilous*, *fragile*, *precarious*, *troubled*, *fraught*, *chaotic*, *volatile*, and *tumultuous*. Iraq's leaders and governing institutions were variously described as *woefully weak*, *squabbling*, *feeble and corrupt*, and far from willing or able to confront looming political challenges. In fact, the *Times* noted, while members of parliament had been drawing their paychecks since the March elections, they had met only once, and that was for less than 19 minutes (T. Williams and Ghazi 2010).

For every attempt by an American official to put a positive spin on the political situation, an alternative—and invariably more negative—interpretation appeared throughout the news outlets' accounts. In a *Post* news report on U.S. hopes for renewed progress in forming a new government, for example, an unnamed American official was quoted as saying that the Obama administration hoped to see an inclusive, representative, and accountable Iraqi government quickly installed; in the next sentence, however, an unnamed Iraqi official remarked that while the U.S. maintained an outward image of calm, the Americans were starting to "pull their hair out" at the political delays (DeYoung and Zacharia 2010). And a *Times* story on Biden's visit to Baghdad that began by quoting his assurance that "We are going to be just fine, they are going to be just fine," immediately noted the continuing political gridlock and a senior national security advisor's far less sanguine acknowledgment that "to build a partnership, you need a partner" (Gordon 2010a).

Engel's assessment of Iraq's current and future political situation for *NBC Nightly News* was no less gloomy:

> Iraq went from a dictatorship run by a single person, Saddam Hussein, to a failed democracy that is run by many different parties, none of which are able to get together right now and create a government. It is—I think if they don't get a government together in the next several months, perhaps by the end of the year, there's a real danger the country could have another episode of civil war. (Engel 2010e)

And even General Petraeus, architect of the surge in Iraq, gave this very tempered appraisal of Iraq's political future in an interview on NBC's *Meet the Press*: "I think the final chapter for Iraq is certainly still to be written. And of course, there's an immediate, pressing issue there, which is the formation of the government" (Petraeus 2010).

News stories about conditions in Iraq were also filled with reminders that violence, although less prevalent than before the surge, continued to be a horrific fact of daily life across the country. Throughout the 60-day period of this study, there were constant reports of casualties from insurgent attacks. "At least 15 people dead in car bombing in Iraq," read one NBC headline from August 4; three days later, another headline stated, "At least 20 people killed in explosions in Basra." "Extremist groups 'very much alive' in Iraq," a *Post* headline in early August declared, and the article went on to note both the scores of people killed within the past two days and the potential for the attacks to be particularly destabilizing during the period of troop drawdown (Londono 2010b).

A *Times* article published the same week likewise claimed that while the earlier carnage had indeed decreased, security was still elusive (Shadid 2010a). In the first week of August alone, the AP ran six different stories on the upsurge in insurgent violence and the toll it was inflicting across the country. On August 8, AP reporter Matthew Lee (2010) wrote that the daily insurgent attacks were preventing Baghdad from regaining even "a semblance of normalcy seven years after the insurgency broke out." And an early September AP article presented yet another "hidden cost" of the war that few outside Iraq might notice or even consider a significant problem: a spike in single women over 30 as seven years of "bloody turmoil" killed many young men and blew apart the country's social networks (Hendawi 2010b).

In mid-August, Fox News's Di-Natale (2010a) offered this troubling assessment of Iraq's security: "Iraq's adversaries are no longer confined to Sunni extremists. Shia terror groups are the new rising threat. Funded by Iran, although their stockpiles are getting seized and overall violence has dropped to around a tenth of what it was a year ago, by any measure, Iraq is fated to further terrorist bloodshed at least for now." Two days later, *Fox News Sunday* commentators suggested that in light of the problematic situation in Iraq, the administration might consider renegotiating the agreement to withdraw all U.S. forces at the end of 2011. It was ridiculous, Bill Kristol declared, to maintain a "dogmatic attachment" to a date certain for the troop removal. And anchor Bret Baier (2010) added the reminder that while in recent months there had been relatively few casualties, violence was now escalating: "Iraq is seeing a lot of deadly attacks. More than 100 people died across Iraq this month. July was Iraq's deadliest month … since 2008."

As the date of the formal U.S. drawdown approached, all five outlets covered a series of coordinated bombings in at least a dozen cities and towns across Iraq. Fox News senior White House correspondent Major Garrett (2010) reported that there had been an "unsettling uptick" in attacks from Baghdad to Basra in southern Iraq to Tikrit in the north. "All these prove that danger not only stalks Iraq but may increase to fill the political vacuum," he warned. A short *Post* news bulletin said that the Islamic State of Iraq, a front organization for al Qaeda in Iraq, had claimed responsibility, and that the attacks contained "bloody reminders" that as U.S. troop levels dwindled, Sunni insurgents remained a "powerful force" in the country ("Al Qaeda Group Asserts Responsibility" 2010). Reporting that insurgents had "deployed their full arsenal" of violence, Shadid (2010e) pointedly commented in the *Times* that the symbolism of the attacks "underscored a theme of America's experience here: its deadlines, including the August 31 date to end combat operations, have rarely reflected the tumultuous reality on the ground."

Journalists from the *Times* and *Post* wove a particularly dismal storyline about the tragic impact of insurgent violence on the fabric of Iraqi society and the ebbing hopes of its citizenry for a peaceful solution. The papers' reports on the problematic security situation in Iraq relied on a variety of sources from ordinary Iraqis to senior U.S. civilian and military officials. Brief vignettes of Iraqi life, all written by correspondents stationed in Iraq, depicted the misery of people across the social spectrum. A *Post* interview with the head of one of Baghdad's "overstretched" police stations, for instance, painted a vivid portrait of existing under a state of constant siege in "a city where almost no one plays by the rules" (Arraf 2010). And an article about a string of bombings across the country contained a shop owner's eyewitness account of a "hellish scene" in Basra: "I saw bodies everywhere, but I didn't know who was dead or alive" (Shadid 2010b).

Similar tales of massacre and destruction permeated most of the papers' security-related news accounts and provided both implicit and explicit criticisms of the administration's narrative of decreasing violence. Quoted in the *Post* about Obama's pledge to turn the page on Iraq, one resident expressed what might well have been the frustration and despair of an entire nation: "What have they left behind them besides widows, orphans, poverty, a destroyed infrastructure, no government, and martyrs?" (Jaffe and Fadel 2010).

In an opinion piece bearing the title "Abandoned in Baghdad," the *Times* highlighted the thousands of Iraqis who had worked on behalf of the American government but who, because of American bureaucratic failures, would be left to suffer at the hands of the insurgents (Sanghvi 2010). A particularly poignant perspective on the toll the war had taken on Iraqis who aided the U.S. military appeared in a *Post* article by a retired Army captain (Hall 2010). Titled "Remembering Roy: In Honor of a Fallen Iraqi Interpreter," the story detailed the dangers faced and ultimate sacrifice paid by a very young interpreter and others like him as they provided invaluable, and largely unrecognized, assistance to the American cause. And a searing image of war's impact on innocent civilians appeared in the second of three articles in the *Times*'s "Left Behind" series, a tale of a room in the Baghdad morgue known as The Missing, and the families who had come for the past seven plus years to see if one of the thousands of unidentified images of the dead displayed there might just be their missing relative. "The horror of this war," the story concluded, "is its numbers, frozen in the portraits at the morgue" (Shadid 2010g).

The frequently quoted assessments of U.S. military officers and troops serving in Iraq often lent little support to the official perspective of steadily improving security. A number of service personnel were quite forthcoming about the problematic security conditions in which they operated and expressed little faith the situation would improve. A *Post* profile of officers who had served multiple tours in Iraq noted that their service had left them both weary and humbled and slow to speak of victory: "I had returned to Iraq thinking I would find massive improvement," one officer admitted, "but what I saw was a state in anarchy" (Jaffe 2010). "August 31 isn't going to look really any different than 1 September," a brigade commander commented in another *Times* story, and a colleague compared the evolution of the U.S. war effort to "spreading peanut butter on the sandwiches he makes for his daughter back home more thinly than she wanted" (Myers 2010b). But a more mixed assessment was provided by a retired chief Marine intelligence officer who told the *Times* that "We opened a Pandora's box. Lots of bad things were flying out of there. But good things are there now too" (Baker 2010b).

Even the senior U.S. commanders in Iraq sometimes hesitated to paint a positive image of security in Iraq. In his first media interview since taking command of U.S. Special Forces in Baghdad, Brigadier General Higgins admitted to the *Post* that al Qaeda in Iraq's "cellular structure" remained "pretty much intact" (Londono 2010b); the paper also quoted an email from the newly appointed top military commander in Iraq, General Stephen Lanza, that the political impasse "fosters and encourages violent extremism," and that he expected attacks to continue until it was resolved (Alwan and Fadel 2010). A *Post* article titled "An Anxious exit for the Iraq War's Last General" noted that the outgoing top commander in Iraq, General Ray Odierno, exited with feelings of accomplishment but also a sense of growing concern over escalating violence amidst no signs of a political breakthrough (Londono 2010d). The *Times* quoted Odierno's admission that "we came in naïve about what the problems were in Iraq; I don't think we understood ... the societal devastation that occurred ... And then we attacked to overthrow the government." Nor, the general continued, did America understand the country's ethnic and sectarian divisions. And when the reporter asked about whether the U.S. had made the country's divisions worse, Odierno bluntly replied, "I don't know" (Shadid 2010f).

Commentaries and editorials in both newspapers also accentuated the theme of Iraq's crumbling economy and infrastructure, the failure of its political class to step up to the plate, the omnipresent violence that threatened to erupt in full-blown civil war, and the suffering that Iraqis still endured. Paul Wolfowitz (2010), architect of the original invasion, wrote in the *Times* that success would be defined "not by what we withdraw, but by what we leave behind," and at a minimum that meant "a stable country, at peace both within its borders and with its neighbors," a condition not even he would claim had yet been achieved. While he similarly argued in a *Post* opinion piece that the U.S. must remain engaged with Iraq, Ryan Crocker (2010), ambassador to Iraq from 2007 to 2009, stated that Iraq still faced great challenges, especially overcoming sectarian divides, stamping out corruption, quelling al Qaeda-sponsored terrorism, and restoring basic services.

A *Times* editorial highlighted the tens of thousands of civilian dead in Iraq; it also noted the failure thus far to move beyond the "stirrings of democratic politics" ("The War in Iraq" 2010). *Post* columnist David Ignatius (2010a) wrote that Iraq's formation of a new government "would tax the patience of the almighty," and in the meantime "the bombs keep going off in Baghdad." While arguing that the level of violence in Iraq had declined, Brookings Institution analyst Kenneth Pollack (2010) also pointed out that "the fear, anger, greed and desire for revenge that helped propel Iraq into civil war in the first place remain just beneath the surface." A board member of Refugees International (Johnstone 2010) reminded the *Post*'s readers of the half a million refugees who had fled Iraq and the even larger number who had been displaced within the country.

A *Post* editorial ("In Iraq, A Long Engagement" 2010) emphasized the "continuing dangers" still lurking in Iraq as insurgent bombings continued and daily brownouts and blackouts represented "an emblem of how life remains maddeningly difficult." An AP analysis of the challenges yet facing the U.S. in Iraq warned that even as the White House eagerly highlighted the drawdown, "the small army of American diplomats left behind is embarking on a long and perilous path to keeping the volatile country from slipping back to the brink of civil war." The reporter's assessment was buttressed by another disheartening quote from Kenneth Pollack: "One of the biggest mistakes that most Americans are making is assuming that Iraq can't slide back into civil war. It can. This thing can go bad very easily" (R. Burns 2010a). The media's consistently downbeat tone about the lives of ordinary Iraqi citizens provided further evidence of journalists' willingness to depart from the official presidential narrative and offer a storyline that differed significantly from the tale that Obama had constructed.

The War's Toll on America

On one subject the media wholeheartedly adopted the official frame: the exemplary performance of U.S. service personnel. Following Obama's lead, the five news outlets paid homage to the tens of thousands of heroic U.S. soldiers who had sacrificed so much since the 2003 invasion. News articles and commentaries frequently cited the president's own words of tribute to the troops. Effusive praise from other administration officials, members of Congress, military commanders, and the journalists themselves also permeated the stories on Iraq. But there was another, far less positive, side to the coverage of America's fighting forces: the many somber assessments of the toll the war had taken on those who fought. All five outlets reported the steadily mounting U.S. deaths as the total crept past 4,400, and the *Times*, the *Post*, and AP published weekly lists of the names of soldiers killed. The *Times* and *Post* were particularly attentive to the plight of the troops and in numerous human interest stories emphasized the emotional and physical scars they and their families bore. And these accounts contained little of the soaring rhetoric the official drawdown narrative had employed to extol the sacrifices of U.S. fighting forces.

In the second of its "Left Behind" series, the *Times* profiled the soldiers of the 3rd Infantry Division, some of whom were on their fourth deployment to Baghdad. The article conveyed the troops' level of exhaustion, their determination to complete their job, but also a pervasive sense that they were not engaged in fighting for a glorious cause. Asked if he thought the children of Iraq now faced a better future, one sergeant responded, "To be honest, I don't really care. As a nation, was it the right thing to do? In the end of the day, when I look back on it, I haven't lost a soldier in my squad. That's what's important to me." Another remarked that "we're not doing this for a victory parade," but became emotional when speaking of how he hoped that his three children would one day be able to say "when America called, we as a family sacrificed" (Myers 2010c).

News articles and op-ed pieces also honed in on the psychological wounds that war had inflicted on the troops. A series of stories highlighted the many struggles Iraq veterans were having with post-traumatic stress disorder, and soldier suicides were also discussed in several reports. Although some articles did mention Obama's promise to provide better services for emotionally troubled vets, they also described America's failures to meet all of their emotional and physical needs. One *Times* story, for instance, detailed the problems in military base towns as thousands of service members flowed back to their home bases. The returns, the authors noted, were moments of celebration and relief, but "tension and peril" most likely lay ahead as suicides, crime, and marital problems usually spiked in the months after a deployment ends (Rafferty and Dao 2010). A *Post* report presented the "hidden costs of war" on those who fought as "hardened glares; tales of comrades' deaths relayed in monotone sentences devoid of emotion; young faces rendered incongruously old" (Londono 2010c).

A brief AP story summarized the findings of a congressional task force report on problems confronting the service branches' suicide prevention programs. Noting that the sharpest increase in recent suicides had been in those services most stretched by America's current wars, the task force called for the Pentagon to create a new high-level office to set strategy and coordinate prevention programs across all military branches. "Rushing to stem historically high rates of military suicides," the article concluded, the service branches had made an "extraordinary effort" to deal with the crisis, but these programs definitely needed to be re-engineered to better meet the soldiers' needs (Jelinek 2010a). Another AP article noted that Marines seemed to be particularly at risk for suicide. As the authors wrote,

> They have been in harm's way for years in two countries, in a branch of the military where toughness and self-reliance have been especially prized for generations. Now the Marines are struggling against an enemy that has entrenched itself over nearly a decade of war: mental illness.
>
> Marines stressed from repeated tours of duty in Iraq and Afghanistan are seeking help like never before, and their suicide rate is the highest in the military after doubling in just the past three years. (Maurer and Watson 2010)

Several editorials bemoaned the recent spike in soldier suicides; one labeled them "doubly tragic casualties of war," a gruesome result of too many repeat deployments and too little time at home between tours of duty ("When Warriors Hurt Themselves" 2010). *Times* columnist Bob Herbert (2010a) described one suicidal incident and then went on to proclaim, "War is a meat grinder for service members and their families. It grinds people up without mercy." In a second column, Herbert (2010b) scolded the president for simply trying to "manage" the war rather than bring it to a definitive conclusion. Such an approach, he declared, was "profoundly disrespectful" to America's fighting forces: "These are real men and women, courageous and mostly uncomplaining human beings that we are sending into the war zones, and we owe them our most careful attention. Above all, we owe them an end to two wars that have gone on much too long."

News reports published after the August 31 withdrawal announcement also reminded readers and viewers that 50,000 U.S. troops still remained in Iraq and that even after combat operations were supposed to have concluded, some American military units would continue to see action and incur casualties. As the *Times* explained, extensive U.S. support to the Iraqi military illustrated the risks American troops still endured in their new advise and assist role (Gordon 2010); the coordinated insurgent attacks underscored, in the words of two other *Times* reporters, "the ambiguous and still-dangerous position for Americans in their role as advisers to Iraq's beleaguered security forces" (Myers and Adnan 2010).

An AP article warned that "the war is not yet over for the remaining troops, who will continue to put themselves in danger on counterterror raids and other high-risk missions that aren't called combat but can be just as deadly," and it went on to quote General Odierno's comment that "There is still danger. There are still going to be people who attack our forces. We all know that" (Jakes 2010b). Other articles noted that the battlefield was not the only arena of worry for the troops. Insurgent attacks and bombings were a constant reminder of lurking dangers even in the most supposedly safe venues, and the *Times* and *Post* reported on health problems the troops would continue to face, including those caused by exposure to the massive open-air pits the military used to burn every conceivable type of waste.

Although most reports on the war's costs to America highlighted the detrimental impact on military personnel, there were a number of brief references in both news and commentaries to the economic and reputational toll Iraq had taken as well. In a *Post* analysis entitled "A War More Costly than we Thought," Nobel prize-winning economist Joseph Stiglitz and policy analyst Linda Bilmes (2010) wrote that their previous estimate of a $3 trillion price tag on Iraq was probably too low because it had ignored the conflict's "most sobering expenses"—a spike in oil prices, a skyrocketing federal debt, the global financial crisis, and the failure to achieve victory in Afghanistan. "It seems clear," these authors concluded, "that without the war, not only would America's standing in the world be higher, our economy would be stronger."

An AP story on the mounting health care expenses for Iraq and Afghanistan veterans cited a warning from Rep. Bob Filner (D-CA), chair of the House Veterans Affairs Committee, that the real costs had not been properly budgeted. "If Americans want to vote for war, the Congress wants to vote for war, that's fine but include the real costs and budget for them," the congressman told reporters. The article also cited Stiglitz and Bilmes, who estimated that the cost of providing vets with lifetime medical costs and disability payments, as well as Social Security payments for the severely disabled, would fall between $589 billion and $934 billion, depending on the length and intensity of the two wars (Jelinek 2010b).

Other news reports detailed various cost overruns and the waste of American taxpayer dollars through incompetence and fraud. Several noted that $1.9 million worth of computers purchased by U.S. taxpayers and intended for Iraqi schoolchildren had instead been auctioned off by Iraqi officials for only a tiny fraction of that amount. "The loss of the computers highlights what have been two flashpoints of controversy during the Iraq war: the accountability of American money and the widespread corruption that many say is one of the biggest challenges to Iraq's future," an AP article concluded (Santana 2010). And already noted was the AP report on the billions in U.S. taxpayer dollars wasted on Iraqi reconstruction projects that were either never completed or shoddily constructed (Gamel 2010).

Yet another AP story highlighted the $5.9 billion the U.S. spent between 2003 and 2009 on private security contractors hired to protect Defense and State department employees. But according to reporter Lara Jakes (2010c), that amount paled in comparison to the reputational hit America took when private security guards working for Blackwater Worldwide opened fire in Baghdad with no apparent provocation and killed 17 Iraqi civilians. Even more damaging to the "U.S. worldwide image" was the detainee abuse at the Abu Ghraib prison outside Baghdad, Jakes concluded. The toll on America's international reputation, especially its effectiveness and ability to think like a global power, was to *Post* analyst Anne Applebaum (2010) also the most far-reaching casualty of the conflict in Iraq: "The overall impression, in Iraq and everywhere else, was of American incompetence—and, after Abu Ghraib, of stupidity and cruelty as well."

The War's Dubious Legacy

While Obama utilized the notion of American exceptionalism to draw some positive conclusions about a conflict he had opposed for years, the five national media outlets embarked on a different interpretive path, and the divide between presidential and media rhetoric was particularly evident as journalists reflected on the wider meaning of war in Iraq. And while Obama pushed for a quick pivot to the future, journalists for these organizations demurred as many engaged in a collective airing of grievances about both their own reportorial performance and the actions of the Bush administration.

A War That Ought Never to Have Been Fought

For a number of reporters and columnists, the drawdown announcement was an opportunity to cast a backward glance at a war they had long opposed. Many of these reflections were intensely personal as some vented more than seven years of pent-up anger while others engaged in agonized soul-searching they believed had been far too long in coming. Examples of the first approach were contained in a number of op-ed pieces. One *Times* editorial ("Leaving Iraq" 2010) indignantly declared Iraq to be "a war that should never have been fought"; a second labeled it "a tragic, pointless war" ("The War in Iraq" 2010). Columnist Frank Rich (2010a) scathingly termed it "this fiasco"; his colleague Bob Herbert (2010a, 2010b) affixed the labels "tragic," "farcical," and "catastrophe"; the *Post*'s Eugene Robinson (2010a) summed up Operation Iraqi Freedom as a "military misadventure"; and *Post* columnist David Ignatius (2010b) wrote of a "false rationale" for war.

Indicative of the "more in sorrow than in anger" style of reflection was a series of articles by *Times* reporters who had spent years on the ground in Iraq. The paper's senior foreign correspondent, John Burns, who had covered the conflict since the 2002 run-up to war, noted that the power of hindsight made it easier to admit "the tragedy that has unfolded since the invasion," and he confessed that few journalists, himself included, foresaw the extent of the violence that would follow the invasion or the "political convulsion" it would cause in Iraq, America, and elsewhere. And, he went on to lament, "We could not know then, though if we had been wiser we might have guessed, the scale of the toll the invasion would unleash" (J. Burns 2010).

Another *Times* reflection by correspondent and author David Sanger (2010) adopted the "what if" approach to his backward-looking gaze upon Iraq: "If only we had not been distracted by Iraq," the "good war" in Afghanistan "might not have gone bad ... If only." And correspondent James Glanz's reflective contribution was a touching eulogy for two young Iraqi journalists whose lives had been brutally cut short in the violence that was a constant fact of life in Baghdad. His heartbreaking tale concluded with these doleful thoughts about the nature of the tragedy the U.S. was leaving in its wake:

> As the American battle ends in Iraq, there are surely new narratives, new conversations, waiting for a country struggling with the devastation of a dictatorship, an invasion, a sectarian war and dreams of a better future. But for Khalid and Fakher and so many others, we leave behind dust, regret and loss, and no words to efface them. (Glanz 2010)

Asked on *The Today Show* about the kind of Iraq from which America was withdrawing, NBC correspondent Engel (2010e) replied that, in his opinion, "Iraq's in a very, very dangerous place." When pressed to answer the question of whether anything positive came from the war, he replied that "Saddam Hussein is gone, and anyone—any Iraqi will tell you that. Saddam really was that bad." But Engel then added that the political structure the U.S. had created to replace him had "failed to deliver on its promises to the people," and had Saddam remained in power he might have moderated and moved in a direction of accommodation, or at the very least have been a boxed in dictator. Equally important, Engel (2010e) went on to say, was that Iran would have been "a lot more contained," and therefore of far less danger than it was currently. And finally, to the question of whether America would be done in Afghanistan had the U.S. not invaded Iraq, Engel responded: "Probably. That was a giant distraction of resources, of intelligence assets. That war would probably be over."

A Clouded War Only History Can Judge

All five news outlets highlighted Defense Secretary Gates' September 1 observations that the war would always be clouded by how it began and that only history could judge whether it was a success. News stories in the *Times* described his comments as "subdued and reflective" and approvingly noted the "markedly anti-triumphal" tone that Gates had adopted (Gordon and Bumiller 2010; Bumiller 2010). An op-ed in the *Post* commented favorably on the appropriateness of his "guarded language" because, as columnist David Ignatius (2010b) opined, "Iraq is in many ways an unfinished war. Its ultimate success or failure won't be clear for some years, when we can see whether Iraq has sustained its new democracy or plunged back into sectarian strife and political chaos." An article from the AP that bore the title "Gates: All is not well as combat role ends" emphasized comments the defense secretary made to an American Legion audience the day before Obama's primetime address. Given the continuing sectarian violence and political paralysis, "I am not saying all is, or necessarily will be, well in Iraq," Gates warned (Gearan 2010).

On the evening of Obama's Oval Office address, Fox News commentators gave the president low marks on progress in Iraq. Charles Krauthammer once again touted the success of the 2007 military surge and Obama's failure to capitalize on it:

> ... all Obama ever wanted to do was end the war. He talks about it now, campaign promise fulfilled, at a time when Iraq doesn't have a government, and a week after al Qaeda in Iraq pulled off simultaneous attacks in 13 cities killing 51 Iraqis, which could not have happened in January when Obama was inaugurated.
>
> He had one task he has not succeeded ... You don't declare an arbitrary milestone on a fixed timetable when you have no Iraqi government and al Qaeda is resurgent. (Krauthammer 2010c)

But Krauthammer and his colleagues gave no indication of how or when the situation in Iraq might improve; their message definitely complemented the wider, predominantly negative, media theme that it was much too soon to declare Iraq even a qualified success.

Obama's official drawdown announcement and the series of events publicizing it also cued the media to undertake some overarching analyses of what Iraq had meant and what lessons the U.S. might draw. This, as we have seen, was the thrust of the administration's end-of-combat narrative. *Times* foreign correspondent Peter Baker summarized the big-picture questions the media sought to answer:

> After hundreds of billions of dollars, more than 4,400 American military deaths and at least 100,000 Iraqi civilian deaths and perhaps many more, was it worth it? Did toppling a dictator and nursing a fledgling if flawed democracy make a difference? And did the United States salvage credibility by sticking it out and finally stabilizing Iraq even if not winning the clear-cut victory originally envisioned? (Baker 2010a)

After carefully parsing of all the administration's public communications about the end of the U.S. combat mission, conducting numerous interviews with American and Iraqi officials, pouring over official documents, reporting on the ground about conditions across Iraq, and questioning hundreds of Iraqi citizens, journalists and columnists across all five media outlets failed to arrive at the conclusions the Obama administration had drawn about what America had accomplished in Iraq. Virtually no news accounts presented Iraq as a current example of successful democracy promotion, nor were the journalists much more sanguine about the possibility for stability and democracy in that strife-torn nation. And except for discussions of heroic U.S. troops, the uplifting rhetoric of American exceptionalism was missing from almost all of the media stories.

There were numerous mentions of Iraq's overall legacy, and the specific term *legacy* was particularly prevalent in the *Times*, appearing in more than 10 percent of the paper's news reports and commentaries. But only rarely did any of the five news outlets' references reflect the official drawdown narrative's optimistic conclusions. Most mentions of Iraq's legacy were embedded in stories of problematic events on the ground and, not surprisingly, the journalists drew very guarded conclusions. Since a major thrust of Obama's Iraq endgame narrative was to emphasize what the conflict had managed to contribute to the wider struggle against terrorist extremism, this aspect of the media storyline also did little to support the official frame the president had constructed.

Frequently the writers decided that it was just not possible to determine what Iraq's legacy might be, although they strongly implied that it would be far from positive. The first of the *Times* articles on what the U.S. left behind, for instance, noted that the "overall legacy of the American invasion today, like that of the war itself, remains a matter of dispute" (Myers 2010a), and a *Times* news analysis about the ongoing political stalemate contained the sobering observation that Iraq's legacy "remains unfinished" (Arango 2010a). At the beginning of August, a *Post* article also on the political impasse noted that Iraq's legacy was still "hanging in the balance" (Londoño 2010a), and a third news analysis published one week later similarly labeled the war's legacy "unsettled" (Arango 2010b).

On other occasions, however, reporters and columnists were more willing to highlight specific facets of Iraq's wider—and unfortunately dubious—legacy. For example, an early August *Times* article on the uptick in violence briefly noted that the cynicism with which Iraqis greeted Obama's forthcoming drawdown announcement was part of a "pervasive legacy" of all the problems they had endured (Shadid 2010a). And an analysis of the Iraqi political elite's inability to reach any sort of political accord contained the assertion that their political failures might become a "lasting American legacy" (Shadid 2010d).

Post reporters Jaffe and Fadel (2010) emphasized the war's "ambiguous outcome," writing that Iraq's political parties remained "incapable of forming a coalition government" and that "remnants of the insurgency remain and are capable of pulling off horrific attacks." Their colleague Ernesto Londoño (2010d) noted that there were still "plenty of milestones to go" in Iraq and quoted General Odierno's far from sanguine statement that "It's going to be three to five years post-2011 before we really understand where Iraq is going and how successful we've actually been in pushing Iraq forward." Writing that "the war in Iraq has been longer, costlier, bloodier and far more unpredictable than most people expected," AP correspondent Jakes concluded that the one enduring legacy of Iraq might be that the U.S. "has learned to be far more careful before declaring victory" (Jakes 2010c).

Even Vice President Biden was compelled to admit that the war's legacy might not be all that the Obama narrative had depicted. In an interview on NBC's *The Today Show* the day after Obama's primetime address, host Matt Lauer questioned whether what America had sacrificed in Iraq was actually worth the terrible toll. While the vice president's very personal response hit all the requisite administration talking points, it injected a note of cautious realism into the previous night's far more soaring presidential narrative about spreading democracy and making America secure:

> Matt, having a son who served here for a year and feeling lucky he came home, and thinking about all those parents who didn't have their child come home, I could never say to those parents it's not worth it. What I have to say is we are committed to making sure the sacrifices they made bear fruit. And the fruit will ultimately be in a stable Iraqi government that's able to stand on their own and in fact is not a threat to its neighbors nor threatened by its neighbors. (Biden 2010c)

Around the time of the president's primetime address, the more positive assessments of Iraq's legacy tended to come from conservative commentators and a few Republican members of Congress who still conflated the war in Iraq with the war on terror. But they too focused on future possibilities rather than current results and were anything but effusive in their assessment of what the U.S. had achieved—or yet might achieve—in Iraq. On NBC's *Meet the Press*, Paul Gigot of the *Wall Street Journal* gave this circumspect reply to moderator David Gregory's query about how victory in Iraq should be defined:

> ... the United States leaving with honor, leaving with dignity, leaving ... a stable, relatively stable government behind, not to say they don't have problems, not to day that they're not disagreeing. This government, disagreements between the two factions, the two people who've figured so closely in the election, is troubling. On the other hand, they're debating, they're not killing one another. We've given them a chance ... And so I think that ... we can still get some strategic benefits from this in terms of a ... democratic government in the Middle East, one that is allied with our interests and can serve our purposes over there if things go ... well in the future. (Gigot 2010)

In interviews with Fox's Greta Van Susteren and on NBC's *Meet the Press*, Senator Lindsay Graham (R-SC), a long-time supporter of the war, also looked to the future rather than the present, and was equally measured about what America might accomplish in Iraq:

> ... we will be safer by how it ends. History will judge us, not by what we did wrong at the beginning, but what we got right at the end ... If it finishes out well and it becomes secure and stable, allied with us on the war on terror—this is the place al Qaeda was beat by fellow Muslims ... America will be safer and history will record this as a big event in the Mideast where a dictatorship was replaced by a democracy in the heart of the Arab world. (Graham 2010)

It is also telling that NBC's Iraq stories on the evening of Graham's interview and for the next three days were only about all that was going wrong at the moment—a series of insurgent attacks, one of which resulted in American deaths. As anchor Brian Williams (2010) reported on September 7, "And in Iraq today, a grim reminder Americans are still in grave danger there." With two U.S. soldiers killed and at least nine others injured, "They are the first U.S. service members to die since President Obama declared the end of the combat operations phase."

In her report on the same deadly incident, Fox News national security correspondent Jennifer Griffin (2010) called it "Just another example that combat in Iraq is far from over." She also noted that, in a separate attack two days earlier, six suicide bombers burst into an Iraqi army headquarters in Baghdad, killing 12 and wounding 36. Two U.S. soldiers helped to kill the attackers, providing proof that troops still in Iraq were there to "do more than just advise and assist" and faced dangers "just as real as if they were in combat." In media accounts, hopeful visions of post-drawdown Iraq thus kept getting trumped by chaotic realities on the ground as event-based reporting from the region drew far more media scrutiny than the hope-infused rhetoric of U.S. leaders, clear evidence that when reality intercedes, the media may not passively repeat the statements of high-ranking official sources.

An editorial in the *Times* the morning after the official drawdown date contained the blunt pronouncement that "the war has not created a new era of democracy in the Middle East—or in Iraq for that matter." Nor, the editorial board went on to say, had the conflict enhanced American security: "In many ways, the war made Americans less safe, creating a new organization of terrorists and diverting the nation's military resources and political will from Afghanistan" ("The War in Iraq" 2010). Perhaps no one news report or op-ed piece better summed up the anger that some media personnel felt upon hearing Obama's hope-infused message about Iraq than the invective *Times* columnist Frank Rich penned five days after the president's Oval Office address. Its concluding paragraph is worth quoting in full:

> And yet here we are, slouching toward yet another 9/11 anniversary, with even our president, an eloquent Iraq war opponent, slipping into denial. Of all the pro forma passages in Obama's speech, perhaps the most jarring was his entreaty that Iraq's leaders 'move forward with a sense of urgency to form an inclusive government that is just, representative, and accountable.' He might as well have been talking about the poisonous political deadlock in Washington. At that moment, there was no escaping the tragic fact that instead of bringing American-style democracy and freedom to Iraq, the costly war we fought there has, if anything, brought the bitter taste of Iraq's dysfunction to America. (Rich 2010a)

The bottom line for so many journalists and commentators covering the war seemed to be that the Iraq conflict remained in a state of suspended animation, a purgatory where neither victory nor defeat could be declared. The brief but pointed words of *Times* correspondent Anthony Shadid seemed to say it all: "The story in Iraq is unfinished, whatever the Obama administration, and the generals and diplomats who do its bidding, may say. The country is neither occupied nor independent, but rather in a limbo whose descriptions are as pliable as the pretexts for the invasion that began America's seven-year involvement here" (Shadid 2010c).

Throughout their many commentaries and news pieces in the period surrounding the official U.S. drawdown from Iraq, the five news outlets ended up advancing an unflattering portrait of a conflict that was far from settled. President Obama's vision of what the war represented was quite thoroughly discussed, dissected, and then found wanting in the pages, websites, and broadcasts of these leading news organizations. For reporters and commentators across the ideological spectrum, a common theme ran throughout accounts of the Iraq war's legacy: To conclude that it represented a successful step in promoting democracy or spreading the cause of freedom was to fly blindly in the face of reality.

* * *

As America moved closer to the Iraq drawdown in late summer 2010, Obama's condemnatory war script had gradually given way to a tale of cautious optimism, and by the time he made the formal announcement of the U.S. troop withdrawal on August 31, references to the problems America had already encountered in the war and the thorny issues yet to be resolved had essentially disappeared from his Iraq narrative. As he had compellingly argued in numerous public statements, it was time to "turn the page" on that misbegotten conflict and move forward with confronting the real national security challenge—the terrorist extremists in Afghanistan and Pakistan. And as the president turned from America's war of choice, he increasingly subsumed the Iraq storyline into the larger frame of Afghanistan as the just and necessary war America still had to fight.

America's leading media organizations, however, were not yet inclined to turn their attention from the Iraq chapter of the national security storyline. Primed by Obama's drawdown announcement, writers for the *New York Times*, *Washington Post*, and Associated Press and correspondents and commentators for NBC News and Fox News seized the opportunity to undertake what most had neglected to do in the months following the 2008 election: scrutinize what was actually happening in Iraq, forecast the likelihood of success, and reflect on the war's wider meaning and legacy. Although they dutifully reported the administration's assessments of the current situation and prospects for progress in Iraq, the journalists looked elsewhere for information, and as they did, they found the official explanation of the drawdown and what America had achieved in Iraq to be wanting.

In the absence of congressional debate and significant elite dissensus on the drawdown, journalists did not engage in the standard practice of relying on official sources on opposing sides of the issue and indexing the level of coverage to the amount of disagreement among those with significant policy-making power. Reporters instead turned to non-Washington sources, and as they sought out Iraqi citizens and officials as well as U.S. troops and their commanders stationed in Iraq, they pieced together a portrait of Iraq far different from the relatively hopeful scenario depicted by the president and his senior lieutenants. Correspondents based in Iraq could also call upon as many as seven and a half years of personal experience with the country and the conflict, and those years of on-the-ground reporting provided ample material for anything but a positive storyline about both the current status of Iraq and what its future might hold. These findings once again provide clear support for Baum and Groeling's (2010) and Glazier and Boydstun's (2012) hypotheses that presidential and media frames of war may differ significantly as over time the gap between what the commander-in-chief asserts to be reality and what reporters observe on the ground widens.

When interviews with beleaguered Iraqis and emotionally and physically scarred U.S. fighting forces were coupled with event-driven reporting that highlighted the dismal political, security, and economic situation in Iraq, the result was a competing media narrative that diverged quite significantly in both tone and content from the official Obama frame. So as the president exhorted America to turn the page on its war of choice and be content with what the conflict had accomplished, journalists from major U.S. media outlets did just the opposite. The result was a torrent of negative news and commentary in the weeks surrounding the end of Iraq combat operations, ample evidence that media independence may occur even in the face of an energetically-promoted presidential narrative. The critical variable, as Bennett and his colleagues (2007) note, is the media's access to credible, and preferably visual, information that clearly contradicts presidential assertions.

A unique facet of the media's Iraq endgame narrative was some prominent journalists' introspective turn, as a number engaged in interrogations of their own reportorial shortcomings, particularly in the early days of the war. These often-anguished moments of intensive self-reflection, criticism, and lament seemed to mirror the wider divisiveness of the war itself, revealing festering emotional sores and a deep sense of guilt that the announcement of the end of combat operations apparently had done little to assuage. The public outpourings of personal emotion also provided clear evidence that contemporary journalists are not content simply to act as scribes dutifully making note of events and issues; the norm today is for reporters to become major actors in their own stories and to insert their self-referential perspectives into news reports as well as commentaries (see, for example, Bennett 2012, ch. 2). And in so doing, members of the media showed little interest in bowing to the Obama narrative that America should pivot to the future and focus on Iraq's promise and potential rather than its dubious present or failed past.

As with Obama's announcement of his surge-then-exit policy for Afghanistan in the fall of 2009, however, limitations to media independence were also apparent in the weeks surrounding the end of the combat mission in Iraq as reporters continued to refrain from interrogating the still-dominant national security frame that Bush had constructed in the days following the 9/11 attacks. Although by this point journalists had followed Obama's lead and mostly cast aside Bush's sweeping global-war-on-terror language, the underlying assumption that America had to maintain its military push against terrorist adversaries went unchallenged in media reports and commentary as the U.S. prepared to leave Iraq.

But the media also made little mention of the Iraq endgame in the context of the wider struggle against terrorism. The war against terrorist adversaries may have remained, in the words of Richard Jackson (2012: 47), an "ever-present interpretive lens" through which leading U.S. media outlets, as well as the president, unhesitatingly presented American national security to their vast audiences, but journalists made few overt references to it either to criticize or praise Obama's drawdown decision or to analyze the wider meaning of the war and its outcome. The war-on-terror narrative remained in the background, providing an uncontested backdrop for the predominantly negative event- and process-driven media coverage of difficulties with the drawdown and the problematic legacy of Iraq. Even for conservative columnists and commentators, Bush's war on terror was not the predominant theme in their Iraq endgame narratives as the five media outlets tended to highlight the same, predominantly negative, storylines.

As numerous studies have demonstrated (see Graber 2010, chs 4 and 5 for examples), the media spotlight is forever restless, and within a month of the official drawdown date, it had once again shifted its focus from Iraq. By the end of September 2010, attention to the conflict-ravaged and politically unstable country where some 50,000 U.S. troops still served dipped even lower than before Obama began his campaign to highlight the end of combat operations. The emotional reportorial outpourings about the meaning of Iraq and the culpability of journalists simply disappeared. For the remainder of the year, news about Iraq would not garner as much as 2 percent of mainstream media coverage and would not constitute any of the top media topics (Project for Excellence in Journalism 2011).

And despite the unleashing of the presidential megaphone and the mighty media pens, American public opinion, so war-weary and disinterested, had not budged one bit over the eight weeks surrounding the troop drawdown announcement. Media cynicism about the future of Iraq was accompanied by a comparable level of public doubt that Obama's hope-infused vision would come to fruition. While Americans continued to support the pullout of U.S. combat brigades, there remained a widespread sense of skepticism about how well the plan might be implemented and significant ambivalence about the entire conflict. Just days after Obama's Oval Office address, a telling two-thirds doubted that the Iraqi government would be able to maintain order once U.S. troops had been removed, and a majority still believed that combat troops would remain past the stated deadline of 2011 (Holsti 2011: 66).

The partisan divide over the wisdom of invading Iraq in the first place also remained as wide in September of 2010 as it had been when Obama assumed office, as even in the wake of his campaign to publicize the possibilities for Iraq to achieve a better future, only 28 percent of members of his own party and 36 percent of Independents stated that the U.S. had done the right thing to go to war (Pew Research Center 2010). Even more sobering was the public response to an August 2010 CBS poll that asked whether the results of the war were "worth the loss of American life and other costs of attacking Iraq?" Here there was much less of a partisan split, as a mere 20 percent of the public concurred that the war was worth the costs, including only 36 percent of Republicans (Holsti 2011: 87). And the public's level of interest in the conflict, so intense and focused just a few years prior, fell to new lows as Iraq became yesterday's news.

By the fall of 2010, neither the public, Congress, nor the mainstream media seemed concerned with further consideration of Iraq, and it was the "let's just put Iraq behind us" aspect of Obama's narrative, not his vision of what the conflict might yet achieve or journalists' impassioned but fleeting critique of that vision, that appeared to have won the day.

Chapter 6
Framing War's Indecisive End

As the 2012 presidential campaign season commenced, Barack Obama once more repeated his signature mantra on the status of America's twenty-first-century military engagements: "We're *turning the page* on a decade of war … Even as our troops continue to fight in Afghanistan, *the tide of war is receding*" (Obama 2012a, emphasis added). But tides flow as well as ebb, and book pages can easily be flipped back and forth. The ambiguity of the president's chosen metaphors thus seemed particularly apt in light of the still-unsettled political and security situation in Iraq and the on-going conflict Obama had labeled America's "war of necessity."

Five months later, in a Memorial Day ceremony commemorating the 50th anniversary of the Vietnam War, Obama noted that due to the "complexity of America's time in Vietnam," historians could not even now agree on precisely when that war began (Obama 2012c). He might just as readily have said the same about the resolutions of America's post-9/11 conflicts. As national security analyst John Nagl wrote the following week in a *New York Times* op-ed column, success in modern counterinsurgency wars is at best "messy and unsatisfying … Rarely, if ever, will they end with a surrender ceremony and look like a conventional victory" (Nagl 2012). Nagl's description of how contemporary wars conclude dovetailed almost exactly with Obama's—as well as Bush's—repeated warnings that America's fight against terrorist aggressors would entail a different kind of war against a different kind of enemy, a type of conflict whose ending would bear little resemblance to the decisive outcomes of World Wars I or II. In such a war, Nagl noted, the best result would be the untidy "sort-of" victory the U.S. had achieved in Iraq; the worst would be comparable to the endpoint of Vietnam— "an abject, helicopters-flying-out-of-Kabul, people-hanging-on-the-skids defeat" (Nagl 2012).

A Narrative of Circumscribed Success

While historians and political analysts have the luxury to conduct extended—and often highly critical—examinations of war's denouement, a president does not. As a conflict winds, however haltingly, to some sort of closure, his task is to remind the public of why war was the only course of action, put the best face on what the nation has accomplished, lavish praise on its heroic fighting forces, and paint a rosy portrait of future possibilities. Once he dons the mantle of commander-in-chief, even a previously outspoken war opponent assumes responsibility for how the conflict proceeds from that point forward, and his narrative may also become the war's defining storyline—or the one that is most fervently contested. He is also the person whom history will credit or condemn for how the war comes to a close. Even if the bulk of a president's agenda focuses on domestic issues, in time of war his legacy may come to rest on the perceived success or failure of his military initiatives. The presidential incentive to present a resonant tale of war's rationale and progress is therefore powerful indeed, a lesson a newly-inaugurated Obama seems quickly to have learned.

Just as in Bush's war-on-terror frame, Obama saw no alternative to waging war against those who attacked the U.S. on 9/11, and years before he raised his hand to take the presidential oath of office he had started to construct a complete and compelling tale of America at war. As we have seen, his storyline differed from his predecessor's in the specific enemies the nation should target, the interrogation tactics it ought to employ, and the choice of words it should use to depict both the enemy and the conflict itself. His was a more nuanced script that sought to limit the scope and time horizon of America's fight against those who sought its destruction, but it was nonetheless a narrative of war.

In the absence of significant political achievements or sustained progress on the ground in Afghanistan during the early months of his presidency, Obama shifted his rhetorical focus from present stumbling blocks to the more positive story of the potential for success as he presented his December 2009 strategy for how to achieve closure in the war. He simultaneously narrowed his definition of what it meant to be victorious, speaking more of disrupting, dismantling, and degrading al Qaeda's capabilities than of decisively defeating the enemy. Admitting that he did not have the luxury of choosing the ideal outcome in Afghanistan over its all-too-messy reality, Obama assured the American public that concrete steps were being taken to establish at least a minimally functioning government and a relatively stable society in a country where such goals had always proved elusive. In Obama's lexicon as in Bush's, failure was simply not an option. In an era of ambiguous end points, however, the president was forced to speak in generalities about how the war would conclude and construct a gauzy vision of future progress.

Even for his much-derided war of choice in Iraq, Obama pursued a strategic rhetorical course: Here, too, he constructed a tale of circumscribed success, folding the misbegotten "bad" war into the "good" war of necessity. By the time Iraq combat operations officially ended in August 2010, Obama had subsumed the story of that second war under the wider frame of Afghanistan, the initial conflict that America had been forced to fight. The man who had gained national visibility with his harsh critique of Bush's foray into Iraq was thereby able to turn the page on that divisive war, hailing the exemplary actions of U.S. troops and even praising the conflict's limited political and security achievements.

While Obama continued to maintain that Iraq had been a diversion from the real mission, he concluded that some good had come from deposing Saddam Hussein and that a democratizing Iraq could become an important ally in the region and a bulwark against extremism. He even made the claim that Iraq's future held some enticing—albeit unrealized—possibilities, especially for enhancing American security and promoting the ideals the U.S. represents. For the most part, however, he was content to highlight Afghanistan and confine Iraq to the rhetorical sidelines as he focused the bulk of his public remarks on the existential struggle against al Qaeda and the Taliban.

It has now become an established annual ritual for the president to deliver a major foreign policy address at the commencement ceremonies of one of America's service academies. Each year the venue rotates, and in May 2012 President Obama delivered his remarks at the U.S. Air Force Academy in Colorado Springs. It was a perfect occasion to unveil the final iteration of his narrative of why America had fought, what Afghanistan and Iraq meant to the nation, how the U.S. was achieving closure in both conflicts, and what this portended for the future. On full display was Obama's framing consistency as he revisited the themes that had become the hallmark of his war rhetoric since he announced his new way forward in Afghanistan and the end of combat operations in Iraq— Afghanistan as a just and necessary war, the need to refocus on the real security threat, the light at the end of the long tunnel of war, and constructing a more secure and democratic world. His uplifting, inspirational tone also recapitulated the relentlessly optimistic message that he had been promoting since taking office: America's best days still lay ahead and mankind's last, best hope would continue to light the path for other nations to follow.

Emphasizing all that had been accomplished during his first term, Obama reminded the 1,100 assembled cadets of the remarkable journey that he, they, and America itself had taken over the course of their undergraduate years. He began with this brief overview:

> Four years ago, you arrived here at a time of extraordinary challenge for our nation. Our forces were engaged in two wars. Al Qaeda, which had attacked us on 9/11, was entrenched in their safe havens. Many of our alliances were strained and our standing in the world had suffered. Our economy was in the worst recession since the Great Depression. Around the world and here at home, there were those that questioned whether the United States still had the capacity for global leadership. (Obama 2012b)

Warming to his tale of war, Obama then noted just how far his nation had traveled in that span of time:

> Today, you step forward into a different world. You are the first class in nine years that will graduate into a world where there are no Americans fighting in Iraq. For the first time in your lives … Osama bin Laden is no longer a threat to our country. We've put al Qaeda on the path to defeat. And you are the first graduates since 9/11 who can clearly see how we'll end the war in Afghanistan. (Obama 2012b)

And to provide a satisfying conclusion to his storyline of both conflicts, the president then heralded the prospect of an ever brighter tomorrow:

So what does all this mean? When you came here four years ago, there were some 180,000 American troops in Iraq and Afghanistan. We've now cut that number by more than half. And as more Afghans step up, more of our troops will come home—while achieving the objective that led us to war in the first place and that is defeating al Qaeda and denying them safe haven. So we aren't just ending these wars, we are doing so in a way that makes us safer and stronger …

For a decade, we have labored under the dark cloud of war. And now we can see a light—the light of a new day on the horizon … (Obama 2012b)

The Indispensable Nation

Throughout the 2012 presidential campaign, conservative pundits and Republican candidate Mitt Romney strongly criticized Obama for his failure to appreciate America's special global standing and its unique history, institutions, and principles. Their most damning piece of evidence was an excerpt from an April 2009 press conference in Strasbourg, France when in response to a reporter's query Obama quipped that "I believe in American exceptionalism, just as I suspect the Brits believe in British exceptionalism and the Greeks believe in Greek exceptionalism" (Obama 2009n). Even though Obama immediately went on to add that "I am enormously proud of my country and its role and history in the world … And I think that we have a core set of values that are enshrined in our Constitution, in our body of law, in our democratic practices, in our belief in free speech and equality that, though imperfect, are exceptional," his initial sound bite had provided the opposition with potent partisan ammunition. It was a verbal misstep the president would not repeat; from that point on, he carefully embedded his war narrative in the notion of America as the indispensable nation on the world stage and touted the reach and impact of its global leadership.

Obama did publicly criticize America for what he saw as occasional failures to live up to its founding principles—important historical shortcomings such as the institution of slavery or, much more recently, the Bush administration's harsh interrogation and detainment policies—that undermined the moral basis of its leadership. As McCrisken (2001) notes, however, a key component of exceptionalist belief is that the U.S. may sometimes be misguided in its policy choices but, always striving for perfection, learns from and invariably corrects its errors. Thus in keeping with his exceptionalist worldview, for every mention of America's past imperfections, Obama inserted numerous references to its stellar accomplishments and unique status as a global exemplar, and spoke passionately of how his policy shifts were bringing U.S. national security policy into line with the nation's fundamental values.

Conservative critics remained unimpressed with what they saw as the president's transparent attempts to paper over his true sentiments about America. For many, the underlying theme of Obama's national security discourse entailed, in the words of the Heritage Foundation's Nile Gardiner, the unacceptable idea that the U.S. was "a flawed nation that must seek redemption for its past 'sins'." The essence of Obama's core message, Gardiner insisted, was nothing less than humiliation of the world's superpower (Gardiner and Roach 2009). In early June 2009, Gardiner published a list of 10 occasions where the new president had managed to express public regret for his country's supposed misdeeds. That most of these apologies came on foreign soil was even further cause for outrage. As Gardiner wrote, in his first four months in office Obama had "already apologized for his country to nearly 3 billion people across Europe, the Muslim world, and the Americas"; the disturbing overall effect of his "relentless penchant for apology-making" had been to "weaken American power on the world stage" (Gardiner and Roach 2009).

Four months later, in the conservative publication, the *Weekly Standard*, Charles Krauthammer wrote a particularly scathing indictment of Obama's vision of America's global role. "If everyone is exceptional, no one is," Krauthammer argued in response to the president's comments about exceptionalism, adding the following caustic observations about Obama's persistent refusal to give the U.S. its proper due:

> Indeed, as he made his *hajj* from Strasbourg to Prague to Ankara to Istanbul to Cairo and finally to the U.N. General Assembly, Obama drew the picture of an America quite exceptional—exceptional in moral culpability and heavy-handedness, exceptional in guilt for its treatment of other nations and peoples. With varying degrees of directness or obliqueness, Obama indicted his own country for arrogance, for dismissiveness and derisiveness (toward Europe), for maltreatment of natives, for torture, for Hiroshima, for Guantanamo, for unilateralism, and for insufficient respect for the Muslim world.
>
> Quite an indictment, the fundamental consequence of which is to effectively undermine any moral claim that America might have to world leadership, as well as any moral confidence that any nation needs to have in order to justify to itself and others its position of leadership. (Krauthammer 2009a)

The subject of Obama's disdain for his country had great staying power among conservative pundits and politicians and would resurface in the 2012 presidential contest in Mitt Romney's oft-repeated claim that Obama's foreign policy initiatives were little more than on-going "apology tour" (see Romney 2010 and 2012 for a more complete exegesis). This criticism would be combined with the emotionally-laden campaign charge that Obama still subscribed to the idea of American decline. Recognizing Republican attempts to capitalize on this issue, Obama delivered a forceful synopsis of his policies to achieve closure in both Iraq and Afghanistan in his Air Force Academy commencement address—embedding it in an even more impassioned defense of the triumph of American primacy under his stewardship. "As we've done the work of ending these wars," he proclaimed, "we've laid the foundation for a new era of American leadership. Let's start by putting aside the tired notion that says our influence has waned or that America is in decline" (Obama 2012b).

As correspondent David Nakamura (2012) noted that day in the *Washington Post*, Obama went to some lengths in his speech to highlight his adherence to American exceptionalism, even pointedly employing those very words. "Never bet against the United States," the president declared, adding that "the United States has been, and will always be, the one *indispensable nation* in world affairs. It's one of the many examples of why *America is exceptional*" (Obama 2012b, emphasis added). To demonstrate that the American model had in no way been eclipsed, Obama also borrowed the twentieth-century descriptor "the American century" and dramatically incorporated it into a vision of his nation's singular role in the new millennium. After enumerating how the U.S. would surmount this century's tough economic times and continuing security challenges, Obama once again emphasized the power of America's values and ideals—and the unbending spirit of its people. As he eloquently concluded:

> I see an American century because of the character of our country—the spirit that has always made us exceptional. It's that simple yet revolutionary idea—there at our founding and in our hearts ever since—that we have it in our power to make the world anew, to make the future what we will. It is that fundamental faith—that American optimism—which says no challenge is too great, no mission too hard. It's that spirit that guides your class: 'Never falter, never fail.' (Obama 2012b)

An intriguing irony is that more than any of his predecessors, Obama made continual reference—both implicitly and explicitly—to the concept of American exceptionalism (see Schlesinger 2011). It was, in fact, a subject he had frequently broached well before announcing his candidacy for president. From his 2002 statement that America had been the "arsenal of democracy" in World War II to his 2004 assertion that nowhere else on earth could so unlikely a person become a candidate for national office to his 2010 invocation of America as the last, best hope of earth, Obama lauded his nation's founding principles, the vast opportunities the U.S. provided, and its moral purpose to serve as a global model.

To Obama's supporters, his Air Force Academy address was the most recent of a long line of heartfelt paeans to America as an exceptional nation; to his political opponents, however, it represented merely the latest election-year political maneuver to distract the public from his far darker conception of the U.S. and its fading global role. The conservative reaction to Obama's 2012 commencement address thus serves as a pointed demonstration of George C. Edwards's (2003, 2009, 2012) admonition about the limits of even the seemingly most resonant presidential frame and most skillfully-delivered presidential oratory: It is almost impossible for the commander-in-chief to reverse the opinions of those whose deep-seated perceptions and beliefs already predispose them to discount his message.

And as my case studies have also shown, Edwards's warning about constraints on the president's ability to persuade is equally applicable to the media's response to his narrative, especially in the latter stages of a long and difficult war.

Presidential and Media Frames of War's End: A Yawning Disconnect

I began this volume by noting that recent research on the dynamics of the presidential/media framing relationship in time of war has uncovered a general pattern: As the situation on the ground departs from the president's initial, rose-tinted narrative of the conflict's success, early positive news coverage grows more negative as it reflects that more unpleasant objective reality. Over time, the presidential and media frames increasingly diverge both in substance and in tone as the commander-in-chief steadfastly maintains his positive storyline while journalists shift their focus to other topics, especially the disgruntled voices of elite opponents and the problematic events of war (see Baum and Groeling 2010; Glazier and Boydstun 2012).

But how do the media react as the conflict actually winds to a conclusion? Remember that by the time Barack Obama took the oath of office, Afghanistan and Iraq had become "old news" in many respects—America had been at war for most of the decade and political allies, adversaries, and the media alike expected the new president to bring closure to both conflicts. As we have seen, the U.S. public was also more than ready for its leaders to put these wars behind them and turn to pressing domestic issues. Might a plausible hypothesis state that as a president unveils a plan to extricate the nation from a necessary but very lengthy conflict and then announces the formal end of combat operations in a second, very divisive war, the media storylines would realign with his narrative? And if the president constructs a positive tale of at least circumscribed success in both these wars, might a further assumption hold that the media tone would move in a distinctly more favorable direction?

But that is not what happened in the case of Afghanistan in late 2009 or Iraq in the summer of 2010. As he presented each of his policy initiatives to bring closure to the war, Obama assiduously promoted what he believed to be a complete, consistent, comprehensible, compelling—and, by the end, overwhelmingly favorable—narrative of why America fought, what had been accomplished, and the brighter future the war made possible. And in each instance, the media declined to accept his version of current reality or his vision for that better tomorrow.

While none of the five media outlets I examined contested Obama's (and Bush's) central premise that war in Afghanistan was both just and necessary, they all privileged a strategic frame of process over substance, conflict and controversy over policy outcome during the two months surrounding the president's December 2009 announcement of his new way forward in the war. The administration's so-called "dithering" on the exit plan, disagreements among his senior national security team, a public split among congressional Democrats, and the failure to guard against terrorist incidents in the air and on a military base became one major component of the media's chosen storyline. The dismal political and security situation in the Af/Pak region comprised a second major media narrative as correspondents based in Kabul and Pakistan highlighted continuing extremist violence in the form of suicide bombings and attacks on mosques, schools, and shops. Hamid Karzai, the Afghan president, was the recipient of repeated media criticism, as his personal idiosyncrasies and corrupt and inefficient government were presented as a glaring contradiction to the uplifting tale of progress and the prospects for democracy that Obama offered.

The media frame of the withdrawal of combat forces from Iraq was even more fraught and negative than that of Afghanistan. The great congressional debates over Bush's war of choice had occurred prior to Obama's term in office, as had the decision to end America's combat operations by 2010. In the absence of significant political controversy in Washington, journalists and media commentators turned to all the problems that Iraq still faced: the shockingly high levels of violence, a political system in seemingly complete disarray, a crumbling infrastructure and an economy in chaos, and a shell-shocked population that felt both hopeless and betrayed. The media also highlighted the horrific toll of war on American troops and their families as well as its negative impact on the nation's economy and global reputation.

Obama's formal announcement of the end of combat operations in Iraq also primed war correspondents and media commentators to reflect on the legacy of a war that some had long opposed and almost all had found to be poorly implemented. In casting a backward glance, there seemed little if anything to celebrate as the war came to an official close. The overarching media sentiment was one of sorrow with more than a little dollop of anger added into the mix. Nor did the future seem much more promising to these journalists as even conservative commentators presented very circumspect storylines about what the U.S. might expect once its troops departed. In late summer 2010, the presidential/media framing divide over Iraq seemed to have become as wide as in the dark days before the surge.

For both Afghanistan and Iraq, all five media outlets—Fox News included—presented quite similar endgame narratives that departed markedly from Obama's sanguine depiction of newly-democratizing nations that would function as bulwarks against extremism. While conservative commentators harped on Obama's failure to give adequate credit to Bush's surge policy in Iraq and complained about the president's rigid adherence to strict timetables for withdrawal, they carefully refrained from sounding a trumpet of victory in either conflict. Even for those who had been the wars' most wholehearted advocates, great caution and concern about the future was the norm.

Obama's eloquent presentations of American exceptionalism also found little media traction during the time frames I examined. With the important exception of continual rhetorical salutes to the heroism and sacrifice of America's fighting forces, reporters and commentators fell silent on this important facet of Obama's war discourse. While his impassioned narrative of American ideals as a model for the world was not disputed in media accounts, neither was it emphasized. The media spotlight shone instead on the numerous political, security, and economic problems both conflicts still presented, evidence of journalists' willingness to construct a counterframe to a presidential narrative that collided with a stark and contradictory reality.

The most successful element of Obama's endgame storyline was the one he wholeheartedly adopted from his predecessor—that America had been forced to engage in military combat against her terrorist adversaries. Even though Obama had re-labeled and narrowed Bush's open-ended war on terror, he—along with Congress and the U.S. foreign policy establishment—never questioned the ongoing need to wage globalized war against those who attacked America on 9/11. And as America exited from Iraq and prepared to depart from Afghanistan, neither did the leading organs of the U.S. mainstream media. Bush's master terror narrative remained essentially intact, firmly ingrained in the American psyche but not even mentioned in any media reports during the time frame under study.

As discussed in my Introduction, this research was informed by three models of the government/media nexus—hegemony, indexing, and cascading activation—as they applied to the presidential frame of war's denouement and the media response. The perseverance of Bush's war-on-terror frame supports, I believe, the hegemony model's perspective that an official narrative will achieve dominance if it is so embedded in a nation's sense of identity and what it values that few if any even think of questioning its assumptions or prescriptions for action. From his first public comments on the 9/11 terrorist attacks, Obama endorsed the Bush worldview of globalized war and constructed a narrative that recapitulated the 43rd president's version of what America represented, why it was attacked, and how it had to respond. And while journalists faulted Iraq as an appropriate target for the war on terror and criticized the implementation and probable long-term outcome of both wars, they too refrained from questioning Bush's core arguments.

My research also demonstrates that, in line with the indexing and cascading models of presidential and media frames, journalists are prepared to contest specific components of the dominant national security narrative even as a conflict concludes. As Bennett et al. (2007, ch. 3) and Entman (2004) argue, such displays of media independence reflect either publicly-expressed opposition within the U.S. political establishment or, in the absence of elite dissensus, event-driven information that contradicts the assertions and interpretations of the presidential narrative. In the time periods under study, there was credible evidence from both conflicts that the U.S. exits were not proceeding smoothly and that the political and security situations in Afghanistan and Iraq diverged significantly from what Obama claimed. Thus even as Bush's broad war-on-terror frame remained ascendant, the media's pessimistic depictions of both wars' denouements obscured the president's far sunnier endgame narratives.

A Slow Fade to Black

Even though Obama primed America's leading media outlets to increase their focus on the endpoints of both wars, journalists' attention quickly moved on to other topics. While media coverage of Afghanistan rose significantly in the weeks leading up to Obama's December 2009 speech on his new surge-then-exit strategy, reaching more than a quarter of the total news hole during the week of his primetime address, the spike in media coverage was short-lived (Project for Excellence in Journalism 2009f). For all his promotional efforts to raise the profile of his new Afghanistan policy, Obama was able to capture significant levels of media interest for only a few weeks and even at that juncture, the content and tone of coverage were far from what the president might have wished. As the Project for Excellence in Journalism (2010a) reported, the major 2009 year-end newspaper story on Afghanistan involved a suicide bomber who infiltrated a CIA base in the eastern part of the country, killing seven Americans in what was described as the deadliest single attack on U.S. intelligence personnel in the eight-year-long war. For the media, this latest in an apparently unending stream of violence represented a far more accurate depiction of reality than all the president's hope-infused words.

By the first week of 2010, Afghanistan had fallen to only about 5 percent of total media stories (Project for Excellence in Journalism 2010b), although the thwarted Christmas day attempt to blow up a Northwest Airlines flight placed the issue of terrorism once more in the headlines. While the war would remain one of the top media stories for 2010, it constituted only 4 percent of the total news hole and media attentiveness would continue to decline, bumping up temporarily as reports of particularly gruesome violence, the WikiLeaks dissemination of thousands of classified war reports, and the removal of General McChrystal as Afghanistan commander crossed the media radar screen (Project for Excellence in Journalism 2010c). For 2011, the story of the killing of Osama bin Laden became a major media event and one of the few times that positive news from Afghanistan outweighed the negative, but other coverage of the war maintained its downward, and predominantly unfavorable, trajectory (Project for Excellence in Journalism 2011).

An even sharper pattern of declining media interest was evident for Iraq. By the time of the 2008 presidential election campaign, Iraq was no longer one of the top foreign policy stories; during the first year of Obama's presidency it accounted for only 2 percent of total news reports, and even as he highlighted the end of combat operations in August 2010, Iraq comprised only 8 percent of the total news hole (Project for Excellence in Journalism 2010d, 2010e). And as I have discussed at length, the tone of the media's Iraq coverage in the weeks surrounding the official drawdown of U.S. forces was consistently negative and veered dramatically from Obama's narrative of cautious optimism. But as the subject of the war drew less and less journalistic scrutiny, the intensity of media criticism also diminished.

Public interest in the conclusion of the wars paralleled the pattern of declining media and political focus. While the U.S. public expressed a renewed interest in both conflicts in the weeks surrounding Obama's televised announcements about the new way forward in Afghanistan and the troop withdrawal in Iraq (Pew Research Center 2009d; Agiesta 2010), the surge in attentiveness was short-lived and rapidly turned to other, more diverting, matters.

In the absence of dramatic, visually enticing "mission accomplished" moments that a nation can celebrate as definitive indicators of military victory, are twenty-first-century wars destined to end with a slow fade to black as politicians, the media, and the public turn their collective gaze from conflicts whose outcomes remain frustratingly unclear and inherently messy and unsatisfying? Will a societal sigh of relief and shrug of indifference replace the ebullient public outpouring of parades, award ceremonies, congratulatory speeches, televised appearances, iconic photographs, and glowing banner headlines that once accompanied the returning troops and their commanders? The evidence I have presented in my two case studies indicates that this was indeed the situation for the U.S. exit from Iraq and the still-in-progress departure from Afghanistan: Even as Obama attempted to achieve closure with a unifying and uplifting narrative of success, the media refused to follow his framing lead, first constructing a far less positive tale of war's end and then virtually banishing the subject from their reportage.

In the weeks following his primetime announcements on Afghanistan and Iraq, the Washington political establishment also made little effort to highlight Obama's tales of what the U.S. had accomplished in its post-9/11 wars. In fact, members of Congress seemed quickly to lose interest in the concluding chapter of either conflict, focusing their rhetorical skirmishes on other domestic and international issues as first the midterm and then the presidential campaign seasons got underway. And in the absence of significant political debate or focused media attention, the U.S. public remained ambivalent and divided about the conflicts' rationales and achievements—although seemingly unified in a desire to put both wars out of their minds as rapidly as possible.

Given the consistent presidential/media framing patterns I uncovered in my case studies, it seems appropriate to offer a prediction for further quantitative analysis: The greater the level of perceived ambiguity surrounding a war's outcome, the greater the disjunction of the final presidential and media frames of the conflict's meaning, accomplishments, and denouement. A corollary predicts that the less satisfying the sense of a war's closure, the more swiftly the media—followed in turn by the president, the Washington political establishment, and the public—will shift their attention to more engaging topics.

Researchers will soon have the opportunity to investigate the framing patterns for the formal end of combat operations in Afghanistan. In the meantime, President Obama still faces some important decisions about the endgame strategy for Afghanistan: What sort of military presence will remain after the 2014 handover to Afghan security? How rapidly will the U.S. reduce its troop force before that date? What will be the role of NATO and other allies? There is also the thorny political issue of congressional reaction, and the possibility of a dramatic divide between—or even within—the two parties over the scope and speed of the drawdown. In other words, there remains the question of whether the withdrawal from Afghanistan becomes a subject of significant elite political controversy and hence a topic of heightened media interest.

If Afghanistan becomes a more divisive issue over the first two years of Obama's second term, my findings suggest that there should be a repeat of media skepticism about the outcome of the once-heralded war and a disinclination to parrot whatever positive spin the president attempts to put on the conflict's formal closure. Negative coverage should then quickly be followed by a shifting of the media spotlight to other issues, events, and personalities. Even if elite U.S. political fights over the post-2014 mission in Afghanistan do not materialize, the results from my two case studies indicate that media coverage will be far from positive in a war where the end point will not see the establishment of a western-style democracy or a more stable political system—or a decisive end to the threat of terrorism. In either case, a sense of media dissatisfaction should prevail and media attention to the war's conclusion should be transitory. As a consequence, a mix of public dismay and disinterest should remain the norm.

What, then, might we expect for presidential and media frames of future international conflicts involving non-state actors? If, as Obama has indicated, such engagements ought to entail a very different form of remote, high-tech warfare, the endgame framing patterns I have observed may not persist beyond America's two post-9/11 wars. A more surgical war fought secretly and in the shadows, far removed from public, media, and congressional gaze, presents a different subject for analysis. And what of highly-publicized presidential appeals for military strikes against violent and repressive regimes that murder their own citizens through the use of outlawed weapons of mass destruction? The evidence from this study suggests that in the near future even glaring examples of heinous state acts may not produce ready acceptance of the president's frame of war. Perhaps it is not beyond the pale to hypothesize that in both such instances the presidential/media framing disconnect may be greater than has been the case for Afghanistan and Iraq as the commander-in-chief cannot bring to bear the powers of the bully pulpit even as war commences, let alone as it moves toward a conclusion.

Bibliography

94 Days: was Obama dithering or decisive? Outlook. *The Washington Post*, 29 November, B4.

A Test for President Karzai. 2009. Editorial. *The New York Times*, 16 December, A42.

Abramowitz, M. 2008. Terrorism fades as issue in 2008 campaign. *The Washington Post* [Online 11 September]. Available at: http://www.washingtonpost.com/wp-dyn/content/article/2008/09/10/10/AR2008091003393.html [accessed 20 May 2009].

Abramowitz, M. and Baker, P. 2007. White House considers next step in Iraq. *The Washington Post*, 27 May, A1.

Abu-Nasr, D. 2009. Airliner plot raises fears about al-Qaida in Yemen. Associated Press, International News, 27 December.

Achenbach, J. 2009. In his slow decision-making, Obama goes with head, not gut. *The Washington Post*, 25 November, A1.

Agiesta, J. 2010. Behind the numbers. *The Washington Post* [Online 16 July]. Available at: http://www.washingtonpost.com/behind-the-numbers/2010/07/public_supportive_of_iraq_afghanistan.html [accessed 1 August 2010].

Alter, J. 2010. *The Promise*. New York: Simon and Schuster.

Al-Qaeda group asserts responsibility for deadly attacks. 2010. *The Washington Post*, 29 August, A15.

Althaus, S. 2003. When news norms collide, follow the leader: new evidence for press independence. *Political Communication*, 20 (4), 381–414.

Alwan, A. and Fadel, L. 2010. Dozens killed, injured in Baghdad suicide bombing. *The Washington Post*, 18 August, A6.

An Afghan strategy. 2009. Editorial. *The Washington Post*, 2 December, A22.

Angle, J. 2009. Fox News all-stars. *Fox Special Report with Bret Baier*, Fox News Network, 28 December.

Anker, E. 2005. Villains, victims and heroes: melodrama, media, and September 11. *Journal of Communication*, 55 (1), 22–37.

Applebaum, A. 2010. Iraq's other casualties: combat has ended, but its costs remain. *The Washington Post*, 30 August, A13.

Arango, T. 2010a. American and Iraqi versions differ in latest chapters of war's story. *The New York Times*, 2 August, A7.

Arango, T. 2010b. US and Iraqi interests may work against withdrawal deadline. *The New York Times*, 11 August, A4.

Arraf, J. 2010. Baghdad police official longs for the rule of law. *The Washington Post*, 19 September, A4.

Artz, L. and Murphy, B. 2000. *Hegemony in the United States.* Thousand Oaks, CA: Sage.

Bacevich, A. 2008a. Surge to nowhere: don't buy the hawk's hype. *The Washington Post*, 20 January, A24.

Bacevich, A. 2008b. *The Limits of Power: The End of American Exceptionalism.* New York: Henry Holt.

Bacevich, A. 2008c. 9/11 plus 7. Webcast video interview [Online 11 September]. Available at: http://www.us.macmillan.com/BookCustomPage.aspx?isbn=9780805088151&mtype=2&m_contentid=283736#video [accessed 15 December 2008].

Bai, M. 2009. Escalations: how Afghanistan might be Vietnam—and Obama the real Kennedy. *The New York Times*, 1 November, MM11.

Baier, B. 2010. Fox News Sunday Roundtable. *Fox News Sunday*, Fox News Network, 15 August.

Baker, P. et al. 2007. Among top officials, "surge" has sparked dissent, infighting. *The Washington Post*, 9 September, A1.

Baker, P. 2009. Inside the situation room: how a war plan evolved. *The New York Times*, 6 December, A1.

Baker, P. 2010a. Obama and the drawdown. *The New York Times*, 22 August, A1.

Baker, P. 2010b. Winning, losing and war. *The New York Times*, 29 August, WK1.

Baker, P. and Cooper, H. 2009. All Afghan war options by Obama aides said to call for more troops. *The New York Times*, 8 November, A8.

Baker, P. and Nagourney, A. 2009. Two messages for two sides. *The New York Times*, 2 December, A1.

Baker, P. and Weisman, J. 2007. Petraeus backs initial pullout. *The Washington Post*, 11 September, A1.

Baker, P. and Zeleny, J. 2008. Obama repeats a campaign staple: time for a change. *The New York Times* [Online 30 October]. Available at: http://www.nytimes.com/2008/10/30/us/politics/30obama.html [accessed 17 November 2008].

Baldor, L. 2007. Bush's Iraq plan draws confrontational opposition from Democrats, some Republicans [Online 12 January]. Available at: http://www.ap.org [accessed 20 January 2007].

Balz, D. 2009. With speech, president makes the conflict truly his own. *The Washington Post*, 2 December, A1.

Baum, M. 2003. *Soft News Goes to War: Public Opinion and American Foreign Policy in the New Media Age.* Princeton, NJ: Princeton University Press.

Baum, M. and Groeling, T. 2010. *War Stories: The Causes and Consequences of Public Views of War.* Princeton, NJ: Princeton University Press.

Benedict, C. et al. 2009. For therapists in the military, painful stories. *The New York Times*, 8 November, A1.

Bennett, W.L. 1994. The news about foreign policy. *Taken by Storm: The Media, Public Opinion, and US Foreign Policy in the Gulf War*, edited by W.L. Bennett and D. Paletz. Chicago: University of Chicago Press, 12–40.

Bennett, W.L. 2012. *News: The Politics of Illusion.* 9th edition. New York: Pearson/Longman.

Bennett, W.L., Lawrence, R., and Livingston, S. 2006. None dare call it torture: indexing and the limits of press independence in the Abu Ghraib scandal. *Journal of Communication*, 56 (3), 467–85.

Bennett, W.L., Lawrence, R., and Livingston, S. 2007. *When the Press Fails: Political Power and the News Media from Iraq to Katrina.* Chicago: University of Chicago Press.

Berger, J. 2009. Giuliani criticizes terror trials in New York. *The New York Times*, 16 November, A1.

Biden, J. 2010a. Transcript of newsmaker interview: Joseph Biden. PBS [Online 1 September]. Available at: http://www.pbs.org/newshour/bb/politics/july-dec10/iraq2_09–01.html [accessed 1 March 2011].

Biden, J. 2010b. Remarks by Vice President Joseph Biden at change of command ceremony for United States Forces-Iraq [Online 1 September]. Available at: http://www.whitehouse.gov/the-press-ovvice/2010/09/01/remarks-vice-president-joseph-biden-change-command-ceremony-united-states [accessed 12 January 2011].

Biden, J. 2010c. Vice President Joe Biden discusses the situation in Iraq. *NBC Today*, NBC News Transcripts, 1 September.

Blackledge, B. 2009. Details emerge about Fort Hood suspect's history. Associated Press, Washington Dateline, 6 November.

Bolton, J. 2009. Report says Obama rejects options presented on Afghanistan. *Fox On the Record with Greta Van Susteren*, Fox News Network, 11 November.

Broder, D. 2009. Enough Afghan debate. *The Washington Post*, 15 November, A23.

Brooks, D. 2007. Obama, gospel and verse. *The New York Times* [Online 26 April]. Available at: http://www.nytimes.com/2007/04/26/opinion/26brooks.html?_r=0 [accessed 1 June 2010].

Brooks, D. 2009. The analytic mode. *The New York Times*, 4 December, A35.

Brooks, D. 2010. Nation building works. *The New York Times*, 31 August, A21.

Brown, A. and Breed, A. 2009. Suspect told "there's something wrong with you." Associated Press, Domestic News, 8 November.

Brummitt, C. 2009. Pakistan's capital city now resembles besieged city. Associated Press, International News, 1 November.

Bumiller, E. 2010. Gates, in Iraq, takes the long view. *The New York Times*, 2 September, A1.

Bumiller, E. and Sanger, D. 2009. 3 Obama advisers lean toward plan for 30,000 more troops for Afghanistan. *The New York Times*, 11 November, A6.

Burns, J. 2007a. US general in Iraq speaks strongly against troop pullout. *The New York Times*, 16 July, A1.

Burns, J. 2007b. For top general in Iraq, role is a mixed blessing. *The New York Times*, 14 August, A1.

Burns, J. 2010. Witnessing the arc of a costly conflict. *The New York Times*, 1 September, A11.

Burns, R. 2007. Iraq options seemed focused on reducing US combat role next year. Associated Press [Online 30 August]. Available at: http://www.ap.org [accessed 10 October 2007].

Burns, R. 2010a. Army of diplomats takes the lead in fractious Iraq. Associated Press, Washington Dateline, 21 August.

Burns, R. 2010b. Analysis: US hopes for Iraq collided with reality. Associated Press, Washington Dateline, 31 August.

Burns, R. and Fuller, B. 2009. Obama's hesitancy on war buildup sends messages. Associated Press, Washington Dateline, 12 November.

Bush, G.W. 2001a. The president's radio address. 15 September. *Weekly Compilation of Presidential Documents*, 37 (38), 1321.

Bush, G.W. 2001b. Remarks to the United Nations General Assembly in New York City. 10 November. *Weekly Compilation of Presidential Documents*, 37 (46), 1638–41.

Bush, G.W. 2003. Address to the nation on Iraq from the USS. *Abraham Lincoln*. 1 May. *Weekly Compilation of Presidential Documents*, 39 (18), 516–18.

Bush, G.W. 2006. The president's radio address. 9 December. *Weekly Compilation of Presidential Documents*, 42 (50), 2148–49.

Bush, G.W. 2007a. Address to the nation on the war on terror in Iraq. 10 January. *Weekly Compilation of Presidential Documents*, 43 (1), 1.

Bush, G.W. 2007b. Address before a joint session of the Congress on the state of the union. 23 January. *Weekly Compilation of Presidential Documents*, 43 (4), 57–64.

Bush, G.W. 2007c. President's news conference. 14 February. *Weekly Compilation of Presidential Documents*, 43 (7), 150–62.

Bush, G.W. 2007d. Remarks to the American Enterprise Institute for Public Policy Research. 15 February. *Weekly Compilation of Presidential Documents*, 43 (7), 165–73.

Bush, G.W. 2007e. Remarks to the National Cattlemen's Beef Association. 28 March. *Weekly Compilation of Presidential Documents*, 43 (13), 377–85.

Bush, G.W. 2007f. Remarks to the World Affairs Council of Western Michigan. 20 April. *Weekly Compilation of Presidential Documents*, 43 (16), 487–502.

Bush, G.W. 2007g. Remarks to the Associated General Contractors of America. 2 May. *Weekly Compilation of Presidential Documents*, 43 (18), 562–74.

Bush, G.W. 2007h. Commencement address at the United States Coast Guard Academy in New London, CT. 23 May. *Weekly Compilation of Presidential Documents*, 43 (21), 665–70.

Bush, G.W. 2007i. Remarks to the Greater Cleveland Partnership, Cleveland OH. 10 July. *Weekly Compilation of Presidential Documents*, 43 (28), 920–37.

Bush, G.W. 2007j. The president's news conference. 12 July. *Weekly Compilation of Presidential Documents*, 43 (28), 944–56.

Bush, G.W. 2007k. Remarks at the Veterans of Foreign Wars national convention in Kansas City, MO. 22 August. *Weekly Compilation of Presidential Documents*, 43 (34), 1107–14.

Bush, G.W. 2007l. Address to the nation on the war on terror in Iraq. 13 September. *Weekly Compilation of Presidential Documents*, 43 (37), 1204–08.

Bush, G.W. 2007m. The president's news conference. 20 September. *Weekly Compilation of Presidential Documents*, 43 (38), 1224–33.

Bush, G.W. 2008a. Address before a joint session of the Congress on the state of the union. 28 January. *Weekly Compilation of Presidential Documents*, 44 (4), 117–25.

Bush, G.W. 2008b. Remarks at the National Museum of the United States Air Force in Dayton, OH. 27 March. *Weekly Compilation of Presidential Documents*, 44 (12), 431–37.

Bush, G.W. 2008c. Remarks on the war on terror. 31 July. *Weekly Compilation of Presidential Documents*, 44 (30), 1080–81.

Bush, G.W. 2008d. Remarks to the community at Fort Campbell, KY. 25 November. *Weekly Compilation of Presidential Documents*, 44 (47), 1453–56.

Bush, G.W. 2008e. The president's radio address. 6 December. *Weekly Compilation of Presidential Documents*, 44 (49), 1492–93.

Bush, G.W. 2008f. Remarks at the United States Military Academy at West Point in West Point, NY. 9 December. *Weekly Compilation of Presidential Documents*, 44 (49), 1503–08.

Bush, G.W. 2008g. Remarks at the United States Army War College in Carlisle, PA. 17 December. *Weekly Compilation of Presidential Documents*, 44 (50), 1542–46.

Bush, G.W. 2009. Farewell address to the nation. 15 January. *Weekly Compilation of Presidential Documents*, 45 (2), 79–82.

Campbell, J., O'Hanlon, M., and Unikewicz, A. 2007. Op.-chart: the state of Iraq, an update. *The New York Times*, 18 March, D1.

Carey, B. et al. 2009. For therapists in the military, painful stories. *The New York Times*, 8 November, A1.

Carragee, K. and Roefs, W. 2004. The neglect of power in recent frame research. *Journal of Communication*, 54, 214–233.

Casey, G. 2009. Army Chief of Staff General George Casey discusses shootings at Fort Hood. *NBC Meet the Press*, NBC News Transcripts, 8 November.

Chandrasekaran, R. 2009. Differing views of new Afghanistan strategy. *The Washington Post*, 26 December, A1.

Cheney, L. 2009. Analysis with Liz Cheney. *Fox Hannity*, Fox News Network, 16 November.

Cheney, R. 2009a. Former VP's remarks prepared for his address to the Center for Security Policy. *Fox News* [Online 21 October]. Available at: http://www.foxnews.com/story/0,2933,569006,00.html [accessed 7 November 2009].

Cheney, R. 2009b. Barack Obama says US will finish job in Afghanistan. *NBC Nightly News*, NBC News Transcripts, 24 November.

Clinton, H.R. 2009a. Secretary of State Hillary Clinton discusses trip to Asia with President Barack Obama and other foreign affairs. *NBC Meet the Press*, NBC News Transcripts, 15 November.

Clinton, H.R. 2009b. Text of Secretary Clinton's prepared testimony. *The New York Times* [Online 3 December]. Available at: http://www.nytimes.com/2009/12/03/world/middleeast/03.policy.clinton.text.html?ref=asia [accessed 4 January 2010].

Clinton, H.R. 2010. A conversation with US Secretary of State Hillary Rodham Clinton. Council on Foreign Relations [Online October 8]. Available at: http://www.cfr.org/diplomacy/conversation-us-secretary-state-hillary-rodham-clinton/p22896 [accessed 3 January 2011].

Cloud, D. and Gordon, M. 2007. Build-up in Iraq needed into '08, US general says. *The New York Times*, 8 March, A1.

Cloud, D. and Shanker, T. 2007. Petraeus warns against quick pullback in Iraq. *The New York Times*, 11 September, A1.

Coe, K., Domke, D., Graham, E., John, S., and Pickard, V. 2004. No shades of gray: the binary discourse of George W. Bush and an echoing press. *Journal of Communication*, 54 (2), 234–52.

Condit, C. 1994. Hegemony in a mass media society. *Critical Studies in Mass Communication*, 11, 205–230.

Constable, P. 2009. As Kabul awaits runoff, 'everything has stopped'; uncertainty slows economy, puts plans and dreams on hold. *The New York Times*, 1 November, A20.

Constable, P. and Partlow, J. 2009. In Kabul, a collective sigh of relief; with Karzai declared winner, many hope political tension is over. *The Washington Post*, 3 November, A8.

Constable, P. and Wilson S. 2009. Challenger poised to quit race; US plays down significance Clinton says departure won't affect vote's legitimacy. *The Washington Post*, 1 November, A1.

Cook, T. 2005. *Governing with the News*. Chicago: University of Chicago Press.

Cooper, H. 2009. Seeking a level in Kabul. *The New York Times*, 12 November, A1.

Cooper, H. and Zeleny, J. 2009. Obama presses Afghan leader on corruption. *The New York Times*, 3 November, A1.

Cooper, M. and Sussman, D. 2008. Voters in poll want priority to be economy, their top issue. *The New York Times* [Online 20 August]. Available at: http://www.nytimes.com/2008/21/us/politics/21poll.html [accessed 1 February 2009].

Crocker, R. 2010. A future to write in Iraq; Washington needs to stay engaged and slow down its clock. *The Washington Post*, 31 August, A17.

DeYoung, K. 2009. With narrow military goals, Obama ups the ante. *The Washington Post*, 2 December, A11.

DeYoung, K. and Zacharia, J. 2010. US hoping for new progress in Iraqi talks. *The Washington Post*, 11 September, A9.

Diehl, J. 2009. Obama's reluctant choice. *The Washington Post*, 15 November, A21.

DiMaggio, A. 2008. *Mass Media, Mass Propaganda: Examining American News in the "War on Terror."* Landham, MD: Lexington Books.
Di-Natale, D. 2010a. Political headlines. *Fox Special Report with Bret Baier*, Fox News Network, 13 August.
Di-Natale, D. 2010b. Political headlines. *Fox Special Report with Bret Baier*, Fox News Network, 18 August.
Dionne, E.J. 2007. Democrats' last best hope. *The Washington Post*, 11 September, A1.
Dionne, E.J. 2009a. A plan C for Afghanistan. *The Washington Post*, 23 November, A19.
Dionne, E.J. 2009b. A Goldilocks strategy. *The Washington Post*, 3 December, A33.
Dionne, E.J. 2010. A speech's tall order. *The Washington Post*, 2 September, A23.
Domke, D. 2004. *God Willing? Political Fundamentalism in the White House, the War on Terror, and the Echoing Press.* London: Pluto.
Domke, D., Graham, E., Coe, K., John, S., and Coopman, T. 2006. Going public as political strategy: the Bush administration, an echoing press, and passage of the Patriot Act. *Political Communication*, 23 (3), 291–312.
Edwards, G. 2003. *On Deaf Ears: The Limits of the Bully Pulpit.* New Haven, CT: Yale University Press.
Edwards, G. 2009. *The Strategic President: Persuasion and Opportunity in Presidential Leadership.* Princeton, NJ: Princeton University Press.
Edwards, G. 2012. *Overreach: Leadership in the Obama Presidency.* Princeton, NJ: Princeton University Press.
Eikenberry, C. 2009. Eikenberry's House testimony on Afghanistan. *The New York Times* [online December 9]. Available at: http://www.nytimes.com/2009/world/asia/09policy.eikenberry.text.html [accessed 4 January 2010].
Elliott, A. 2009. Complications grow for Muslims serving nation. *The New York Times*, 9 November, A1.
Engel, R. 2009. Treating short-tempered troops. *NBC Nightly News*, NBC News Transcripts, 12 November.
Engel, R. 2010a. Life in Baghdad very difficult. *NBC Nightly News*, NBC News Transcripts, 2 August.
Engel, R. 2010b. Iraq: the long way out: Awakening forces concerned about their future after US combat troops leave Iraq. *NBC Nightly News*, NBC News Transcripts, 14 August.
Engel, R. 2010c. The long way out: suicide bomber attacks as US soldiers pull out. *NBC Nightly News*, NBC News Transcripts, 17 August.
Engel, R. 2010d. Richard Engel gives his take on what type of Iraq will be left after US troops leave. *NBC Today*, NBC News Transcripts, 31 August.
Engel, R. 2010e. Richard Engel on the cost of changes wrought by the Iraq war. *NBC Nightly News*, NBC News Transcripts, 31 August.
Entman, R. 2003. Cascading activation: contesting the White House's frame after 9/11. *Political Communication*, 20 (4), 415–32.

Entman, R. 2004. *Projections of Power: Framing News, Public Opinion, and US Foreign Policy.* Chicago: University of Chicago Press.

Entman, R. and Page, B. 1994. The news before the storm: the Iraq War debate and the limits to media independence. *Taken by Storm: The Media, Public Opinion, and US Foreign Policy in the Gulf War*, edited by W.L. Bennett and D. Paletz. Chicago: University of Chicago Press, 82–101.

Esch, J. 2010. Legitimizing the "war on terror": political myth in official-level rhetoric. *Political Psychology*, 31 (3), 357–91.

Eshbaugh-Soha, M. and Peake, J. 2011. *Breaking Through the Noise: Presidential Leadership, Public Opinion, and the News Media.* Stanford, CA: Stanford University Press.

Fadel, L. 2010a. In Iraq, a precarious time plagued by "what ifs": as US troops depart, country faces instability and political impasse. *The Washington Post*, 22 August, A10.

Fadel, L. 2010b. As Obama declares end of combat in Iraq, its citizens move forward with uncertainty. *The Washington Post*, 1 September, A8.

Farhan, H. 2010. Quotation of the day. *The New York Times*, 2 August, A2.

Farnsworth, S. and Lichter, R. 2006. *The Mediated Presidency: Television News and Presidential Governance.* Landham, MD: Rowman and Littlefield.

Feller, B. 2009. Obama warns Afghan president: time for new chapter. Associated Press, Washington Dateline, 2 November.

Filkins, D. 2009a. Qaeda had role in attack on UN staff, official says. *The New York Times*, 1 November, A12.

Filkins, D. 2009b. With troops, a demand for Afghans to step up fight. *The New York Times*, 2 December, A1.

Filkins, D. and Rubin, A. 2009. Karzai rival said to be planning to quit runoff. *The New York Times*, 1 November, A1.

Flaherty, A. and Gearan, A. 2009. Skeptical Dems resign themselves to Obama war plan. Associated Press, Washington Dateline, 2 December.

Friedman, T. 2007. Remember Iraq. *The New York Times*, 24 October, A21.

Fuller, B. and Gearan, A. 2009. Official: Obama wants his war options changed. Associated Press, Washington Dateline, 12 November.

Gallup. 2007a. Gen. David Petraeus better known, better liked after last week [Online 19 September]. Available at: http://www.gallup.com/poll/28726/Gen-David-Petraeus-Better-Known-Better-Liked-After-Last-Week.aspx [accessed 18 October 2007].

Gallup. 2007b. Gen. Petraeus buys time for Iraq war, but not support [Online 19 September]. Available at: http://www.gallup.com/poll/28726/Gen-Petraeus-Buys-Time-Iraq-War-Support.aspx [accessed 18 October 2007].

Gallup. 2008a. Nearly half of US adults now applaud the Iraq surge [Online 31 July]. Available at: http://www.gallup.com/poll/109165/Nearly-Half-US-Adults-Now-Applaud-Iraq-Surge.aspx [accessed 15 September 2008].

Gallup. 2008b. Gallup's pulse of democracy: the war in Iraq [Online 15 December]. Available at: http://www.gallup.com/poll/1633/Iraq.aspx [accessed 8 January 2009].

Gamel, K. 2010. AP Impact: US wasted billions in rebuilding Iraq. Associated Press, Business News, 30 August.

Gardiner, N. and Roach, M. 2009. Barack Obama's top 10 apologies: how the president has humiliated a superpower. The Heritage Foundation [Online 2 June]. Available at: http://www.heritage.org/Research/Europe/wm2466.cfm [accessed 4 December 2011].

Garrett, M. 2010. Political headlines. *Fox Special Report with Bret Baier*, Fox News Network, 23 August.

Gates, R. 2009a. Remarks of Secretary of Defense Robert M. Gates [Online 27 January]. Quoted in: Tyson, *The Washington Post*. Available at: http://www.washingtonpost.com/wp-dyn/content/article/2009/01/27/AR2009012700472.html [accessed 31 March 2009].

Gates, R. 2009b. Statement of Secretary of Defense Robert M. Gates, Senate Armed Services Committee [Online 27 January]. Available at: www.armed-services.senate.gov/statement/2009/January/Gates01-27-09.pdf [accessed 31 March 2009].

Gates, R, 2009c. Statement of Secretary of Defense Robert M. Gates, Senate Armed Services Committee [Online 2 December]. Available at: www.armed-services.senate.gov/statement/2009/December/Gates12-02-09.pdf [accessed 4 January 2010].

Gates, R. 2010a. Remarks as delivered by Secretary of Defense Robert M. Gates, Milwaukee, Wisconsin [Online 31 August]. Available at: http://www.defense.gov/speeches/speech.aspx?speechid=1500 [accessed 1 February 2011].

Gates, R. 2010b. Press availability with Secretary Gates from Ramadi, Iraq [Online 1 September]. Available at: http://www.defense.gov/transcripts.aspx?transcriptid=4678 [accessed 1 March 2011].

Gearan, A. 2009a. AP source: US envoy objects to troop increase. Associated Press, Washington Dateline, 12 November.

Gearan, A. 2009b. Analysis: US works with and around Afghan leader. Associated Press, Washington, Dateline, 19 November.

Gearan, A. 2009c. Obama speech next week: more troops for Afghan. Associated Press, Washington Dateline, 24 November.

Gearan, A. 2010. Gates: all is not well as combat role ends. Associated Press, Domestic News, 31 August.

Gearan, A. and Flaherty, A. 2009. Obama will unveil Afghan troops move at West Point. Associated Press, Washington Dateline, 26 November.

Gearan, A. and Hurst, 2009. AP sources: US troops likely for Afghan in January. Associated Press, Washington Dateline, 10 November.

Gearan, A. and Jakes, L. 2009. New Afghan violence makes Obama decision tougher. Associated Press, Washington Dateline, 6 November.

Gearan, A. and Loven, J. 2009. White House braces for tough sell on Afghan policy. Associated Press, Washington Dateline, 24 November.

Gershkoff, A. and Kushner, S. 2005. Shaping public opinion: the 9/11-Iraq connection in the Bush administration's rhetoric. *Perspectives on Politics*, 3 (3), 525–37.

Gerson, M. 2009a. Obama the undecider. *The Washington Post*, 20 November, A25.

Gerson, M. 2009b. Obama's case to make. *The Washington Post*, 4 December, A27.

Gibson, C. 2008. Transcript: Charlie Gibson interviews President Bush [Online December 1]. Available at: http://www.abcnews.go.com/WN/Politics/Story?id=6356046&page=1 [accessed 18 December 2008].

Gigot, P. 2010. The Wall Street Journal's Paul Gigot discusses the mosque at Ground Zero and other issues. *NBC Meet the Press*, NBC News Transcripts, 22 August.

Gitlin, T. 2003. *The Whole World is Watching*. Berkeley: University of California Press.

Glanz, J. 2010. What was lost. *The New York Times*, 1 September, A11.

Glazier, R. and Boydstun, A. 2012. The president, the press, and the war: a tale of two framing agendas. *Political Communication*, 29 (4), 428–46.

Goler, W. 2009. Political Headlines. *Fox Special Report with Bret Baier*, Fox News Network, 2 September.

Goler, W. 2010. Political headlines. *Fox Special Report with Bret Baier*, Fox News Network, 2 August.

Goode, E. 2009. When minds snap. *The New York Times*, 8 November, WK1.

Gordon, M. 2010a. Biden visits Iraq for major step in troop pullout and to meet gridlocked leaders. *The New York Times*, 31 August, A8.

Gordon, M. 2010b. In an Iraqi operation, a clearer picture of American support. *The New York Times*, 14 September, A10.

Gordon, M. and Bumiller, E. 2010. In Baghdad, US officials take note of milestone. *The New York Times*, 2 September, A4.

Graber, D. 2010. *Mass Media and American Politics*. 8th edition. Washington, DC: CQ Press.

Graham, L. 2010. Senator Lindsey Graham discusses midterm elections and other issues. *NBC Meet the Press*, NBC News Transcripts, 5 September.

Gramsci, A. 1971. *Selections for the Prison Notebooks*, edited by Q. Hoare and G.N. Smith. London: Lawrence and Wishart.

Gregory, D. 2007. *NBC Nightly News*, NBC News Transcripts, 11 September.

Gregory, D. 2009a. *NBC Meet the Press*, NBC News Transcripts, 1 November.

Gregory, D. 2009b. David Gregory on Obama's Afghanistan plan. *NBC Nightly News*, NBC News Transcripts, 1 December.

Griffin, J. 2010. Political Headlines. *Fox Special Report with Bret Baier*, Fox News Network, 7 September.

Guthrie, S. 2009. President Obama set to announce decision on Afghanistan within the week. *NBC Today*, NBC News Transcripts, 24 November.

Hall, B. 2010. Remembering Roy: in honor of a fallen Iraqi interpreter. *The Washington Post*, 29 August, B1.

Hall, S., Critcher, C., Jefferson, T., Clark, J., Rogers, B. 1978. *Policing the Crisis.* London: Macmillan.
Hallin, D. and Gitlin, T. 1994. The Gulf War as popular culture and television drama. *Taken by Storm: The Media, Public Opinion, and US Foreign Policy in the Gulf War*, edited by W.L. Bennett and D. Paletz. Chicago: University of Chicago Press, 149–63.
Hayes, S. 2009. Fox News all-stars. *Fox Special Report with Bret Baier*, Fox News Network, 28 December.
Hayes, S. 2010. Fox News all-stars. *Fox Special Report with Bret Baier*, Fox News Network, 3 August.
Heintz, J. 2009. US troop deaths soared in Afghanistan in 2009. Associated Press, International News, 31 December.
Hefling, K. 2009. Shortage of military therapists creates strain. Associated Press, Washington Dateline, 7 November.
Hendawi, H. 2010a. High Iraq deaths cast doubt on US stability talk. Associated Press, International News, 1 August.
Hendawi, H. 2010b. Female, single, over 30: Iraqis count cost of war. Associated Press, International News, 6 September.
Herbert, B. 2009a. Stress beyond belief. *The New York Times*, 7 November, A23.
Herbert, B. 2009b. A tragic mistake. *The New York Times*, 1 December, A35.
Herbert, B. 2010a. The lunatic's manual. *The New York Times*, 3 August, A23.
Herbert, B. 2010b. We owe the troops an exit. *The New York Times*, 31 August, A24.
Herman, E. and Chomsky, N. 2002. *Manufacturing Consent: the Political Economy of the Mass Media.* New York: Pantheon.
Herzenhorn, D. 2007. On war funding, Democrats have a day of disagreement. *The New York Times*, 2 October, A1.
Hiding behind the general. 2007. Editorial. *The New York Times* [Online 9 September]. Available at: http://www.nytimes.com/2007/09/09/opinion/09sun1.html [accessed 12 September 2007].
Hoekstra, P. 2009. Interview with Pete Hoekstra. *Fox Hannity*, Fox News Network, 10 November.
Holsti, O. 2011. *American Public Opinion on the Iraq War.* Ann Arbor, MI: University of Michigan Press.
Holt, L. 2009a. Obama getting closer to making decision on troop levels in Afghanistan. *NBC Nightly News*, NBC News Transcripts, 1 November.
Holt, L. 2009b. Barack Obama says US will finish job in Afghanistan. *NBC Nightly News*, NBC News Transcripts, 24 November.
The horror at Fort Hood. 2009. Editorial. *The New York Times*, 7 November, A22.
Hull, A. and Priest D. 2009. At Walter Reed, a palpable strain on mental-health system. *The Washington Post*, 7 November, A1.
Hume, B. 2009. Fox News Sunday Roundtable. *Fox News Sunday*, Fox News Network, 1 November.
Hulse, C. 2007. Disappointed democrats map withdrawal strategy. *The New York Times*, 13 September, A1.

Hulse, C. and Shanker, T. 2007. The struggle for Iraq: in Senate, allies of Bush attempt to halt Iraq vote. *The New York Times*, 31 January, A1.

Hutcheson, J., Domke, D., Billeaudeaux, A., and Garland, P. 2004. US national identity, political elites, and a patriotic press following September 11. *Political Communication*, 21 (1), 27–50.

Hutchison, K.B. 2009. Senators' opinions. *NBC Meet the Press*, NBC News Transcripts, 22 November.

Ignatius, D. 2009a. The real Afghan strategy; will Obama give it a chance? *The Washington Post*, 1 November, A29.

Ignatius, D. 2009b. Afghan tribes to the rescue? *The Washington Post*, 22 November, A21.

Ignatius, D. 2009c. Surge, then leave. *The Washington Post*, 2 December, A23.

Ignatius, D. 2010a. Patient diplomacy—with an asterisk. *The Washington Post*, 19 August, A17.

Ignatius, D. 2010b. Awaiting a verdict in Iraq. *The Washington Post*, 2 September, A23.

In Iraq, a long engagement; it's in America's interest to play a continuing role. 2010. Editorial. *The Washington Post*, 31 August, A16.

In plain sight? Editorial. *The Washington Post*, 12 November, A20.

Iraq Study Group. 2006. *The Iraq Study Group Report* [Online, 6 December]. Available at: http://www.usip.org/iraq_study_group_report/report/1206/index.html [accessed 18 December 2006].

Iyengar, S. and McGrady, J. 2007. *Media Politics: A Citizen's Guide*. New York: W.W. Norton.

Jackson, R. 2005. *Writing the War on Terrorism: Language, Politics and Counterterrorism*. Manchester, UK: Manchester University Press.

Jackson, R. 2011. Culture, identity and hegemony: continuity and (the lack of) change in US counterterrorism policy from Bush to Obama. *International Politics*, 48 (2/3), 390–411.

Jaffe, G. 2010. Iraq conflict leaves officers weary and humbled. *The Washington Post*, 30 August, A14.

Jaffe, G. and Fadel, L. 2010. In Iraq, clear signs of a new US mission. *The Washington Post*, 2 September, A8.

Jaffe, G. and Kessler, G. 2009. General offers assurances on Afghan war. *The Washington Post*, 9 December 2009.

Jaffe, G., Wilson, S., and DeYoung, K. 2009. US envoy resists increase in troops. *The Washington Post*, 12 November, A1.

Jakes, L. 2009. White House: Afghan troop decision within weeks. Associated Press, Washington Dateline, 1 November.

Jakes, L. 2010a. Bomber kills 61 Iraqis in recruitment drive. Associated Press, International News, 17 August.

Jakes, L. 2010b. Remaining US troops still face danger in Iraq. Associated Press, International News, 24 August.

Jakes, L. 2010c. Looking at lessons that can be learned from Iraq. Associated Press, International News, 27 August.

Jakes, L. and Santana, R. 2010. Iraq says it's independent as US ends combat. Associated Press, International News, 31 August.

Jelinek, P. 2010a. Report: military needs new office to stem suicides. Associated Press, Washington Dateline, 24 August.

Jelinek, P. 2010b. Study: vets' health costs could top $900 billion. Associated Press, Business News, 29 September.

Johnston, D. and Schmitt, E. 2009. Little evidence of terror plot in base killings. *The New York Times*, 8 November, A1.

Johnston, D. and Shane, S. 2009. US was aware of suspect's tie to Yemeni cleric. *The New York Times*, 10 November, A1.

Johnstone, L.C. 2010. What we owe the Iraqis. *The Washington Post*, 10 September, A27.

Jones, J. 2010. Americans see US as exceptional; 37% doubt Obama does. Gallup.com [Online 22 December]. Available at: http://www.gallup.com/poll/145358/Americans-Exceptional-Doubt-Obama.aspx?utm_source=email2Ba%2Bfriend&utm_medium=email&utm_campaign=sharing&utm_term=Americans-Esceptional-Doubt-Obama&utm_content=morelink [accessed 1 January 2011].

Judt, T. 2008. What have we learned, if anything? *New York Review of Books* [Online 1 May]. Available at: http://www.nybooks.com/articles/archives/2008/may/01/what-have-we-learned-if-anything [accessed 10 July 2011].

Kagan, F. 2007. Plan B? Let's give plan A some time first. *The New York Times*, 6 May, D4.

Kagan, F. 2009. Interview with Fred Kagan. *Journal Editorial Report*, Fox News Network, 5 December.

Kagan, R. 2007. The "surge" is succeeding. *The Washington Post*, 11 March, D3.

Kane, P. 2009. Pelosi says she will not seek votes for troop surge; speaker also warns of 'serious unrest' over war in Afghanistan. *The Washington Post*, 17 December, A4.

Kaplan, F. 2009. Obama's War and Peace: how Obama accepted the Nobel Peace Prize while escalating the war in Afghanistan. *Slate Magazine* [Online 10 December]. Available at: http://www.slate.com/articles/news_and_politics/war_stories/2009/12/obamas_war_and_peace.html [accessed 5 May 2010].

Kernell, S. 2007. *Going Public: New Strategies of Presidential Leadership.* 4th edition. Washington, DC: CQ Press.

King, E. and Wells, R. 2009. *Framing the Iraq War Endgame: War's Denouement in an Age of Terror.* New York: Palgrave-Macmillan.

King, P. 2009. Congressman Peter King discusses how the president is handling the current threat to airlines by terrorists. *NBC Today*, NBC News Transcripts, 29 December.

Khan, H. and Brulliard, K. 2009. Doubts abound among people of S. Waziristan; few willing to back army. *The Washington Post*, 1 November, A19.

Kornblut, A. 2010. Obama speech on Iraq carries some pitfalls. *The Washington Post*, 31 August, A9.

Kornblut, A. and Ignatius, D. 2009. Discussion of Obama's announcement on Afghanistan. *NBC Chris Matthews Show*, NBC News Transcripts, 29 November.

Krauss, C. and Dao, J. 2009. Details trickle out as Army tests sole-killer theory. 2009. *The New York Times*, 7 November, A1.

Krauthammer, C. 2009a. Decline is a choice: the new liberalism and the end of American ascendancy. *Weekly Standard* [Online 19 October]. Available at: http://www.weeklystandard-com/author/charles-krauthammer [accessed 7 January 2010].

Krauthammer, C. 2009b. Fox News all-stars. *Fox Special Report with Bret Baier*, Fox News Network, 2 November.

Krauthammer, C. 2009c. Medicalizing mass murder. *The Washington Post*, 13 November, A21.

Krauthammer, C. 2009d. Fox News all-stars. *Fox Special Report with Bret Baier*, Fox News Network, 24 November.

Krauthammer, C. 2009e. Fox News all-stars. *Fox Special Report with Bret Baier*, Fox News Network, 2 December.

Krauthammer, C. 2009f. Uncertain trumpet. *The Washington Post*, 4 December, A27.

Krauthammer, C. 2010a. Fox News all-stars. *Fox Special Report with Bret Baier*, Fox News Network, 2 August.

Krauthammer, C. 2010b. Fox News all-stars. *Fox Special Report with Bret Baier*, Fox News Network, 12 August.

Krauthammer, C. 2010c. Fox News all-stars. *Fox Special Report with Bret Baier*, Fox News Network, 31 August.

Krebs, R. and Jackson, P. 2007. Twisting tongues and twisting arms: the power of political rhetoric. *European Journal of International Relations*, 13 (1), 35–66.

Krebs, R. and Lobasz, J. 2007. Fixing the meaning of 9/11: hegemony, coercion and the road to war in Iraq. *Security Studies*, 16 (3), 409–51.

Kristol, W. 2009. A war president. *The Washington Post*, 2 December, A23.

Kuypers, J., Cooper, S., and Althouse, M. 2008. The president and the press: a rhetorical framing analysis of George W. Bush's speech to the United Nations on November 10, 2001. *American Communication Journal*, 10 (3). Available at: http://www.ac-journal.org/journal/pubs/2008/Fall [accessed 12 September 2012].

Kuypers, J., Cooper, S., and Althouse, M. 2012. George W. Bush, the American press, and the initial framing of the war. *The George W. Bush Presidency: A Rhetorical Perspective*, edited by R. Denton. Lanham, MD: Lexington Books, 89–112.

Landler, M. and Zeleny, J. 2009. Ambassador's views show sharp Afghanistan divide. *The New York Times*, 13 November, A12.

The least bad plan. 2007. Editorial. *The Washington Post* [Online September 13]. Available at: http://www.washingtonpost.com/wp/dyn/content/article/2007/09/13/AR2007091302342.html [accessed 20 September 2007].

Leaving Iraq. 2010. Editorial. *The New York Times*, 28 August, A18.

Lee, M. 2010. US commander says Iraqis ready to handle security. Associated Press, Washington Dateline, 8 August.

Lewis, D. 2009. Political headlines. *Fox News Special Report with Bret Baier*, Fox News Network, 2 November.

Liasson, M. 2008. The anatomy of McCain's stump speech. *All Things Considered* [Online 27 October]. Available at: http://www.npr.org/templates/story/story.php?storyId=96187955 [accessed 12 November 2008].

Lieberman, J. 2009. Interview with Senator Lieberman. *Fox News Sunday*, Fox News Network, 8 November.

Limbaugh, R. 2009. Interview with Rush Limbaugh. *Fox News Sunday*, Fox News Network, 1 November.

Lipset, S. 1996. *American Exceptionalism: A Double-Edged Sword.* New York: W.W. Norton.

Livingston, S. and Bennett, W.L. 2003. Gatekeeping, indexing, and live event news: is technology altering the construction of news? *Political Communication*, 20 (4), 363–80.

Londono, E. 2010a. Political Impasse in Iraq deepens; US fears further unrest. *The Washington Post*, 1 August, A1.

Londono, E. 2010b. Extremist groups "very much alive" in Iraq. *The Washington Post*, 9 August, A8.

Londono, E. 2010c. A truly historic end to 7 years of war. *The Washington Post*, 19 August, A1.

Londono, E. 2010d. An anxious exit for the Iraq war's last general. *The Washington Post*, 5 September, B1.

Londono, E. and Paley, A. 2008. Western journalists in Iraq stage pullback of their own. *The Washington Post*, 11 October, A1.

Loven, J. 2009. Analysis: a war strategy with echoes of Bush. Associated Press, Washington Dateline, 2 December.

Maceda, J. 2009. Taliban claims responsibility for suicide bombing in Afghanistan that killed eight American CIA employees. *NBC Today*, NBC News Transcripts, 31 December.

Massing, M. 2004. *Now They Tell Us: The American Press and Iraq.* New York: New York Review of Books.

Matthews, C. 2009. Discussion of Obama's announcement on Afghanistan. *NBC Chris Matthews Show*, NBC News Transcripts, 29 November.

Maurer, K. and Watson, J. 2010. Marines pour resources into mental health care. Associated Press, Domestic News, 25 August.

McCain, J. 2009. Political headlines. *Fox Special Report with Bret Baier*, Fox News Network, 11 November.

McChesney, M. 2002. September 11 and the structural limitations of US journalism. *Journalism After September 11*, edited by B. Zelizer and Allen. New York: Routledge, 91–100.

McChrystal, S. 2009. Statement of General Stanley A. McChrystal, USA Commander, NATO International Security Assistance Force, House Armed Services Committee. *The New York Times* [Online 8 December]. Available at: http://www.graphics8.nytimes.com/packages/pdf/world/2009/20091208POLICY-MCCHRYSTAL.pdf [accessed 4 January 2010].

McConnell, M. 2010a. Interview with Mitch McConnell. *Fox News Sunday*, Fox News Network, 1 August.

McConnell, M. 2010b. Press release: the surge worked [Online 2 August]. Available at: http://www.mcconnell.senate.gov/public/index.cfm?p=PressReleases&ContentRecord_id=7947db2a-008-4e11-8cbf-ed0620ebeaContentType_id=c19bc7a5-2bb9-4a73-b2ab-3c1b5191a72b&Group_id=0fd6ddca-6a05-4b26-8710-a0b7b59a8f1f&MonthDisplay=8&YearDisplay=2010 [accessed 12 February 2011].

McCrisken, T. 2001. Exceptionalism. *Encyclopedia of American Foreign Policy*, 2nd edition, edited by A. DeConde and R. Burns. NY: Scribner's, 63–80.

McCrisken, T. 2012. Ten years on: Obama's war on terrorism in rhetoric and practice. *International Affairs*, 87 (4), 781–801.

McKinley, J. and Dao, J. 2009. After years of growing tensions, 7 minutes of bloodshed. *The New York Times*, 9 November, A1.

McMahon, R. 2008. The campaign and foreign policy. *The Washington Post* [Online 3 November]. Available at: http://www.washingtonpost.com/wp-dyn/content/article/2008/11/03/AR2008110301607 [accessed 21 November 2008].

Mermin, J. 1999. *Debating War and Peace: Media Coverage of US Intervention in the Post-Vietnam Era*. Princeton, NJ: Princeton University Press.

Meyers, S. and Thee, M. 2007. Americans feel military is best at ending the war. *The New York Times*, 10 September, A1.

Miklaszewski, J. 2007. *NBC Nightly News*, NBC News Transcripts, 10 September.

Miklaszewski, J. 2009a. *NBC Meet the Press*, NBC News Transcripts, 1 November.

Miklaszewski, J. 2009b. More details about alleged Fort Hood shooter, Nidal Hassan. *NBC Nightly News*, NBC News Transcripts, 6 November.

Miklaszewski, J. 2009c. *NBC Today*, NBC News Transcripts, 25 November.

Milbank, D. 2007. The general does battle with … a broken mike. *The Washington Post*, 11 September, A1.

Miller, J. 2009. White House stimulus report. *Fox Hannity*, Fox News Network, 2 November.

Mitchell, A. 2009. Roundtable of NBC News' Andrea Mitchell and Jim Miklaszewski and author Jon Krakauer discusses Afghanistan. *NBC Meet the Press*, NBC News Transcripts, 1 November.

MoveOn.org. 2007. General Petraeus or General Betray Us? *The New York Times* [Online September 10]. Available at: http://www.moveon.org [accessed 12 October 2007].

Mr Obama's task. Editorial. *The New York Times*, 19 November, A34.

Mullen, M. 2009. Text of Admiral Mullen's prepared testimony [Online 3 December]. Available at: http://www.nytimes.com/2009/12/03/us/politics/03mullentxt.html?ref=asia [accessed 3 January 2010].

Murtha, J. 2007. Murtha reacts to president's veto threat [Online 4 April]. Available at: http://www.house.gov/apps/list/press/pa12_murtha/pr040407war.html [accessed 12 May 2007].

Myers, S. 2010a. What is left behind: a benchmark of progress, electrical grid fails Iraqis. *The New York Times*, 2 August, A1.

Myers, S. 2010b. Exit strategy, meet your challenge: Iraq. *The New York Times*, 8 August, WK3.

Myers, S. 2010c. As Iraq war winds down, soldiers say they had a job to do. *The New York Times*, 20 August, A1.

Myers, S. and Adnan, D. 2010. Attack shows lasting threat to US in Iraq. *The New York Times*, 6 September, A1.

Myers, S. and Cooper, H. 2009. In Baghdad, Obama presses Iraq's leaders to unite factions. *The New York Times* [Online 7 April]. Available at: http://www.nytimes.com/2009/04/08/world/middleeast/09obama.html?_r=0 [accessed 12 July 2009].

Nacos, B. 2007. *Mass-Mediated Terrorism: The Central Role of the Media in Terrorism and Counterterrorism*, 2nd edition. Landham, MD: Rowman and Littlefield.

Nagl, J. 2012. The age of unsatisfying wars. *The New York Times* [Online 6 June]. Available at: http://www.nytimes.com/2012/06/07/opinion/the-age-of-unsatisfying-wars.html [accessed 10 June 2012].

Nagourney, A. and Sussman, D. 2009. Poll finds support for Obama's plan for Afghanistan mixed with skepticism. *The New York Times*, 10 December, A8.

Nakamura, D. 2012. Obama touts American exceptionalism, end of wars in Air Force graduation speech. *The Washington Post* [Online 23 May]. Available at: http://www.washingtonpost.com/politics/obama-touts-american-exceptionalism-end-of-wars-in-air-force-graduation-speech/2012/05/23/gJQANN2zkU_story.html [accessed 1 June 2012].

Napolitano, J. 2009. Secretary of Homeland Security Janet Napolitano discusses national security in the wake of a terror arrest aboard a plane bound for Detroit. *NBC Meet the Press*, NBC News Transcripts, 27 December.

Nearing the End. 2008. Editorial. *The New York Times* [Online 9 October]. Available at: http://www.nytimes.com/2008/10/09/opinion09thu1.html [accessed 4 February 2009].

Niebuhr, R. 1952. *The Irony of American History*. New York: Charles Scribner's Sons.

Norris, P., Kern, M., and Just, M. 2003. Framing terrorism. *Framing Terrorism: the News Media, the Government, and the Public*, edited by P. Norris, M. Kern, and M. Just. New York: Routledge, 3–26.

Now Yemen. 2009. Editorial. *The New York Times*, 31 December, 26A.

Obama, B. 2002. Remarks of Illinois State Sen. Barack Obama against going to war with Iraq [Online 2 October]. Available at: http://www.barackobama.com/pdf/warspeech.pdf [accessed 10 October 2008].

Obama, B. 2004. Transcript: Illinois Senate candidate Barack Obama [Online 27 July]. Available at: http://www.washingtonpost.com/ac2/wp-dyn/articles/A19751-2004Jul27.html [accessed 10 October 2008].

Obama, B. 2005. Moving forward in Iraq [Online 22 November]. Available at: http://www.obamaspeeches.com/040-Moving-Forward-in-Iraq-Chicago-Council-on-Foreign-Relations-Obama-Speech.htm [accessed 10 October 2008].

Obama, B. 2006. A way forward in Iraq [Online 20 November]. Available at: http://www.barackobama.com/2006/11/20/a-way-foward-in-Iraq.php [accessed 11 October 2008].

Obama, B. 2007a. Floor statement on Bush's decision to increase troops in Iraq [Online 19 January]. Available at: http://www.obamaspeeches.com/096-Floor-Statement-on-Presidents-Decision-to-Increase-Troops-in-Iraq [accessed 12 October 2008].

Obama, B. 2007b. Barack Obama's campaign speech [Online 10 February]. Available at: http://www.guardian.co.uk/world/2007/feb/10/barackobama [accessed 12 October 2008].

Obama, B. 2007c. Remarks of Senator Barack Obama on the Iraq war [Online 21 March]. Available at: http://www.usliberals.about.com/od/extraordinaryspeeches/a/ObamaIraqWar.htm [accessed 12 October 2008].

Obama, B. 2007d. Remarks at the Chicago Council on Global Affairs [Online 13 April]. Available at: https://www.my.barackobama.com/page/content/fppcga [accessed 5 January 2009].

Obama, B. 2007e. Renewing American leadership. *Foreign Affairs*, 86 (4), 2–16 [Online July 2007]. Available at: http://www.jstor.org/stable/20032411 [accessed 8 January 2009].

Obama, B. 2007f. Obama's speech at Woodrow Wilson Center [Online 1 August]. Available at: http://www.cfr.org/us/-election-2008/obamas-speech-woodrow-wilson-center/p13974 [accessed 8 January 2009).

Obama, B. 2007g. Barack Obama's foreign policy speech. Council on Foreign Relations [Online 2 October]. Available at: http://www.cfr.org.us-election-2008/barack-obamas-foreign-policy-speech [accessed 8 January 2009].

Obama, B. 2008a. Remarks of Senator Barack Obama: "The world beyond Iraq" [Online 19 March]. Available at: https://mybarackobama.com/page/content/fiveyearslaterspeech [accessed 8 January 2009].

Obama, B. 2008b. My plan for Iraq. *The New York Times* [Online 14 July]. Available at: http://www.nytimes.com/2008/07/14/opinion/obama.html [accessed 1 August 2008].

Obama, B. 2008c. Obama's remarks on Iraq and Afghanistan. *The New York Times* [Online 15 July]. Available at: http://www.nytimes.com/2008/07/15/us/politics/15text-obama.html?pagewanted=all&_r=0 [accessed 1 August 2008].

Obama, B. 2008d. Obama's speech in Berlin. *The New York Times* [Online 25 July]. Available at: http://www.nytimes/com/2008/07/25/us/politics/25obama.html?pageswanted=all [accessed 1 August 2008].

Obama, B. 2008e. Plan for ending the war in Iraq [Online January 2008]. Available at: http://www.barackobama.com/issues/Iraq/index.php [accessed 1 November 2008].

Obama, B. 2009a. President Barack Obama's inaugural address [Online 20 January]. Available at: http://www.whitehouse.gov/blog/inaugural-address [accessed 30 January 2009].

Obama, B. 2009b. Remarks at the State Department [Online 22 January]. *The American Presidency Project*, edited by G. Peters and J. Woolley. Available at: http://www.presidency.ucsb.edu/ws/?pid=85694 [accessed 30 January 2011].

Obama, B. 2009c. Obama's Al Arabiya interview [Online 27 January]. Available at: http://www.whitehouse.gov/blog_post/PresidenttoMuslimWorldAmericansarenotyourenemy/ [accessed 5 February 2009].

Obama, B. 2009d. Anderson Cooper 360 interview with President Barack Obama [Online 3 February]. Available at: http://www.transcripts.cnn.com/TRANSCRIPTS/0902/03/acd.01.html [accessed 5 February 2009].

Obama, B. 2009e. Interview with Peter Mansbridge of Canadian Broadcasting Company [Online 17 February]. *The American Presidency Project*, edited by G. Peters and J. Woolley. Available at: http://www.presidency.ucsb.edu/ws/?pid=85784 [accessed 20 February 2011].

Obama, B. 2009f. Address before a joint session of the Congress [Online 24 February]. *The American Presidency Project*, edited by G. Peters and J. Woolley. Available at: http://www.presidency.ucsb.edu/ws/?pid=85753 [accessed 1 March 2011].

Obama, B. 2009g. Remarks of President Barack Obama responsibly ending the war in Iraq [Online 27 February]. Available at: http://www.whitehouse.gov/the_press_office/Remarks-of-President-Obama-Responsibly-Ending-War-in-Iraq [accessed 1 March 2009].

Obama, B. 2009h. Newsmaker: Obama outlines goals for Afghanistan, Iraq [Online 27 February]. Available at: http://www.pbs.org/newshour/bb/politics/jan-june09/obamainterview_02–27.html [accessed 1 March 2009].

Obama, B. 2009i. Interview with Master Sergeant rusty Barfield of the Pentagon Channel [Online 27 February]. *The American Presidency Project*, edited by G. Peters and J. Woolley. Available at: http://www.presidency.ucsb.edu/ws/?pid=85804 [accessed 1 March 2011].

Obama, B. 2009j. Remarks at the National Defense University [Online 12 March]. *The American Presidency Project*, edited by G. Peters and J. Woolley. Available at: http://www.presidency.ucsb.edu/ws/?pid=85854 [accessed 20 March 2011].

Obama, B. 2009k. Interview with Steve Kroft on CBS News' "60 Minutes" [Online 22 March]. *The American Presidency Project*, edited by G. Peters and J. Woolley. Available at: http://www.presidency.ucsb.edu/ws/?pid=85895 [accessed 20 March 2011].

Obama, B. 2009l. Remarks by the president on a new strategy for Afghanistan and Pakistan [Online 27 March]. Available at: http://www.whitehouse.gov/the_press_office/Remarks-by-the-President-on-a-New-Strategy-for-Afghanistan-and-Pakistan [accessed 1 April 2009].

Obama, B. 2009m. Interview with Bob Schieffer on CBS News' "Face the Nation" [Online 29 March]. *The American Presidency Project*, edited by G. Peters and J. Woolley. Available at: http://www.presidency.ucsb.edu/ws/?pid=85929 [accessed 20 March 2011].

Obama, B. 2009n. Remarks on American exceptionalism. Quoted in: Benen, S. 2009. Political animal. *Washington Monthly* [Online 5 April]. Available at: http://www.washingtonmonthly.com/archives/individual/2009_04/017614.php [accessed 1 June 2009].

Obama, B. 2009o. Remarks by President Barack Obama in Prague [Online 5 April]. Available at: http://www.whitehouse.gov/the_press_office/Remarks-By-President-Barack-Obama-in-Prague-As-Delivered [accessed 10 April 2009].

Obama, B. 2009p. Remarks by the president on national security [Online 21 May]. Available at: http://www.whitehouse.gov/the_press_office/Remarks-by-the-President-on-National-Security-as-delivered [accessed 24 May 2009].

Obama, B. 2009q. Remarks by the president on a new beginning [Online 4 June]. Available at: http://www.whitehouse.gov/the-press-office/remarks-president-cairo-university-6-04-09 [accessed 10 June 2009].

Obama, B. 2009r. Transcript: Terry Moran interview President Obama [Online 23 July]. Available at: http://www.abcnews.go.com/Politics/story?id=8156230&page=5#.T8JpmMWE605 [accessed 10 May 2011].

Obama, B. 2009s. Remarks by the president on the post-9/11 GI Bill [Online 3 August]. Available at: http://www.whitehouse.gov/the-press-office/remarks-president-post-911-gi-bill-george-mason-university [accessed 15 May 2011].

Obama, B. 2009t. Obama delivers remarks at the VFW national convention [Online 17 August]. Available at: http://www.washingtonpost.com/wp-dyn/content/article/2009/08/17/AR2009081701657.html [accessed 15 May 2011].

Obama, B. 2009u. Remarks by the president to the United Nations General Assembly [Online 23 September]. Available at: http://www.whitehouse.gov/the_press_office/Remarks-by-the-President-to-the-United-Nations-General-Assembly [accessed 1 October 2009].

Obama, B. 2009v. The president's weekly address [Online 7 November]. *The American Presidency Project*, edited by G. Peter and J. Woolley. Available at: http://www.presidency.ucsb.edu/ws/?pid=86866 [accessed 12 March 2011].

Obama, B. 2009w. Remarks at a memorial service at Fort Hood [Online 10 November]. *The American Presidency Project*, edited by G. Peter and J. Woolley. Available at: http://www.presidency/ucsb.edu/ws/?pid=86870 [accessed 12 March 2011].

Obama, B. 2009x. Remarks by the president on Veterans Day [Online 11 November]. Available at: http://www.whitehouse.gov/the-press-office/2011/11/11/remarks-president-veterans-day [accessed 13 November 2009].

Obama, B. 2009y. Remarks at a town hall meeting and a question-and-answer session in Shanghai, China [Online 16 November]. *The American Presidency Project*, edited by G. Peter and J. Woolley. Available at: http://www.presidency.ucsb.edu/ws/?pid=86909 [accessed 10 July 2011].

Obama, B. 2009z. Interview with Chip Reid on CBS' "Early Show" [Online 18 November]. *The American Presidency Project*, edited by G. Peter and J. Woolley. Available at: http://www.presidency.ucsb.edu/ws/?pid=86949 [accessed 10 July 2011].

Obama, B. 2009aa. Interview with Chuck Todd on NBC's "Today" [Online 18 November]. *The American Presidency Project*, edited by G. Peter and J. Woolley. Available at: http://www.presidency.ucsb.edu/ws/?pid=86950 [accessed 10 July 2011].

Obama, B. 2009bb. Interview with Ed Henry on CNN's "The Situation Room" [Online 18 November]. *The American Presidency Project*, edited by G. Peter and J. Woolley. Available at: http://www.presidency.ucsb.edu/ws/?pid=88331 [accessed 10 July 2011].

Obama, B. 2009cc. Interview with Major Garrett of Fox News [Online 18 November]. Available at: http://www.politics.blogs.foxnews.com/2009/11/18/major-garrett-interviews-president-obama-transcript [accessed 10 July 2011].

Obama, B. 2009dd. The president's news conference with Prime Minister Manmohan Singh of India [Online 24 November]. *The American Presidency Project*, edited by G. Peter and J. Woolley. Available at: http://www.presidency.ucsb.edu/ws/?pid=86929 [accessed 10 July 2011].

Obama, B. 2009ee. Remarks by the president in address to the nation on the way forward in Afghanistan and Pakistan [Online 1 December]. Available at: http://www.whitehouse.gov/the-press-office/remarks-president-address-nation-way-forward-afghanistan-and-pakistan [accessed 3 December 2009].

Obama, B. 2009ff. Remarks by the President at the Acceptance of the Nobel Peace Prize [Online 10 December]. Available at: http://www.whitehouse.gov/the-press-office/remarks-president-acceptance-nobel-peace-prize-as-delivered [accessed 12 December 2009].

Obama, B. 2009gg. Interview with Steve Kroft on CBS' "60 Minutes" [Online 13 December]. *The American Presidency Project*, edited by G. Peter and J. Woolley. Available at: http://www.presidency.ucsb.edu/ws/?pid=88330 [accessed 12 July 2011].

Obama, B. 2009hh. Interview with Jim Lehrer on PBS' "The News Hour" [Online 23 December]. *The American Presidency Project*, edited by G. Peter and J. Woolley. Available at: http://www.presidency.ucsb.edu/ws/?pid=88328 [accessed 12 July 2011].

Obama, B. 2009ii. Remarks on improving homeland security in Kaneohe, Hawaii [Online 28 December]. *The American Presidency Project*, edited by G. Peter and J. Woolley. Available at: http://www.presidency.ucsb.edu/ws/?pid=58054 [accessed 12 July 2011].

Obama, B. 2010a. Remarks by the president on strengthening intelligence and aviation security [Online 7 January]. Available at: http://www.whitehouse.gov/the-press-office/remarks-president-strengthening-intelligence-and-aviation-security [accessed 6 January 2011].

Obama, B. 2010b. Remarks by the president in state of the union address [Online 27 January]. Available at: http://www.whitehouse.gov/the-press-office-/remarks-president-state-union-address [accessed 6 January 2011].

Obama, B. 2010c. Remarks by the president to the troops [Online 28 March]. Available at: http://www.whitehouse.gov/the-press-office/remarks-president-troops [accessed 6 January 2011].

Obama, B. 2010d. Remarks by the president at the United States Military Academy at West Point commencement [Online 22 May]. Available at: http://www.whitehouse.gov/the-press-office/remarks-president-united-states-military-academy-west-point-commencement [accessed 6 January 2011].

Obama, B. 2010e. Remarks by the president at Disabled Veterans of America conference in Atlanta, Georgia [Online 2 August]. Available at: http://www.whitehouse.gov/the-press-office/remarks-president-disabled-veterans-america-conference-atlanta-georgia [accessed 6 January 2011].

Obama, B. 2010f. Weekly address: President Obama: as the combat mission in Iraq ends, we must pay tribute to those who have served [Online 28 July]. Available at: http://www.whitehouse.gov/the-press-office/2010/08/28/weekly-address-president-obama-combat-mission-iraq-ends-we-must-pay-tribute [accessed 6 January 2011].

Obama, B. 2010g. Remarks by the president during Fort Bliss army base visit [Online 31 August]. Available at: http://www.whitehouse.gov/the-press-office/2010/08/31/remarks-president-during-fort-bliss-army-base-visit [accessed 6 January 2011].

Obama, B. 2010h. Remarks by the president in address to the nation on the end of combat operations in Iraq [Online 31 August]. Available at: http://www.whitehouse.gov/the-press-office/2010/08/31/remarks-president-address-nation-end-combat-operations-iraq [accessed 6 January 2011].

Obama, B. 2010i. Remarks by the president at the Pentagon Memorial [Online 11 September]. Available at: http://www.whitehouse.gov/the-press-office/2010/09/11/remarks-president-pentagon-memorial [accessed 6 January 2011].

Obama, B. 2010j. Remarks by the president to the United Nations General Assembly [Online 23 September]. Available at: http://www.whitehouse.gov/the-press-office/2010/09/23/remarks-president-united-nations-general-assembly [accessed 6 January 2011].

Obama, B. 2010k. Remarks by the president on the Afghanistan-Pakistan annual review [Online 16 December]. Available at: http://www.whitehouse.gov/the-press-office/2010/12/16/statement-president-afghanistan-pakistan-annual-review [accessed 6 January 2011].

Obama, B. 2011a. Remarks by President Obama in address to United Nations General Assembly [Online 21 September]. Available at: http://www.whitehouse.gov/the-press-office/2011/09/21/remarks-president-obama-address-united-nations-general-assembly [accessed 3 November 2011].

Obama, B. 2011b. Remarks by the president on ending the war in Iraq [Online 21 October]. Available at: http://www.whitehouse.gov/the-press-office/2011/10/21/remarks-president-ending-war-iraq [accessed 21 November 2011].

Obama, B. 2011c. Remarks by the president on Veterans Day [Online 11 November]. Available at: http://www.whitehouse.gov/the-press-office/2011/11/11/remarks-president-veterans-day [accessed 21 November 2011].

Obama, B. 2011d. President Obama and the First Lady speak to troops at Fort Bragg [Online 14 December]. Available at: http://www.whitehouse.gov/photos-and-video/video/2011/12/14/president-obama-and-first-lady-speak-troops-fort-bragg [accessed 21 November 2011].

Obama, B. 2012a. Remarks by the president on the Defense Strategic Review [Online 5 January]. Available at: http://www.whitehuse/gov/photos-and-video/2012/01/05/president-obama-speaks-defense-strategic-review#transcript [accessed 20 July 2012].

Obama, B. 2012b. Remarks by the president at the Air Force Academy Commencement [Online 23 May]. Available at: http://www.whitehouse.gov/the-press-office/2012/05/23/remarks-president-air-force-academy-commencement [accessed 20 July 2012].

Obama, B. 2012c. Remarks by the president commemorating Memorial Day [Online 28 May]. Available at: http://www.whitehouse.gov/the-press-office/2012/05/28/remarks-president-commemorating-memorial-day [accessed 20 July 2012].

O'Donnell, K. 2009. Senate and House question Obama's war council over timing of troop withdrawal. *NBC Nightly News*, NBC News Transcripts, 2 December.

O'Hanlon, M. and Pollack, K. 2007. A war we just might win. *The New York Times*, 30 July, D3.

Oppel, R. and Bumiller, E. 2009. Afghanistan's president says army will need allies' help until 2024 or longer. *The New York Times*, 9 December, A16.

O'Reilly, B. 2009a. What has Obama accomplished so far? *O'Reilly Factor*, Fox News Network, 4 November.

O'Reilly, B. 2009b. Impact. *O'Reilly Factor*, Fox News Network, 6 November.

Pace, J. and Loven, J. 2010. Obama salutes promised end of US combat in Iraq. Associated Press, Domestic News, 2 August.

Partlow, J. 2009a. UN's Afghanistan mission moving workers for safety; many will be sent out of country in wake of deadly Kabul attack. *The Washington Post*, 6 November, A12.

Partlow, J. 2009b. In Afghanistan, Taliban surpasses al-Qaeda; shifting power dynamic could influence where US focuses firepower. *The Washington Post*, 11 November, A1.

Pelosi, N. 2007. Pelosi: Iraq resolution will signal a change in direction and bring our troops home safely and soon [Online 16 February]. Available at: http://www.house.gov/pelosi/press/releases/Feb07/IraqSpeech16.html [accessed 3 March 2007].

Pelosi, N. and Reid, H. 2007. Congressional leaders call on president to reject flawed Iraq troop surge [Online 5 January]. Available at: http://www.house.gov/pelosi/press/releases/Jan07/Iraq.html [accessed 3 March 2007].

Peters, R. 2009. Impact. *The O'Reilly Factor*, Fox News Network, 6 November.

Petraeus, D. 2010. General Petraeus discusses issues in Afghanistan. *NBC Meet the Press*, NBC News Transcripts, 15 August.

Pew Research Center. 2003. After Hussein's capture [Online 18 December 2003]. Available at: http://www.people-press.org/2003/12/18/after-husseins-capture/ [accessed 8 January 2009].

Pew Research Center. 2007a. Public sees progress in war effort [Online 27 November]. Available at: http://www.people-press.org/2007/11/27/public-sees-progress-in-war-effort [accessed 28 December 2007].

Pew Research Center 2009a. Obama's approval rating slips amid division over economic proposals [Online 16 March]. Available at: http://www.people-press.org/2009/03/16/obamas-approval-rating-slips-amid-division-over-economic-proposals/ [accessed 12 January 2011].

Pew Research Center 2009b. Most say they lack background to follow Afghan news [Online 22 October]. Available at: http://www.people-press.org/2009/10/22/most-say-they-lack-background-to-follow-afghan-news [accessed 12 January 2011].

Pew Research Center. 2009c. Public divided over Afghan troop requests, but still sees rationale for war [Online 5 November]. Available at: http://www.pewresearch.org/2009/11/05/public-divided-over-afghan-troop-requests-but-still-sees-ratioale-for-war [accessed 12 January 2011].

Pew Research Center. 2009d. News interest in Afghanistan surges [Online 10 December]. Available at: http://www.people-press.org/2009/12/10/news-interest-in-afghanistan-surges [accessed 12 January 2011].

Pew Research Center. 2010. Perceptions of economic news remain mixed [Online 9 September]. Available at: http://www.people-press.org/2010/09/09/perceptions-of-economic-news-remain-mixed/ [accessed 12 July 2011].

Pincus, W. 2009a. Bad Karzai, good Karzai. *The Washington Post*, 24 November, A17.

Pincus, W. 2009b. If it is to be fought, it ought to be paid for. *The Washington Post*, 1 December, A23.

Pollack, K. 2010. 5 myths about leaving Iraq. *The Washington Post*, 22 August, B3.

President Karzai's second term. Editorial. *The New York Times*, 3 November, A28.

Project for Excellence in Journalism. 2008a. Iraq war coverage plunges [Online 25 March]. Available at: http://www.journalism.org/node/10345 [accessed 30 April 2008].

Project for Excellence in Journalism. 2008b. Why news of Iraq dropped [Online 26 March]. Available at: http://www.journalism.org/node/10365 [accessed 7 May 2008].

Project for Excellence in Journalism. 2008c. Winning the media campaign [Online 22 October]. Available at: http://www.journalism.org/node/13307 [accessed 10 November 2008].

Project for Excellence in Journalism. 2009a. Geithner's plan drives the economic narrative [Online 29 March]. Available at: http://www.journalism.org/index_report/news_coverage_index_march_23_29 [accessed 5 January 2011].

Project for Excellence in Journalism. 2009b. Health care, Afghanistan emerge as the summer's big stories [Online 23 August]. Available at: http://www.journalism.org/index_report/pej_news_coverage_index_august1723_2009 [accessed 5 January 2011].

Project for Excellence in Journalism. 2009c. For the first time, Afghanistan tops the week's news [Online 11 October]. Available at: http://www.journalism.org/index_report/pej_news_coverage_index_october_511_2009 [accessed 11 January 2011].

Project for Excellence in Journalism. 2009d. The Army base massacre dominates the week [Online 8 November]. Available at: http://www.journalism.org/index_report/pej_news_coverage_index_november_28_2009 [accessed 11 January 2011].

Project for Excellence in Journalism. 2009e. Fort Hood fallout leads the news again [Online 15 November]. Available at: http://www.journalism.org/index_report/pej_news_coverage_index_november_915_2009 [accessed 11 January 2011].

Project for Excellence in Journalism. 2009f. Afghanistan dominates while two scandals fascinate [Online 6 December]. Available at: http://www.journalism.org/node/18564 [accessed 11 January 2011].

Project for Excellence in Journalism. 2010a. The near-miss plane plot leads newspaper headlines [Online 3 January]. Available at: http://www.journalism.org/node/18833 [accessed 17 January 2010].

Project for Excellence in Journalism. 2010b. From Detroit to Yemen, terror tops the news agenda [Online 10 January]. Available at: http://www.journalism.org/node/18920 [accessed 18 January 2010].

Project for Excellence in Journalism. 2010c. Afghanistan tops the news [Online 1 August]. Available at: http://www.journalism.org/index_report/pej_news_coverage_index_july_26 august_2010 [accessed 5 August 2010].

Project for Excellence in Journalism. 2010d. Mosque controversy, Iraq War dominate the news [Online 22 August]. Available at: http://www.journalism.org/index_report?iraq_war_dominate_news [accessed 1 September 2010].

Project for Excellence in Journalism. 2010e. A near-miss hurricane tops the news [Online 5 September]. Available at: http://www.journalism.org/index_report/pej_news_coverage_index_august_30september_3_2010 [accessed 10 September 2010].

Project for Excellence in Journalism. 2011. Year in News 2011 [Online 21 December]. Available at: http://www.journalism.org/node/27799 [accessed 7 January 2012].

Project for Excellence in Journalism. 2012. The state of the news media 2012 [Online 19 March]. Available at: http://www.stateofthemedia.org [accessed 23 March 2012].

Raftery, I. and Dao, J. 2010. After Iraq, troops fill base towns. *The New York Times*, 21 August, A10.

Raghaven, S. 2007. Weighing the surge: the US war in Iraq hinges on the counterinsurgency strategy of Gen. Petraeus. *The Washington Post*, 4 September, A1.

Reagan, R. 1987. Address before a joint session of Congress on the state of the union [Online 2011]. *The American Presidency Project*, edited by G. Peters and J. Woolley. Available at: http://www.presidency.ucsb.edu/ws/index.php?pid=34430 [accessed 7 September 2012].

Reid, R. 2009a. Analysis: with few options, US accepts Karzai. Associated Press, International News, 1 November.

Reid, R. 2009b. Analysis: US low on options in Afghanistan. Associated Press, International News, 12 November.

Reid, R. and Brummitt, C. 2009. Obama's Afghan plan represents high-stakes gamble. Associated Press, International News, 2 December.

Reid, R. and Gannon, K. 2009. Afghan corruption tough to combat. Associated Press, International News, 3 November.

Rich, F. 2009. The missing link from Killeen to Kabul. *The New York Times*, 15 November, WK10.

Rich, F. 2010a. Freedom's just another word. *The New York Times*, 5 September, WK8.

Rich, F. 2010b. Time for this big dog to bite back. *The New York Times*, 12 September, WK11.

Ricks, T. 2007a. General may see early success in Iraq: but sharp rise in insurgent violence could soon follow, official says. *The Washington Post*, 23 January, A1.

Ricks, T. 2007b. Bush leans on Petraeus as war dissent deepens. *The Washington Post*, 15 July, A1.

Robinson, E. 2009a. Failing the troops at Fort Hood. *The Washington Post*, 10 November, A15.

Robinson, E. 2009b. Down the wrong path in Afghanistan. *The Washington Post*, 4 December, A27.

Robinson, E. 2010a. Obama's winning streak. *The Washington Post*, 20 August, A23.

Robinson, E. 2010b. The fog at war's end. *The Washington Post*, 31 August, A17.

Rodman, P. and Shawcross, W. 2007. Defeat's killing fields. *The New York Times*, 7 June, A25.

Rojecki, A. 2008. Rhetorical alchemy: American exceptionalism and the war on terror. *Political Communication*, 25 (1), 67–88.

Romney, M. 2010. *No Apology: The Case for American Greatness.* New York: St Martin's Press.

Romney, M. 2012. Mitt Romney's speech on foreign policy at the Virginia Military Institute: prepared remarks. *The Washington Post* [Online 8 October]. Available at: http://www.washingtonpost.com/2012–10–08/politics/35499325_1-vmi-graduates-virginia-military-institute-foreign-policy [accessed 7 November 2012].

Romney prods Obama to decide Afghan strategy now. 2009. Associated Press, Washington Dateline, 2 November.

Rove, K. 2009. Analysis with Karl Rove. *Fox on the Record with Greta Van Susteren*, Fox News Network, 10 November.

Rubin, A. 2009a. After siege at Afghan guesthouse, UN decides to move 600 workers temporarily. *The New York Times*, 6 November, A6.

Rubin, A. 2009b. Prospect of more US troops worries a wary Afghan public. *The New York Times*, 7 November, A1.

Rutenberg, J. and Healy, P. 2007. Democrats are unified in opposition to troop increase, but split over what to do about it. *The New York Times*, 15 January, A1.

Sanger, D. 2007. Bush adds troops in bid to secure Iraq. *The New York Times*, 11 January, A1.

Sanger, D. 2009a. Buttressing a tainted ally. *The New York Times*, 2 November, A1.

Sanger, D. 2009b. One decision, many messages. *The New York Times*, 25 November, A14.

Sanger, D. 2010. Rethinking a war's what-ifs. *The New York Times*, 1 August, WK1.

Sanger, D. 2012. *Confront and Conceal: Obama's Secret Wars and Surprising Use of American Power.* New York: Crown.

Sanger, D. and Rutenberg, J. 2007. In address, Bush insists US must not fail in Iraq. *The New York Times*, 24 January, A1.

Sanger, D. and Shanker, T. 2007. General's Iraq progress report has competition. *The New York Times*, 24 June, A1.

Sanghvi, S. 2010. Abandoned in Baghdad. *The New York Times*, 31 August, A21.

Santana, R. 2010. US: $1.9M in computers for kids missing in Iraq. Associated Press, International News, 27 August.

Schlesinger, R. 2011. Obama has mentioned 'American Exceptionalism' more than Bush. *US News and World Report* [Online 31 January]. Available at: http://www.usnews.com/opinion/blogs/robert-schlesinger/2011/01/31/obama-has-mentioned-american-exceptionalism-more-than-bush [accessed 12 February 2011].

Schmitt, E. 2009. Jetliner plot demonstrates growing ability of al Qaeda affiliates to stage attacks. *The New York Times*, 31 December, A12.

Schmitt, E. and Cooper, H. 2009. Pressure builds in Congress as Obama nears Afghanistan troop plan. *The New York Times*, 24 November, A10.

Schweid, B. 2010. Analysis: Obama runs risk by withdrawing troops. Associated Press, Washington Dateline, 3 August.

Sewall, S. 2007. He wrote the book. Can he follow it? *The Washington Post*, 25 February, A1.

Shadid, A. 2010a. As Obama talks peace, many Iraqis are unsure. *The New York Times*, 4 August, A4.
Shadid, A. 2010b. Dozens are killed in a string of bombings and other attacks across Iraq. *The New York Times*, 8 August, A9.
Shadid, A. 2010c. Western clocks, but Middle Eastern time. *The New York Times*, 15 August, WK1.
Shadid, A. 2010d. Hapless elites, growing fear. *The New York Times*, 18 August, A1.
Shadid, A. 2010e. Militants show might, striking in 13 Iraq cities. *The New York Times*, 26 August, A1.
Shadid, A. 2010f. Commander sees delay for new Iraqi government. *The New York Times*, 30 August, A8.
Shadid, A. 2010g. Restoring names to war's unknown casualties. *The New York Times*, 31 August, A1.
Shadid, A. 2010h. After years of war in Iraq, few see a brighter future. *The New York Times*, 1 September, A10.
Shane, S. and Dao, J. 2009. Tangle of clues about suspect at Fort Hood. *The New York Times*, 15 November, A1.
Shane, S. and Johnston, D. 2009. Accused gunman's exchanges with cleric raised questions, not alarms. *The New York Times*, 12 November, A24.
Shawn, E. 2009. Political Headlines. *Fox Special Report with Bret Baier*, Fox News Network, 23 November.
Shear, M. 2007. Vietnam shades Warner's Iraq stand; silent then, senator won't be this time. *The Washington Post*, 28 January, A1.
Shear, M. and Kane, P. 2009. President vs. party on troop increase; caucus wouldn't back a costly expansion of Afghan war. *The Washington Post*, 26 November, A1.
Sidoti, L. 2007. McCain assails Democrats on war in Iraq. Associated Press [Online 11 April]. Available at: http://www.ap.org [accessed 16 April 2007].
Smith, S. 2009. Suspected Ft Hood shooter still alive. *Fox On the Record with Greta Van Susteren*, Fox News Network, 5 November.
Something for everyone. 2010. Editorial. *The Washington Post*, 2 September, A22.
Stanley, A. 2007. Winning the hearing battle with no sound coming out. *The New York Times*, 11 September, A10.
Stiglitz, J. and Bilmes, L. 2010. A war more costly than we thought. *The Washington Post*, 5 September, B4.
Stoddard, A.B. 2010. Fox News all-stars. *Fox Special Report with Bret Baier*, 12 August.
Stolberg, S. and Myers, S. 2007. Limited pullout is middle way on Iraq, Bush will say. *The New York Times*, 13 September, A1.
Stolberg, S. and Cooper, H. 2009. Obama speeds troops and vows to start pullout in 2011. *The New York Times*, 2 December, A1.
The Afghan decision; President Obama must convince the world that he himself is convinced. 2009. Editorial. *The Washington Post*, 29 November, A20.
The Afghanistan speech. 2009. Editorial. *The New York Times*, 2 December, A34.

The road home. 2007. Editorial. *The New York Times* [Online 8 July]. Available at: http://www.nytimes.com/2007/07/08/opinion/08sun1.html?pagewanted=all [accessed 10 July 2007].

Toal, G. 2009. "In no other country on earth": the presidential campaign of Barack Obama. *Geopolitics*, 14 (2), 376–401.

Todd, C. 2009a. Hamid Karzai to remain president of Afghanistan. *NBC Nightly News*, NBC News Transcripts, 2 November.

Todd, C. 2009b. Obama to unveil reasoning behind strategy in Afghanistan. *NBC Nightly News*, NBC News Transcripts, 1 December.

The trouble with Yemen; How to fight al-Qaeda's Arabian offshoot. 2009. Editorial. *The Washington Post*, 30 December, A12.

Tyndall, A. 2010. Tyndall report: 2009 year in review [Online January]. Available at: http://www.tyndallreport.com/yearinreview2009/ [accessed 30 March 2010].

Tyndall, A. 2011. Tyndall Report: 2010 year in review [Online January]. Available at: http://www.tyndallreport.com/yearinreview2010/ [accessed 1 March 2011].

Tyson, A. 2007. Top US officers see mixed results from Iraq "surge." *The Washington Post*, 22 April, A1.

Tyson, A. 2009a. Gates predicts "slog" in Afghanistan. *The Washington Post*, 28 January, A1.

Tyson, A. 2009b. Fort Hood has felt the strain of repeated deployments; base leads Army posts in number of suicides since Iraq invasion. *The Washington Post*, 6 November, A8.

Unconnected dots, again: on the Northwest bomber, the administration had been warned. 2009. Editorial. *The Washington Post*, 28 December, A14.

Varney, S. 2009. What is Obama's strategy in Afghanistan? *Fox Hannity*, Fox News Network, 24 November.

Vieira, M. and Russert, T. 2007. *NBC Today Show* [online 14 September]. Available at: http://www.today.msnbc.msn.com [accessed 21 September 2007].

Vogt, H. and Gearan, A. 2009. Karzai's election increases pressure on Obama. Associated Press, International News, 2 November.

The war in Iraq. 2010. Editorial. *The New York Times*, 1 September, A22.

The war that didn't bark. 2008. Editorial. *The Washington Post* [Online 4 November]. Available at: http://www.washingtonpost.com/wp-dyn/content/article/2008/11/03/AR2008110302030.html [accessed 20 November 2008].

West, B. 2009a. Topic A. *The Washington Post*, 8 November, A25.

West, B. 2009b. Afghanistan strategy review. *Fox Hannity*, Fox News Network, 13 November.

Western, J. 2005a. *Selling Intervention and War: The Presidency, the Media, and the American Public.* Baltimore, MD: Johns Hopkins University Press.

Western, J. 2005b. The war over Iraq: selling war to the American public. *Security Studies*, 14 (1), 106–39.

When warriors hurt themselves. 2010. Editorial. *The New York Times*, 2 September, A34.

Will, G. 2009a. Unicorns in Kabul; Karzai is making "dithering" look like wisdom. *The Washington Post*, 4 November, A25.

Will, G. 2009b. This will not end well. *The Washington Post*, 3 December, A33.

Williams, B. 2007. *NBC Nightly News*, NBC News Transcripts, 11 September.

Williams, B. 2010. *NBC Nightly News*, NBC News Transcripts, 7 September.

Williams, B. and Miklaszewski, J. 2007a. *NBC Nightly News*, NBC News Transcripts, 20 April.

Williams, B. and Miklaszewski, J. 2007b. *NBC Nightly News*, NBC News Transcripts, 4 June.

Williams, T. and Ghazi, Y. 2010. Half a year after voting, Iraq waits for a government on a long vacation. *The New York Times*, 27 September, A7.

Wilson, S. and Blake, A. 2010. Obama reminds veterans he's beginning war's end; US forces in Iraq will change from combat operations to exit plan. *The Washington Post*, 3 August, A8.

Wilson, S. and Chandrasekaran, R. 2009. Karzai is wild card for US strategy; reelected leader could undermine Obama's efforts in Afghanistan. *The Washington Post*, 3 November, A1.

Wilson, S., Johnson, C., and Hsu, S. 2009. Probe of suspect's motive begins; web postings spur questions. *The Washington Post*, 7 November, A1.

Wishful thinking on Iraq. 2007. Editorial. *The Washington Post* [Online 12 July]. Available at: http://www.washingtonpost.com/wp-dyn/content/article/2007/07/11/AR2007071102042.html [accessed 21 July 2007].

Wolfowitz, P. 2010. In Korea, a model for Iraq. *The New York Times*, 31 August, A21.

Woodward, B. 2008. *The War Within*. New York: Simon and Schuster.

Woodward, B. 2010. *Obama's Wars*. New York: Simon and Schuster.

Woodward, C. 2007a. US choices dwindle if Iraq war plan fails. Associated Press [Online 13 January]. Available at: http://www.ap.org [accessed 2 February 2007].

Woodward, C. 2007b. Amid the tempest over Iraq, Gen. David Petraeus a force of calm. Associated Press [Online 10 September]. Available at: http://www.ap.org [accessed 15 September 2007].

Wright, R. 2009. Who created Major Hasan? *The New York Times*, 22 November, WK11.

Zacharia, J. 2010. A hazy vision of the US role ahead in Iraq. *The Washington Post*, 25 September, A6.

Zaller, J. and Chiu, D. 1996. Government's little helper: US press coverage of foreign policy crises, 1945–1991. *Political Communication*, 13 (4), 385–405.

Zeleny, J. 2009. Obama purposely taking time on troop decision. *The New York Times*, 13 November, A14.

Index

9/11
    depth of exceptional grievance 139
    media narrative for 10–11

Abramowitz, Michael 77
Achenbach, Joel 92
Afghanistan
    circumscribed success, Obama's narrative of 177–9
    comparison to Vietnam 68
    corruption in 86–7
    criteria for victory in 60–61
    declining media interest 2009 onwards 186
    escalation, arguments against 68–9
    as forgotten issue to 2009 77–8
    high level of media attention given to 81
    increased US troop presence 62–3, 66–8
    Iraq War, consequences of for 118
    meaning of conflict in 69
    near future likely media coverage 187–8
    negative media coverage during 2009 79–80
    new strategy for 58–61, 62–71
    political discussions over in US 63
    presidential elections 81–3
    public opinion on 80
    refocus on at end of Iraq War 135–9
    rise in interest in 2009 78
    support for new strategy 70–71
    surge and exit from 62–6
    victory redefined 71–3
    violence in 81–5
Althaus, Scott 9
Angle, Jim 103
Anker, Elizabeth 6–7
Arango, Tim 152, 153–4

Associated Press (AP)
    Christmas airline bomber incident 103
    consequences of losing in Iraq 32
    continuing violence in Iraq 159, 162
    coverage of news by 15
    deliberative process of Obama 91, 92
    dubious legacy of Iraq 167, 169
    economic/reputational toll of Iraq War 165
    Hasan, Fort Hood attack by 96–7
    high level of attention given to Afghanistan 81
    hope, triumph over reality in Iraq 156
    inadequacies of Iraq drawdown narrative 150
    Karsai as problematic ally 86–7
    lack of progress in Iraq 151–2
    mental health of military personnel 96–7
    Pakistan 83–4
    Petraeus's congressional testimony 34–5
    political conditions in Iraq 158
    on the surge in Iraq 29, 30
    surge-then-exit policy, strategy behind 104, 105, 106, 108–9, 110, 111
    toll of war on Iraq 157–8
    toll on military personnel of Iraq War 164–5
    violence in Afghanistan 83, 84
axis of evil (phrase) 5–6

Bacevich, Andrew 5, 7, 38, 43
Bai, Matt 105
Baier, Bret 160
Baker, Peter 105, 108, 110–11, 168
Balz, Dan 108
Baum, Matthew 11–12, 17
Bennett, W. Lance 3, 10, 85, 89, 185

Biden, Joe 128, 131, 132, 134, 135, 140, 169–70
Blake, Aaron 150
Boehner, John 89, 129
Bolton, John 93, 152
Boydstun, Amber 12, 17, 135
Broder, David 90
Brooks, David 109, 155–6
Brummit, Chris 84
Bumiller, Elisabeth 105
Burns, John 166
Burns, Robert 92, 156
Bush, George W.
　comparison with Obama on terrorism 50, 74–5
　consequences of losing in Iraq 31–2
　Iraq as war on terror 39–42
　on MoveOn.org advertisement 26
　Petraeus as savior of the surge 25–6, 33
　surge narrative on Iraq 21–4
　surge on Iraq and the media 36–42
　UN declaration 5

cascading activation model of government/media nexus 17, 185
Casey, George 98
Chandrasekaran, Rajiv 104, 111
Cheney, Liz 102
chosen nation, America as 5
　see also exceptionalism
Christmas airline bomber incident 101–3
Clinton, Hilary 66, 71, 87
communication of frames 7–10
Constable, Pamela 82
Cooper, Helene 86, 88, 105
Cornyn, John 111
corruption in Afghanistan 86–7
counterframes 17
　on Iraq 26–8, 38–9
Crocker, Ryan 162

Dao, James 99
Declining Frame Alignment hypothesis 12
Delahunt, Bill 111
democracy, surge narrative on Iraq 24
DeYoung, Karen 108
Di-Natale, Dominic 152, 160
Diehl, Jackson 90

Different Framing Dynamics hypothesis 12
Dionne, E.J. 35–6, 106, 111–12, 156
dissemination of frames 7–10

Edwards III, George C. 4, 7, 8
Eikenberry, Karl 70–71, 87
Elasticity of Reality hypothesis 11
elections in Afghanistan 81–3
Elliott, Andrea 98
end of war
　circumscribed success, Obama's narrative of 177–9
　media disconnect with presidential frames 183–5
　as messy and unsatisfying 177
　narrative 13–14
　as slow fade to black 187
　see also Iraq
Engel, Eliot 111, 152
Engel, Richard 96, 150–51, 154–5, 159, 167
Entman, Robert 3–4, 7, 8, 28
Esch, Joanne 6–7
event-driven news 17
exceptionalism
　American 4–7
　closing argument on Iraq War 141–3
　and Obama 46–50, 180–83
　Obama on the military as exemplars of 61–2
　rationale for war 4–7
　refocus on Afghanistan at end of Iraq War 137–9
　surge narrative on Iraq 24
　thanks given to Iraq military personnel 132

Fadel, Leila 153, 169
Filkins, Dexter 85, 110
Fort Hood attack
　Jihadist connection 97–101
　mental health of Hasan 95–7
Fox News
　Christmas airline bomber incident 102
　continuing violence in Iraq 160
　deliberative process of Obama 93–4
　dubious legacy of Iraq 168, 171
　increased coverage on Iraq drawdown 148–9

Jihadist connection with Fort Hood
  attack 99–101
lack of progress in Iraq 151, 152, 153
perceptual gulf between US and Iraq
  155
surge-then-exit policy, strategy behind
  106, 109
frames
  acceptance of dominant frame 8
  communication of 7–10
  construction of 3–4
  contests between 7–8
  counterframes 17
    Iraq 26–8, 38–9
  media departures from official
    narrative 11–13, 183–5
  presidential narrative of war as 2–3
  rhetorical coercion 8
Framing Stickiness hypothesis 11
Fuller, Ben 92

Gamel, Kim 157–8
Gannon, Kathy 87
Gardiner, Nile 181
Garrett, Major 160160
Gates, Robert 61, 69–70, 134, 140–41, 167
Gearan, Anne 86, 87, 91
Gerson, Michael 90, 109
Gibbs, Robert 91
Gigot, Paul 170
Giuliani, Rudolph 102
Glanz, James 167
Glazier, Rebecca 12, 17, 135
Goler, Wendell 153
Goode, Erica 96
government/media nexus, models of
  16–17, 185
Graham, Lindsay 170
Gregory, David 36, 82, 87, 98, 107
Griffin, Jennifer 171
Groeling, Tim 11–12, 17
Guthrie, Savannah 92, 94, 107

Hasan, Nidal Malik, Fort Hood attack
  Jihadist connection 97–101
  mental health of 95–7
Hayes, Stephen 103, 151
Hefling, Kimberly 96

hegemony model of government/media
  nexus 16, 185
Hendawi, Hamza 150
Herbert, Bob 95, 109, 164, 166
Hoekstra, Pete 100–101
Holt, Lester 86, 107
home-grown terrorism 95–103
Hume, Brit 85
Hutchison, Kay Bailey 89

Ignatius, David 104, 110, 162, 166, 167
indexing model of government/media
  nexus 16–17, 185
Iraq
  abandoned construction projects 157–8
  benefits to of war 133–5
  circumscribed success, Obama's
    narrative of 177–9
  closing argument on war, Obama's
    141–3
  consequences of losing in 31–3
  continuing violence in 159–62
  costs of war for people of 134
  costs of war for US 165
  counterframes on 26–8
  declining interest in 37–8
  declining media interest 2009 onwards
    186
  dissenting accounts over 38
  divergence of official/media narrative
    172–3
  dubious legacy of 166–72
  economic conditions 157–8
  economic/reputational toll on US
    165–6
  exit strategy, Obama's 123–8
  hope, triumph over reality 155–6
  hope, triumph over reality in 155–6
  inadequacies of drawdown narrative
    149–56
  introspective turn of media 173
  lack of attention in 2008-9 147–8
  lack of progress in, media on 149–53
  legacy of war in 140–41
  lessons from failures in 57–8, 117–18
  media departures from official
    narrative 12–13
  near future likely coverage 187–8

new relationship after war 130
new strategy for 116–23
as not part of war on terror 26–7
Obama's criticism of war in 115, 118–20, 122–3
perceptual gulf between US and 153–5
Petraeus as savior of the surge 25–6
political conditions 158–9
political motivation to drawdown 151–2
political solution to war, Obama's call for 120–21
post-Iraq vision, Obama's 127–8
presidential campaign discourse prior to elections 146–7
promises and responsibilities as theme 128–31
public support and opinion on 145–6
refocus on Afghanistan at end of war 135–9
as straining US military 30–31
success in, lack of definition in 24
supporting role in security discourse 126–7
surge narrative on 21–4
  president and the media 36–42
thanks given to military personnel 131–3
themes of narrative of 128–43
toll of war on 157–62
toll of war on America 163–6
toll on military personnel 163–5
troop surge, Obama's opposition to 119
unwinnable, conflict as 27–8
war as catastrophic 121–2
as war on terror 39–42
war-on-terror not focus with media 173–4
war that ought never to have been fought 166–7

Jackson, Richard 6–7, 16, 74, 139, 173–4
Jaffe, G. 169
Jakes, Lara 91, 104, 165
Jihadist connection with Fort Hood attack 99
Judt, Tony 7

Kagan, Fred 109
Karsai, Hamid 85–8
King, Peter 102
Kornblut, Anne 93, 153
Krauthammer, Charles 93, 99, 107, 109, 151, 155, 181
Kristol, William 109, 160
Kroft, Steve 60

Landler, Mark 105
Lauer, Matt 92
Lee, Matthew 159
Lehrer, Jim 60
Lewis, Dana 82
Lieberman, Joseph 100
Limbaugh, Rush 93
Londono, Ernesto 169
Loven, Jennifer 108–9

Maceda, Jim 84
Mansbridge, Peter 60
McCain, John 89, 123
McChrystal, Stanley 70
McConnell, Mitch 129, 151
McCrisken, Trevor 5, 6, 74, 180
media
  9/11, narrative for 10–11
  Christmas airline bomber incident 101–3
  consequences of losing in Iraq 31–3
  corruption in Afghanistan 86–7
  declining interest in Afghanistan and Iraq 186
  deliberative process of Obama 89–94
  departures from official narrative 11–13, 172–3
  disconnect with presidential frames 183–5
  dissenting accounts over Iraq 38–9
  divergence from official narrative on Iraq 172–3
  elections in Afghanistan 81–3
  end of war narrative 13–14
  event-driven news 17
  government/media nexus, models of 16–17, 185
  Hasan, Fort Hood attack by 95–101
  high level of attention given to Afghanistan 81

home-grown terrorism 95–103
hope, triumph over reality in Iraq 155–6
inadequacies of Iraq drawdown narrative 149–56
increased coverage on Iraq drawdown 148–9
introspective turn of on Iraq 173
on Iraq 12–13
Karsai as problematic ally 85–8
lack of progress in Iraq 149–53
mental health of military personnel 95–7
narratives of war 10–13
near future likely coverage 187–8
negative coverage during 2009 79–80
negativity due to reality/rhetoric divide 112
perceptual gulf between US and Iraq 153–5
Petraeus's congressional testimony 33–6
president and the surge narrative on Iraq 36–42
prior to surge announcement 28–9
procedures for covering stories 9
rise in interest in Afghanistan and terrorism in 2009 78
on the surge in Iraq 28–36
surge-then-exit policy, strategy behind 104–12
terrorism and Afghanistan as forgotten issue to 2009 77–8
time as a variable 17
toll of war on Iraq 157–62
violence in Afghanistan 81–5
war-on-terror not focus with Iraq 173–4
medical care for veterans 130
mental health of military personnel 95–7, 163–4
Miklaszewski, Jim 30, 82, 92, 98, 107
military personnel
  medical care for veterans 130
  mental health of 95–7
  thanks given to 131–3
  toll on of Iraq War 163–5
Miller, Judith 93

Mitchell, Andrea 86
Mohammed, Khalid Sheikh, criminal trial of 101–2
MoveOn.org advertisement 26
Mullen, Michael 70
Murtha, John 27
Muslims, reassurance addressed to by Obama 54
Myers, Steven 152, 157

Nagl, John 177
Nagourney, Adam 108
Napolitano, Janet 102
narratives of war
  dissemination of 7–10
  end of war 13–14
  Iraq War, themes of 128–43
  media's 10–13
  oppositional, on Iraq 26–8
  presidential 2–3
  surge narrative on Iraq 21–4
    media on 28–36
    media reports prior to 28–9
NBC
  continuing violence in Iraq 159
  deliberative process of Obama 92–3
  dubious legacy of Iraq 169–71
  Hasan, Fort Hood attack by 96
  high level of attention given to Afghanistan 81
  inadequacies of Iraq drawdown narrative 150–51
  increased coverage on Iraq drawdown 148–9
  Iraq War ought never to have been fought 167
  Jihadist connection with Fort Hood attack 98
  Karsai as problematic ally 86
  lack of progress in Iraq 152
  mental health of military personnel 96
  perceptual gulf between US and Iraq 154–5
  Petraeus's congressional testimony 35, 36
  political conditions in Iraq 158–9
  on the surge in Iraq 30

surge-then-exit policy, strategy behind 106
violence in Afghanistan 82–3, 84
Negativity hypothesis 11
New York Times
    Christmas airline bomber incident 102
    consequences of losing in Iraq 31–2
    continuing violence in Iraq 159, 160, 161, 162
    coverage of news by 15
    deliberative process of Obama 91, 93–4
    dubious legacy of Iraq 166–7, 168–9, 171
    Hasan, Fort Hood attack by 95–6
    high level of attention given to Afghanistan 81
    hope, triumph over reality in Iraq 155–6
    increased coverage on Iraq drawdown 148–9
    Iraq War ought never to have been fought 166–7
    Jihadist connection with Fort Hood attack 97–8, 99, 101
    Karsai as problematic ally 85–6, 88
    lack of progress in Iraq 152, 153
    mental health of military personnel 96
    perceptual gulf between US and Iraq 153–4, 155
    Petraeus's congressional testimony 35
    political conditions in Iraq 159
    on the surge in Iraq 29, 30–31
    surge-then-exit policy, strategy behind 105, 108, 109–10, 110–11, 111
    toll of war on Iraq 157
    toll on military personnel of Iraq War 163, 164
    violence in Afghanistan 83, 84

Obama, Barack
    circumscribed success in Afghanistan and Iraq, narrative of 177–9
    comparison with Bush on terrorism 50, 74–5
    deliberative process of 89–94
    and exceptionalism 180–83
    exceptionalism of USA 46–50
    force, need for 56–7
    integrated, overarching strategy, need for 47–8
Iraq War
    benefits to Iraq of war 133–5
    as catastrophic war 121–2
    closing argument on 141–3
    criticisms of 115, 118–20, 122–3
    evolving interpretation of 133–4
    exit strategy 123–8
    legacy of 140–41
    new strategy for 116–23
    political solution, call for 120–21
    promises and responsibilities as theme for Iraq 128–31
    refocus on Afghanistan at end of 135–9
    thanks given to military personnel 131–3
    themes of narrative of 128–43
    troop surge, opposition to 119
lessons from failures in Iraq 117–18
narrative of war 2–3
negative media coverage during 2009 79–80
philosophy of war 56–7
on post-9/11 wars 1–2
post-Iraq vision 127–8
public support for strategy 113
support for fight against terrorism 45–6
surge-then-exit policy, strategy behind 104–12
terrorism as one of many dangers faced 46
themes in 2009 narrative
    Afghanistan, increased US troop presence 62–3, 66–8
    Afghanistan, new strategy for 58–61, 62–71
    arguments against escalation in Afghanistan 68–9
    comparison of Vietnam to Afghanistan 68
    criteria for victory in Afghanistan 60–61
    just and necessary war 52–7
    lessons from failures in Iraq 57–8
    meaning of Afghanistan conflict 69

military as exemplars of
    exceptionalism 61–2
Muslims, reassurance addressed
    to 54
new approach to terrorism 58–61
omnipresent threat of terrorism
    73–4
support for new Afghanistan
    strategy 70–71
surge and exit from Afghanistan
    62–6
victory redefined 71–3
"war on terror," replacement of
    phrase 53–4, 59
unsavory wartime actions by USA,
    policy changes on 54–5
O'Donnell, Kelly 111
O'Reilly, Bill 93, 100

Pakistan
    new strategy for 59
    as refuge for militants 83–4
Partlow, Joshua 83
Pelosi, Nancy 27, 106, 111
Peters, Ralph 100
Petraeus, David H. 159
    congressional testimony, media
        portrayal of 33–6
    consequences of losing in Iraq 33
    as embodiment of the surge 25–6
    MoveOn.org advertisement 26
Pincus, Walter 88
Pollack, Kenneth 162
presidential elections in Afghanistan 81–3
psychological health of military personnel
    95–7, 163–4

Reagan, Ronald 5
Reid, Harry 27
Reid, Robert 87, 88
research questions 18, 81, 148
rhetorical coercion 8
Rich, Frank 101, 156, 166, 171
Ricks, Thomas 30, 33
Robinson, Eugene 98, 109–10, 156, 166
Romney, Mitt 89
Rove, Karl 100
Rubin, Alissa 83, 85

Sanger, David 29, 85–6, 105, 107, 166–7
Schweid, Barry 151
Shadid, Anthony 153, 155, 171
Shane, Scott 99
Shawn, Eric 102
Slaughter, Louise 111
Stoddard, A.B. 155
stress suffered by military personnel 95–7
suicide prevention programs 164
surge narrative on Iraq
    Bush on 21–4
    counterframes to 26–8
    declining media interest 37–8
    dissenting accounts over 38
    media on 28–36
    media reports prior to 28–9
    Petraeus as embodiment of 25–6
    president and the media 36–42

television news
    Christmas airline bomber incident
        102–3
    continuing violence in Iraq 159, 160
    coverage by 15–16
    deliberative process of Obama 92–3
    dubious legacy of Iraq 168, 169–71
    high level of attention given to
        Afghanistan 81
    Iraq War ought never to have been
        fought 167
    Jihadist connection with Fort Hood
        attack 98, 99–100
    lack of progress in Iraq 151, 152, 153
    perceptual gulf between US and Iraq
        154–5
    Petraeus's congressional testimony
        35, 36
    political conditions in Iraq 158
    on the surge in Iraq 30
    surge-then-exit policy, strategy behind
        106, 109
    violence in Afghanistan 82–3
terrorism
    as forgotten issue to 2009 77–8
    home-grown 95–103
    Iraq as war on terror 39–42
    negative media coverage during 2009
        79–80

new approach to 58–61
omnipresent threat of 73–4
rise in interest in 2009 78
time as a variable 17
Todd, Chuck 64, 86, 107
Tyson, Ann 95

United States of America
as benevolent world policeman 6
as chosen nation 5
exceptionalism of 4–7, 24
good/evil struggle, international conflict as 5–6
superiority of institutions of 7
toll of Iraq War on 163–6
victimhood, sense of 6–7

victimhood, sense of in USA 6–7
Vietnam, comparison to Afghanistan 68
violence in Afghanistan 81–5
Vogt, Heidi 86

war on terror
Iraq as 39–42
Iraq as not part of 26–7
replacement of phrase by Obama 53–4
staying power of narrative of 112–13
Washington Post
Christmas airline bomber incident 103
consequences of losing in Iraq 32
continuing violence in Iraq 159, 161, 162
deliberative process of Obama 90–91, 92, 93–4
dubious legacy of Iraq 166, 167, 169
economic/reputational toll of Iraq War 165
exceptionalism, Obama and 182
Hasan, Fort Hood attack by 95, 96

high level of attention given to Afghanistan 81
hope, triumph over reality in Iraq 155–6
inadequacies of Iraq drawdown narrative 149–50
increased coverage on Iraq drawdown 148–9
Iraq War ought never to have been fought 166–7
Jihadist connection with Fort Hood attack 97, 98–9, 99
Karsai as problematic ally 87, 88
lack of progress in Iraq 153
mental health of military personnel 95, 96
perceptual gulf between US and Iraq 154, 155
Petraeus's congressional testimony 33, 34, 35–6
political conditions in Iraq 158–9
on the surge in Iraq 29, 31
surge-then-exit policy, strategy behind 104, 105, 106, 108, 109–10, 111–12
toll on military personnel of Iraq War 163
violence in Afghanistan 81–2, 82–3
Wells, Robert A. 13, 34
West, Bing 99
Will, George 90, 109
Williams, Brian 170–71
Wilson, Scott 104, 150
Wolfowitz, Paul 162
Woodward, Bob 43
Wright, Robert 101

Zacharia, Janine 153
Zeleny, Jeff 86, 91, 105